Laurence O'Neill (1864-1943)

Lord Mayor of Dublin (1917-1924)

Patriot and Man of Peace

Laurence O'Neill (1864-1943)

Lord Mayor of Dublin (1917-1924)

Patriot and Man of Peace

....

Thomas J. Morrissey, S.J.

Dublin
Dublin City Council
2014

First published 2014 by
Dublin City Council
c/o Dublin City Library and Archive
138-144 Pearse Street
Dublin 2

Comhairle Cathrach
Bhaile Átha Cliath
Dublin City Council

Decade of Commemorations

www.dublincommemorates.ie

Designed by Yellowstone Communications Design
Indexed by Julitta Clancy
Printed by Hudson Killeen

PRINt
IRISH
CLÓBHUAILE
IN ÉIRINN

ISBN – Hbk: 978-1-907002-12-0
ISBN – Pbk: 978-1-907002-13-7

Distributed by
Four Courts Press
Malpas Street
Dublin 7
www.fourcourtspress.ie

Contents

PART III
A Long Epilogue, 1925-1943

Author's Introduction

Over the years, in my reading and research of the period 1913 to 1924, the name of Laurence O'Neill came up time and again; not least, of course, in his summoning and chairing of the national convention against conscription which united all shades of national opinion. Unfortunately, there did not seem to be sufficient material for a biography. Then, happily, I learned of family papers, which were kindly made available to me by Mrs Nuala O'Neill and her son John. They came in the form of three large scrapbooks for the years 1917-1919. They also contained, however, letters and reminiscences covering those and later years. It was evident that Laurence had in mind publishing a Memoir. It never happened, partly because of the political sensitivity of the 1920s and 1930s. From all the available material there emerged a figure of no great external distinction, but a man able to charm people in Britain and the United States of America as well as in Ireland, a gifted orator, diplomat and negotiator, who sought to lessen unemployment, assist the poor, and enable the citizens of Dublin to live as securely as possible despite the contending forces of the Westminster Government and of the Irish Republic.

At the conclusion of this book, there are many grounds for acknowledgement. First, my thanks are due to Nuala and John O'Neill, without whom this work would not have been undertaken. As with all my previous publications, I am particularly indebted to the Jesuit Provincial for encouraging my research and giving me space and opportunity to pursue it, and to my Jesuit community at Manresa, the Jesuit Centre of Spirituality, Clontarf, for their support and patience. I am greatly indebted also to the three readers of the original text, each of whom generously brought to it their special expertise: Maria Mullen, Dr. Fergus O'Donoghue, S.J., and Dr Mary Clark. To Dr Clark, too, belongs the credit of bringing the book to the attention of the Dublin City Council as a worthy tribute to one of the city's greatest lord mayors, a Patriot and Man of Peace. I feel honoured to have the book supported by Dublin City Council for publication through Dublin City Library and Archives and I am grateful to Assistant City Manager Brendan Kenny, Executive Manager Vincent Norton, and Dublin City Librarian Margaret Hayes, for making this possible. My special thanks goes to the Lord Mayor of Dublin, Councillor Oisin Quinn, for hosting the book-launch and for contributing a preface to the volume.

At an early stage in my approach to the book, I received valuable assistance from a keen local historian, John O'Neill of Malahide, and also from Sheila Carden, biographer of Alderman Tom Kelly. During the years of preparation, I have experienced the support of the staff of many institutions: The National Library of Ireland, the Dublin City Library and Archives, Pearse Street, the archivists of University College Dublin, the National Archives of Ireland, and the ever helpful librarians at Miltown Park Library. I am grateful to Seamus Helferty, Principal Archivist, UCD and to Dr. Deirdre McMahon, Mary Immaculate College, for their kind assistance in captioning the front cover illustration. Photography by Alastair Smeaton greatly enhanced the book. I am grateful to the National Library of Ireland for permission to reproduce photographs from their collections and wish to acknowledge the assistance of Glenn Dunne, Keith Murphy and Berni Metcalfe in this regard. My thanks also go to Raidio Telefis Eireann for permission to reproduce photographs from the Cashman Collection. Nearer home, at Manresa, my on-going thanks to Eileen Toomey and Valerie Corrigan for their bountiful copying of manuscripts; and to Cormac McConnell, whose unfailing courtesy, interest in history, and computing skills overcame many obstacles.

It only remains to thank and compliment Dr Clark on her work in publishing this book, to pay tribute to the designers, Yellowstone Communications Design, to the indexer Julitta Clancy and to wish the distributors, Four Courts Press, every success in making Laurence O'Neill more widely known not only in Ireland but in Britain and USA.

Thomas J. Morrissey, S.J

Preface

Laurence O'Neill (1864-1943) was Lord Mayor of Dublin during key years in modern Irish history, 1917 – 1924. During these troubled years he held the confidence of his fellow councillors and was hailed in ballad as the greatest lord mayor since Daniel O'Connell. He combined charm with oratorical gifts, political skill, mediating skills in industrial disputes, and a strong social conscience. From 1917 to 1919 Dublin Corporation had a major voice and leadership role in the absence of an Irish parliament. Hence, in 1917, O'Neill as Lord Mayor convened and chaired the Mansion House Conference against Conscription and through his friendship with Archbishop Walsh of Dublin helped to win the support of the Catholic hierarchy and thereby united all shades of nationalist opinion against conscription.

As Lord Mayor in those years one of O'Neill's major aims was to preserve the city from bloodshed and violence. A constitutional nationalist himself, he was friendly with de Valera and Michael Collins, the Dail met in the Mansion House Round Room, and republican leaders secretly found shelter there during the Troubles; at the same time, O'Neill cultivated the good will of successive Viceroys, Chief Secretaries, and Commanders-in-chief. One of these last, General Bryan Mahon, an Irishman, became both a friend and admirer. Subsequently, Lloyd George's emissary in Ireland, Alfred Cope, worked with O'Neill to bring about a truce.

Laurence O'Neill was born in Kings Inn Street, Dublin in 1864, the son of a potato and corn merchant. The family came from the Portmarnock area, Co. Dublin, and had a house and land there. After a few years at Belvedere College, he went into the family business and, in his spare time became an avid cyclist, competing in events across the country. Subsequently he was prominent in the Irish Cycling Association and represented that body at international conferences in several European countries. He was elected to the Corporation in 1910, and in subsequent years his concern for the welfare of workers won him the gratitude of Jim Larkin's union. In 1916 he was wrongfully imprisoned, an experience which gave him empathy with political prisoners and enabled him to be a successful negotiator between them and the authorities, especially in cases of hunger strike. In 1920 he pursued Lloyd George through Wales to Chequers seeking a reprieve for Kevin Barry. O'Neill was a leading figure in the Irish White Cross Relief organisation established to assist families in distress because of the Troubles, and he made a successful visit to USA to ensure the assistance of the American White Cross.

O'Neill was elected to the first Dail after the Treaty. A serious prolonged illness rendered him unable to compete in the next election. In 1924 the Free State Government disbanded Dublin Corporation on vague grounds of corruption and inefficiency. O'Neill was expressly excluded from any criticism and was offered chairmanship of the Commission that was appointed to run the city. He refused Mr Cosgrave's offer, saying that he saw no grounds for disbandment and that it would be disloyal to his colleagues to accept the position. This decision left him in financial straits, as his business was not going well due to his long involvement in public affairs. With Mr Cosgrave's support he was elected to the Senate. Under de Valera's Government, he was appointed to the Seanad and proved an eloquent member until the Seanad was disbanded in 1936. By then his business had finally collapsed, largely, according to his son, because of his support for labour. In 1941 he was appointed to a reconstituted Seanad by de Valera, and died unexpectedly two years later. Dignatories from different political allegiances, including de Valera and Cosgrave, attended the funeral. O'Neill was buried in the Portmarnock area, where he had lived continually in his later years. He had four children, two sons and two daughters. One son, William, became a medical doctor in England. The other son, John, worked in the business and when that collapsed the only work available was a minor position in Dublin Corporation. Of the girls, Mary married a solicitor in Ballina, Co. Mayo; Annie, who stayed with her father, was obliged after his death to join her sister in the West of Ireland. Despite the decline in position and livelihood, all the family retained warm memories of their father.

Dublin's historic Mansion House has been a focus for Irish history for nearly three hundred years. As this biography shows, Lord Mayor O'Neill worked tirelessly and selflessly behind the scenes to ensure that the people of this great city remained safe and well in a time of upheaval which was unprecedented in its long history. O'Neill has not until now received the credit which was his due. In 1924 Alfred Cope assured Laurence O'Neill: 'When the true history comes to be written, you …will stand out in strong light among the few who worked wholeheartedly and disinterestedly to promote your country's welfare…' This important biography, by Thomas J. Morrissey S.J., restores O'Neill to his rightful place as a champion of liberty, justice and national pride – an outstanding Lord Mayor. I congratulate the author on his original and painstaking research which has uncovered an untold story and given new insight into a hidden part of Dublin's history. He is a distinguished historian and biographer and his care and attention to detail, allied to his warm interest in people, make this book both authoritative and accessible.

Dublin City Council is proud to publish this biography as a tribute to Lord Mayor O'Neill and as a significant contribution to the Decade of Commemorations, 1913-1923.

Oisin Quinn, Lord Mayor of Dublin
The Mansion House, Autumn 2013.

List of Illustrations

PART I

A Long Prologue

"Seek the beginnings, learn from whence you came,
And know the various earth from which you are made."

[Edwin Muir. *The Journey Back*]

Laurence O'Neill, 1864-1943
Lord Mayor of Dublin, 1917-1924
Patriot and Man of Peace

1.

Early Years in City and County

Laurence O'Neill, the future lord mayor of Dublin, was born Laurence Neil, on 4 March 1864, at 7 King's Inn Street, a Georgian residence on the north side of Dublin's River Liffey. His father was John Neil, of that address, a potato factor or merchant.[1] In the earlier years of the nineteenth century it was not unusual for Irish families, wishing to advance socially/commercially, to drop the O or the Mac prefix to their names. This is likely to have happened with Laurence's antecedents. By the 1870s, however, the family had reverted to the original name. When Laurence married on 22 February 1886, he, and his father, signed themselves O'Neill.[2]

Setting the scene

The marriage certificate gave Laurence's address as Airfield, St. Doloughs, in the district of Malahide. His was one of a number of O'Neill families possessing land in the Kinsealy/ Malahide/Portmarnock area of north County Dublin. Laurence's great-grandfather, Patrick O'Neill, appears to have been a farmer there in 1786.[3] The land was part of a terrain rising from the sea coast; an eminently healthy and desired location during the nineteenth century when Dublin suffered from cholera and smallpox epidemics and, subsequently, was ravaged by tuberculosis. By 1900 the city had the highest death-rate in Britain and Ireland, and the fifth highest recorded in the world.[4]

Laurence's father, John, married Mary Murphy, the daughter of a farmer in the Portmarnock area. In addition to land there, John, as indicated above, had accommodation and a business in King's Inn Street. His wife's mother, Harriet Murphy, lived close by at 8 Britain Street.[5] There were two other children to the marriage, James and Mary. James is mentioned as a witness at Laurence's wedding. Mary married a Mr Kelly. Nothing further is recalled of them in family papers or by surviving family members.[6]

Of Laurence's youth little is known. It seems likely that he spent much of the school year in the city. The only reference to his formal education is that he was educated by the Christian Brothers at primary level and then attended Belvedere College, run by the Irish Jesuits, at Great Denmark Street, no more than ten minutes walk from his home. Information on his time there is meagre. He is recalled as small in stature, but alert and energetic and particularly successful in the new sport of cycling.[7] It is likely, nevertheless, that he developed two of his distinctive future talents at the college. Belvedere, like most Jesuit colleges in Britain and Ireland, gave attention to drama and public speaking. In debating societies, run according to parliamentary procedures, pupils were encouraged to enunciate clearly and to argue logically. The debates frequently centred on a chosen motion. At a certain time in the year, there was a public debate at which parents and some prominent citizens were present. The chosen speakers were divided into Government, defending the motion, and Opposition, against it, and each speaker was encouraged to prepare his own speech. For such public occasions, however, the assistance of teachers was readily available. The debating process aimed at enabling students to speak with confidence in public.

Laurence O'Neill, whether or not he participated in school debating, was to become an articulate public speaker, at ease in debate and with a dramatic quality that enhanced his argument and his reputation as an orator. He grew up at a time when public speaking was highly regarded. The memory was cherished of great Irish orators such as Henry Grattan, Henry Flood, and especially Daniel O'Connell, and public interest was stimulated by the reporting of speeches at Westminster, and of those made at political hustings and at meetings of public bodies such as the Dublin City Council. While there is no record of Laurence's participation in drama productions at Belvedere, his interest in drama was evidenced by a reference in his papers to his taking part in Shakespeare's *King John*, presented by "the Literary and Dramatic Class, 1877-1878, of the Academy of Mount Carmel, 41 Dominick Street". The play was performed in "the presence of the Right Hon. the Lord Mayor", and "L. O'Neill" is mentioned as playing two minor roles – the "English Herald" and "Citizen of Angiers".[8]

Like many pupils of the time, Laurence probably left school at fifteen or sixteen years. He moved into his father's flourishing business. Despite his own comfortable situation and educational opportunity, he could not avoid being conscious of, and affected by the poverty, unemployment, squalor and slums that were part of Dublin during most of his life. He lived close to some of the worst examples of it. Virulent poverty and "tenementation" were evident in nearby Brunswick Street, North King's Street, and Queen's Street. All round the O'Neill premises there were patent distinctions between people: those who were poverty-stricken, those who were permanently unemployed, those living in temporary employment from day to day, those fortunate enough to have steady jobs – but among these last there were also notable gradations: they included labourers and the many assistants and clerks; the artisan class, who were viewed as fulfilling an important role in the city's industrial life; and the various members of the middle and upper-middle class, including the representatives of the legal profession who frequented King's Inn Street.

Adding to the variety of people and employments familiar to the O'Neill children was the nearby Smithfield area with its celebrated, bustling markets. The hay and horse markets drew large crowds. The horse fairs, in particular, attracted all classes of people, not only from Dublin and other counties but from overseas. Buyers came from Britain and mainland Europe. It was the age of horse-transport, and of the horse for work on the farm and in world armies. Laurence and neighbouring children grew up to the everyday sight and smell of horses, and occasionally experienced consternation and fear as horses ran wild, out of control, slipping and skidding on the cobblestones.[9] In Smithfield, farmers strode with their whips tied in bandolier fashion over their shoulders; many availing of the unpretentious eating houses and sleeping accommodation facilitating them and visiting dealers. There, and in the neighbouring streets, coach builders, harness makers, farriers, and potato and corn factors, like John O'Neill, lived above or adjoining their work premises.[10] Dublin into the first quarter of the twentieth century had a strong agricultural presence. Farm labourers and field workers lived in the heart of the city, as well as "cow-keepers", cattle-drovers, shepherds and herdsmen.[11]

Against this background, it is not surprising that in later years Laurence O'Neill manifested an ease with all classes of people and a deep empathy for the poor. Among the badly-off for whom he displayed special concern were the drovers and farm labourers who brought animals and goods to market for their employers and, after perhaps a fifteen or sixteen hour day, were paid not more than 14 shillings a week.[12] As a member of the Dublin City Council, he was to make a special effort to alleviate their situation.

Marriage and family

On 26 February 1886, Laurence married Anne Fottrell, from St. Doloughs, Balgriffin, the daughter of William Fottrell, a local farmer. She, like Laurence, was 22 years of age. Their marriage was celebrated at the small Catholic church of Kinsealy.[13] It proved a close and abiding one.

Fifteen years later, when they were both aged thirty-seven, the public census (1901) gave their address as 18 King's Inn Street; adding that they had four children – Mary aged 15, John aged 11, William 9, and Annie 5. All the children, except Annie, could read and write, but no member of the family had knowledge of the Irish language.[14] At the next census, 1911, the year after Laurence's election to the Dublin City Council, the family's address was 45 Smithfield. By then, Laurence, his children, and the house-keeper, Mrs Kate Delany, were described as speaking Irish and English. The mother, Anne O'Neill, however, spoke only English. At that stage, the eldest daughter, Mary, aged 23, was studying medicine, her brother, John, 21, was an auctioneer, while William,

19, and Annie 15, were represented as "scholars". It was observed that six children had been born to Laurence and Anne, but only four had survived. Of the four, Mary did not qualify as a doctor. She married a Mr Carrig, a solicitor in Ballina, County Mayo. Her younger brother, William, however, did become a medical doctor and practised in England, while Annie never married and lived with her parents.

Political background

Laurence's decision to go forward for election to Dublin Corporation was influenced by his political affiliations and the history of events between Britain and Ireland during his lifetime. It seems likely, indeed, that there was a lively interest in politics in the O'Neill household. Later, Laurence would assert proudly that he was the son of a Fenian.[15] There is no evidence, however, of his father being imprisoned for his views. Land and Politics were in the air as Laurence grew up. In 1870, when he was six, Prime Minister Gladstone brought in a land act that weakened landlord control over their property, and the same year Isaac Butt founded the Home Rule Party. Two years on, a major blow to landlord political power was delivered by the Secret Ballot Act, which liberated tenant voters. These events provoked major political and agrarian outcomes in Ireland during Laurence's teenage years. He was thirteen when Parnell took control of the Irish Parliamentary Party. On 19 December 1880, when he was sixteen, Lawrence joined the Land League at a meeting in Baldoyle, County Dublin, which was chaired by Thomas Sexton, M.P., and had Michael Davitt as one of its principal speakers. Parnell supported the League and availed of it as a lever towards Home Rule. Laurence greatly admired "the Chief", and many years later would claim that in his public career he had been guided by the political principles of Parnell.[16]

In the years prior to Laurence's wedding, the dream of Home Rule appeared about to be realised as Gladstone and Parnell moved closer politically. In the month of his marriage, February 1886, the public demand for self-government was at such a pitch that many Catholic bishops joined in a declaration that 'Home Rule alone can satisfy the wants, the wishes, as well as the legitimate aspirations of the Irish people'.[17]

During his public career, Laurence O'Neill was to refer to himself a number of times as a "parnellite" (seeking Home Rule or political independence by constitutional means); but to what extent he participated politically in the years from 1886-1900 is not known. In the first decade of the new century, however, he was a dedicated supporter of John Redmond. The reality of the support is indicated by an envelope in his family papers containing 5 linen badges signifying that he was "steward" at "Home Rule Demonstrations" on 31 March, 1912, and at a "Home Rule Convention" on 23 April 1912.[18]

Despite strong nationalist convictions, he did not allow politics to damage his relations with members of the extensive unionist community. Unionists continued to hold a dominant position in business and many sporting organisations well into the twentieth century. Laurence for many years was a member of the Irish Cycling Association, in which he met with unionists from Britain and all parts of Ireland and shared a spirit of comradeship with many of them. He was a well-known and successful competitor under the rules of the Association, and subsequently was a prominent and popular figure in the administration of the sport and as a representative of the I.C.A. at international gatherings. The Association was composed of clubs from all over the country, each of which had an elected committee whence a representative or representatives were sent to a central committee. In this arena there was competition for position and influence, and in it Laurence O'Neill demonstrated ambition and honed his political skills. The years of cycling and committee work also helped to develop him personally and socially.

Notes

1   General Registry Office Dublin, Births, Deaths and Marriages, vol. 2, p. 501. Laurence's birth was registered at the North Dublin City Union, on 14 March 1864.

2   Idem. Marriage certificate, vol. Jan-March 1886, p.399

3   Source: Nuala and John O'Neill, keepers of the family papers

4   Mary Daly. "Dublin Life" in Tom Kennedy ed. *Victorian Dublin* (Dublin), p. 79. See also Ruth McManus. *The Background to Modern Town Planning and Suburban Development* (Dublin), p. 461, Appendix 1.

5   General Registry Office. Laurence's birth, vol.2, p. 501

6   Nuala and John O'Neill, already mentioned, keepers of family papers.

7   *The Belvederian,* Summer 1919, "News of Our Past".

8   O'Neill Family Papers (ONFP)

9   Mary Roche, "Horse Handlers" in Kevin C. Kearns. *Streets Broad and Narrow, Images of Vanishing Dublin* (Dublin 2000), p. 137; Paddy Crosbie. "Clamour on Cobblestones", idem, p. 98

10   Moira Lysaght. "Smithfield Side-Shows", idem, p.168.

11   Catriona Crowe ed. *Dublin 1911* (Dublin 2011), p. 174

12   H. Geraghty. *William Patrick Partridge and his Times* (Dublin 2003), p. 184.

13   Marriage Certificate, vol. 2, p. 399

14   Census of Ireland 1901. Form A, the night of 31 March 1901.

15   Seanad Debates, vol. 19, p. 1575

16   O'Neill's speech at the Municipal Council, 24 Jan. 1916. Dublin City Archives (DCA), Mins. Municipal Council, pp. 82-4. Report of the speech in the *Daily Express* in a column entitled "By the Man in the Gallery".

17   Abp. Walsh-Gladstone, 17 Feb. 1886; *Freeman's Journal,* 22 Feb.1886

18   L.O'Neill Family Papers (ONFP)

Laurence O'Neill, 1864-1943
Lord Mayor of Dublin, 1917-1924
Patriot and Man of Peace

2.
Cyclist and Administrator

O'Neill competed on the special tracks in Dublin: at the Royal Dublin Society, Ballsbridge, at Lansdowne Road, and the grass track in Dublin University as well as other venues which held cycling competitions as part of their sports days. He became an active member of the Wanderers Cycle Club, established in 1884, first as a cyclist and later as administrator.

A pen-picture of developments in cycling and its growing popularity as a sport and leisure activity was provided by the *Irish Cyclist and Athlete* journal in its first Christmas edition, 1885-1888.[1] Reviewing the 1885 season, it observed that the number of riders had increased steadily. Tricycling, too, was becoming popular: 'whole families of the upper and more influential classes have adopted *en masse*'.[2] Various issues of the journal conveyed the enthusiasm of participants in verse form.[3]

Laurence O'Neill's contribution to cycling, and especially to the Wanderers Club, went far beyond enjoying the activity for its social and healthful benefits. This was made clear in an extant celebratory speech at the club. The speaker, referring to Mr O'Neill, proclaimed: 'As you are all aware, he has during the past year, and particularly in the inter-club competition, carried off the laurels of victory, and raised the Wanderers Club to a place of high distinction, thus rendering it the envy of other cycle associations who, unfortunately for themselves, cannot boast a member of such cycle celebrity as Mr O'Neill'. The pride they all felt in his great achievement, led the speaker to express his esteem in a substantial way. They all hoped that 'this small testimonial of his athletic prowess' would act 'as a further incentive' to Mr O'Neill 'to re-double his efforts during the coming year and earn for himself international laurels'.[4]

By the early 1890s, O'Neill seems to have cut back on competitive cycling and turned his attention increasingly to administering the club. On 6 April 1892, he was a Wanderers' delegate at the ordinary meeting of the council of the Irish Cyclists Association.[5] Although he continued to compete for the club, he no longer did so with his former commitment. Nevertheless, on 7 August 1895, at Balbriggan Sports, he managed to come third in both a 3 and 5 mile race; and on 28 August, in a handicap race at Jones's Road, Dublin, he finished third in a 10 mile event.[6]

By then, cycling had become a widespread past-time. There were said to be even more women than men cycling. Members of the nobility were mentioned as taking up the activity,[7] the Lord Lieutenant was mentioned as cycling in the Phoenix Park[8], and Dr Walsh, Archbishop of Dublin, cycled to meetings in Maynooth, and during holidays in Germany rode up to 100 kilometres on some days.[9] The cycling craze had spread across Europe. Cycle manufacturers were prepared to offer subsidies to riders who promoted their products; a situation that threatened to undermine the amateur status of cyclists participating in amateur competitions. It became a critical and emotional issue, in which O'Neill became actively involved.

A zealous and assertive official

Already in January 1894, amateurism was declared 'practically dead in England' and the National Cyclist Union (NCU) was seeking to revive it by having an obligatory system of registration.[10] In Ireland, however, amateurism was believed to flourish. O'Neill, after being elected to the registration committee of the Irish Cycling Association (ICA), showed himself more than zealous in defending the reputation of Irish amateurs. He strongly opposed a motion by Dr F.F. McCabe, at a monthly ICA meeting, that their delegate to the international meeting be instructed to vote that the section defining amateurism, which excluded the receiving of remuneration, be eliminated, because he was aware of many established Irish riders who were subsidised. O'Neill fervently defended the purity of Irish sport, and declared McCabe's motion unwise and unnecessary. The motion was defeated.[11]

The registration council of the British NCU acted very severely towards breaches of amateurism. Men were suspended on suspicion, refused a hearing, and not informed of the charges made against them.[12] O'Neill disagreed with this procedure, and he was elected unanimously to the appeals section of the Irish Registration Committee following his declaration that he would 'not confirm the refusal of any certificate on mere suspicion', and would 'only be guided by such evidence as was laid before the registration committee'.[13]

In that context, he was a leading voice in opposing the NCU's condemnation of the popular Irish cyclist, R. J. Macredy, as a "professional". At the council meeting of the ICA, he proposed that as Macredy was under the jurisdiction of the ICA his case should be referred to that body.[14] In support of the motion, he dwelt eloquently on Macredy's career as an amateur sportsman and pointedly asked what was behind the condemnation. Was it a case of anti-Irish prejudice? 'The meeting applauded loudly as he drawled in his own inimitable style – "You may break, you may scatter, the barrel if you will, but the scent of the herring will cling to it still".' 'The fate of Macredy today', he pointed out, 'might be the fate of their chairman tomorrow if this "Bossism" was to be allowed to continue. When did an Irishman become an Englishman? It was the grossest piece of impertinence to interfere in this way with an Irish rider. Even granting their (English) jurisdiction, Mr Macredy had committed no offence. They had the statements of Mr Macredy himself, and that of the chairman of the Pneumatic Tyre Company that he had never, individually or officially, subsidised or sanctioned the subsidising of amateurs.' 'The plain issue before the Association,' O'Neill concluded was – 'Were Irish cyclists to be ruled by the ICA or by a foreign body?'[15] Despite the chairman, J. W. Baynham, questioning whether it was desirable to oppose the NCU, the motion was passed with great applause.[16]

There was much criticism of the ICA in cycling magazines and in the Dublin branch of the organisation. Those in power were said to have 'disgraced the ICA management during the last twelve months and rendered Dubliners the laughing-stock of the rest of the country'.[17] From some of his comments,[18] it was evident that O'Neill agreed with such criticism, nevertheless, he continued to play a prominent part in the association as a delegate from the Wanderers Club. Despite his small stature and rather unimpressive appearance, O'Neill's articulacy, and his ability to relate easily to people, unionist or nationalist, Protestant or Catholic, ensured his progress in the organisation. He was elected as one of the Irish delegates to the World Amateur Cycling Championships from 1895 to 1899. His family papers contain mementoes in the form of five gold medals, with the flags of the competing nations in their distinctive colours ranged round and protruding from each medal, and on the reverse side there is noted, in turn - 'Delegate: 1895 Cologne; 1896 Copenhagen; 1897 Glasgow; 1898 Vienna; 1899 Paris'. In May 1898, a 'hearty vote of thanks' was accorded him by the general council of the ICA 'for his valuable services on the International Board'.[19]

By that date, his 34th year, Laurence O'Neill had travelled more than most of his contemporaries, and had made friends and acquaintances with people from several countries and from different religious traditions. On 24 January 1898, he was elected president of Wanderers Cycling Club[20], and the following month he represented the club on the central council of the ICA at the association's annual general meeting, during which a complete set of rules and regulations for the ICA was adopted.[21] Two years later, on 14 February 1900, he became president of the central district council of the association. The occasion was overcast, however, by the death of his father.[22] The Association's influence extended into local politics. In January 1901, it intervened in the election to the Dublin Municipal Council. Candidates were approached for their views on certain desired reforms, such as the proper laying and maintenance of streets and tramlines. Previous efforts had led to 'the passing of a universal lighting regulation'.[23] The number of people cycling had become such a feature of city life that the great majority of the candidates approached were prepared to give a written pledge of support for the reforms.

St John Gogarty on O'Neill

A less than favourable description of Laurence in these years was conveyed in the unsympathetic memoirs of Oliver St. John Gogarty, medical doctor, poet, cyclist and *poseur*. He recalled 'Larry O'Neill' as 'a dark, serious, tubby little man all in black, black knickerbockers, and black-a-vised – but there was cotton wool in his ear'. Gogarty conceded that O'Neill, during a race over which he presided in the Phoenix Park, 'suspended me for bad language at the Furzy Glen corner where all the cyclists from Ulster crashed'.[24]

Despite Gogarty's cameo, Laurence O'Neill, in the role of chairman or president, learned to carry authority lightly but firmly, and to combine eloquence, folksy humour, and a spirit of independence, with an almost old-fashioned gentlemanly courtesy that softened criticism. The spirit of independence was to be given vigorous expression during 1901 in the case of two Irish cyclists, who were banned from amateur competition by the English and Scottish cycling associations.

Confrontation and division

O'Neill and the Central District Council claimed that there was no proof of professionalism on the part of the two men, Messrs Pease and Reynolds.[25] At a special meeting of the general council of the ICA, it was decided not to send a team to the United Kingdom Championships in Glasgow because the suspension of Pease and Reynolds on 'general charges without proof' had violated and nullified the agreement between the NCU, the Scottish Association (SCU), and the ICA. The rift continued into 1904 after Pease and Reynolds had ceased to compete.[26] The English and Scottish unions complained that the ICA had not given the required three months notice before ending the agreement, while the ICA demanded an apology for the unjustified condemnation of two of their members.

At the annual general meeting of the general council of the ICA, on 23 March 1904, Mr R. McCann moved a motion that 'in order to remove the unfortunate dispute' the ICA would 'express regret for breaking the agreement without tendering the three months notice stipulated in the same'. In support of the motion he emphasised the damage that had occurred to public support and attendances 'by not having competitors from England and Scotland at Irish meetings'. O'Neill saw the proposal as capitulation and vigorously opposed it. 'If the motion were passed and the apology tendered, the association would know him no more'. The motion was lost by three votes. In subsequent discussion, it was decided to write to the secretary of the *Union Cycliste International* for affiliation to that body. The chairman of the general council of the ICA, Mr. C.P. Redmond, then requested that he be permitted to act as delegate of the ICA at a meeting in London to decide upon the terms of a settlement. This was agreed provided he acted with the assistance of three other members, Messrs Low, Rennie, and Laurence O'Neill. At the London meeting, Mr Redmond did not consult with his colleagues, Messrs Low, Rennie and O'Neill. Nevertheless, on 27 July 1904 the *Irish Cyclist* paid tribute to his bringing the dispute to an end.

The central district council of the ICA, however, was not happy with the agreement. Laurence O'Neill 'voiced what was probably a general feeling of the delegates of the centre by saying that ...Mr Redmond had acted illegally and against the proposals of the general council, and that he had been hoodwinked into agreeing with what he knew to be false and untrue, and he hoped they were not going to allow the president of their centre, that is to say, Mr O'Neill himself, to be insulted by being left out of the conference.' The district council passed a motion stating that Redmond acted illegally in not calling on Low, Rennie, and O'Neill, and that a special meeting of the general council be called to discuss the matter.[27]

Weariness with the dispute, however, was perceptible. The *Irish Cyclist* noted that the Ulster and South East district centres were for the agreement. At the special meeting of the general council of the ICA, in November 1904, Mr R. McCann presided in the absence of Mr Redmond, who was stated to be ill. 'The settlement of the international dispute' was approved, but the recommendation was made that the delegates add a clause to the agreement putting the onus of proof on the association calling in question the amateur status of any rider, and requiring the evidence to be submitted to the association issuing the licence... sixteen days before the meeting...'[28] The meeting followed up this rearguard action with the assertive appointment of L. O'Neill and C.P. Redmond to the international board!

By 1906, the tension between the three international cyclist bodies had passed. In June of that year, the British Empire Championships were held in Dublin, hosted by the ICA. At the dinner closing the championships, Mr McCann, presiding, proposed the first toast "to the King", and then 'Mr Larry O'Neill, in an excellent speech, proposed the toast of "the SCU and the NCU". He dealt in sympathetic terms with the cordial relations at present existing between the three bodies, and the healthy rivalry which had resulted, and he offered a hearty welcome to the SCU and NCU representatives who were present there that evening. They were all united under the one banner, they all worshipped at the one shrine, viz. the sport of cycling, "irrespective of politics or religion".[29]

The GAA ban

The reference to 'politics or religion' carried a particular poignancy and weight in that year, for in January 1906, the Gaelic Athletic Association, at its convention in Thurles, resolved that clubs affiliated to the GAA could no longer hold races under the auspices of the ICA. 'At the same meeting, a resolution was passed declaring that any athletes competing at a sports meeting organised by the police, military or navy shall not be eligible to compete at a GAA meeting.'[30]

The ban inevitably weakened the sport of cycling in Ireland, dividing registered cyclists into two camps. At the annual general meeting in April 1906, O'Neill reviewed the position of the ICA. There had been a falling off in the number of affiliations, which was a matter of regret but unavoidable in the circumstances. He paid tribute to the Irish Amateur Athletic Association, 'the members of which had gone even further in their support of the ICA than they had promised'.[31] On 27 June 1906, it was observed that 'not a single racing man of repute' had 'raced at GAA meetings'.[32] Nevertheless, the split continued and was destined to expand as things Gaelic were increasingly intertwined with being "Irish" as distinct from "Foreign".

Various developments

The arrival of a new mode of transport, the motor car, generated much enthusiasm in the early years of the new century. In 1903 the international Gordon-Bennett Motor Race, was held in County Kildare. It attracted contestants from all over Europe and received world-wide publicity.[33] The cars were weighed-in at the Royal Irish Automobile Club, Dawson Street, Dublin,[34] of which O'Neill later, and perhaps then, was a member. The following year he experienced motor racing nearer home, on the "velvet strand" at Portmarnock. Among the international contestants was a former winner of the Gordon-Bennett race, Selwyn F. Edge. Speed trials were organised by the Royal Irish Automobile Club in September 1904. The cars had two miles of smooth sand on which to race. The event attracted around 5,000 people from all sections of society. [35]

The years 1900-1910 were marked by a swirl of developments likely to influence O'Neill and his family. Enthusiasm for the Irish language brought about its academic recognition; the long struggle for university education for the majority of the population resulted in the National University Act; social developments were heralded by the Land Act of 1903, the arrival of James Larkin and the foundation of the Irish Transport and General Workers' Union, and the Housing of the Working Class Act, which increased the powers of local authorities to deal with Dublin's appalling housing problem. On the political side, Arthur Griffith's Sinn Féin appeared in 1906, with its emphasis on national pride and self-reliance, while the Irish Parliamentary Party grew in strength to the point of obtaining from Prime Minister Asquith, in December 1909, the promise of self-government for Ireland. Two months later, following the general election, January-February 1910, the Irish Party held the balance of power in the House of Commons. That year, Laurence O'Neill embarked on a public career. He sought election to the Dublin City Council.

In his favour was the likely support of the nationalist party machine, his gregarious personality, and a certain amount of public recognition as cyclist and businessman, and as the eloquent president of a fairly widely known organisation. A key consideration in O'Neill's going forward had to be the support of his able, adaptable wife, and the circumstance that their children were at an age when they were not likely to be unsettled by his involvement in public life.

Laurence O'Neill's career provides some clues to the motivational factors in his decision. He was endowed with abundant energy. His active involvement in the world of cycling made it evident that he needed more to occupy him than running a business. Although he demonstrated enterprise early on, and had the reputation of being a successful businessman, he had no desire to accumulate wealth. On the contrary, he was almost a spendthrift with what he had. O'Neill had a strong social conscience and also liked to be appreciated as munificent. In 1908 he had donated some of his land for a nine-hole golf course for the local community in Portmarnock. He was also drawn to public life by the skills he had acquired, and the success he enjoyed in the committees of the ICA, and by his awareness of his own capacity compared to a number of the city councillors he knew. And there was the attraction of the City Council itself, with its long history, and the fact that, in the absence of an Irish parliament, it had, on occasion, a country-wide standing and influence. In addition, it was proving a testing ground for future members of a Home Rule parliament; and, above all, it was responsible for the upkeep of the city, the welfare of its citizens, especially the poorer ones, and the promotion of business.

Laurence O'Neill's development as a public figure, and his contribution to Irish history, came through his association with Dublin Corporation. It is important, therefore, to recall at this point something of its more recent history prior to 1910, and to examine its structures, powers and responsibilities.

Notes

1   National Library of Ireland (NLI). Ir.CB 0518

2   Idem, p. 19

3   NLI. Ir. CB 0518

4   ONFP

5   NLI. ILB 05

6   *Irish Cyclist* July-Dec. 1895

7   Idem, 23 Jan 1895

8   Idem, 30 Jan. 1895

9   T.J. Morrissey. *William J. Walsh, Archbishop of Dublin,1841-1921* (Dublin 2000), pp. 173ff

10   Editorial in *Irish Cyclist*, 3 Jan. 1894

11   *Irish Cyclist,* Oct-Dec. issue, 14 Nov. 1894, p.64

12   Idem, vol. x, no. 50, 10 Oct. 1894

13   *The Irish Wheelman,* Wed. 12 June 1895, p. 907

14   *Irish Cyclist,* 5 June 1895, p. 880

15   Idem, 12 June 1895, p. 908

16   Idem, p. 909

17   Idem, 12 Feb. 1896, Editorial, p.457

18   Idem, Oct-Dec issue 1894. Letter to editor by O'Neill on 9 Nov. critical of Dr McCabe and the registration committee of the ICA

19   Idem, 11 May 1898, p. 1234

20   Idem, 2 Feb, 1898

21   Idem, 23 Feb. 1898, pp.823-4

22   Idem, 28 Feb. 1900, noted that Wanderers Club, on 27 February, passed a vote of condolence to him on his father's death.

23   Idem, 2 Jan. 1901, p. 67

24   *It Isn't This Time of Year at all* (N.Y. ed. 1954), p. 74; London ed. p.43

25   *Irish Cyclist*, 14 Aug. 1901, pp. 843-4

26   Idem, 17 Feb. 1904, in editorial on "The International Position".

27   Idem, 17 Aug. 1904

28   Idem, 20 Nov. 1904

29   Idem, 11 July 1906. The Irish did poorly in the championships, none reaching the semi-finals.

30   Idem, 31 Jan. 1906. The same meeting also placed a ban on Rugby, Association Football, Hockey, as imported games.

31   Idem, 25 April 1906

32   Idem, 27 June 1906

33   E.E. O'Donnell,S.J. *The Annals of Dublin* (Dublin 2008), p.159. The event was reported for the French press by a young James Joyce.

34   Idem.

35   Derek Stanley. *North Dublin from the Liffey to Balbriggan*, Images of Ireland series, p. 94

3.
Aspects of Dublin Corporation, 1900-1914

In Laurence O'Neill's life time, the social and political composition of Dublin Corporation underwent a major change. Into the 1860s, the city council had a powerful unionist, largely Protestant representation, which included the city's most prosperous business men, but by the end of the next decade a nationalist majority, mainly Catholic, had taken control of municipal affairs.[1]

The metamorphosis reflected the expanse of assertive nationalist feeling in the country, and the departure of thousands of unionists to the suburbs. The drift of the better-off to the suburbs was a European phenomenon prompted, among other factors, by an idyll of country life and the desire to escape from the poverty and health hazards of life in the inner city. The "other factors" in Ireland were a mixture of economics, politics and religion. In the suburbs, many of the well-to-do had their own townships, with their own government, their commissioners, their own services, and their own rating system[2]. Many of them worked in the city, benefited from its services, but paid little in return. This was greatly resented by municipal council members seeking to run the city. Their resentment was magnified by the fact that two of the most successful suburbs, Pembroke, and Rathmines, were situated just outside the city boundary.

In major cities in Britain the problem would have been solved by extending the city boundary. This had been recommended for Dublin by a government report in 1880, but when the corporation attempted the annexation in 1899, it met with unionist resistance which the Government did not wish to override. Rathmines's commissioners canvassed wider unionist support. Edward Carson and Colonel Sanderson, later so prominent against Irish Home Rule, rallied with the political argument that what was at issue was not the economic needs of the city, but the overriding and marginalising of efficient and loyal unionists by corrupt and inefficient nationalists.[3] The denigration of members of the corporation as corrupt and inefficient was a feature of comment in the *Irish Times* and other unionist papers, and it found further ammunition in the 1898 Local Government Act which abolished all special property qualifications for holding office, and opened the municipal council not just to grocers and small merchants, but to social revolutionaries or others who had no business experience and would be expected to squander taxpayers' money.

The political fears behind the criticism were intensified by the corporation's history of provocative manifestations of nationalism, which did little to solicit government support. Thus, in 1885 the members of the city council refused an address of welcome to the Prince of Wales, and two years later elected as lord mayor, T.D. Sullivan, then serving a prison term for his activities during the Plan of Campaign. There was also a nationalist assertion in the erection of public statues to O'Connell, Smith-O'Brien and Parnell, while showing reluctance towards commemorations for Queen Victoria and Prince Albert and eventually locating their statues away from public thoroughfares.[4]

The 1898 Local Government Act both terminated the current corporation and, as mentioned, required an election to a new body under a broadened franchise. Nearly 120 candidates stood for sixty vacancies. Although membership rose to eighty after 1910, the results of the January 1898 election broadly mirrored the kind of body that Laurence O'Neill was to join. Forty-five of the sixty seats were occupied by nationalists (generally supporters of the Irish Parliamentary Party). The remaining seats were shared by unionists, who had seven, and labour, with eight. The success of labour in topping the poll in three of the fifteen electoral wards, and thereby becoming aldermen,[5] occasioned additional concern to the *Times* at this irrational support for revolutionaries. The men elected were, in fact, moderate tradesunionists.[6]

The nationalists met with new political opposition following the foundation of Arthur Griffith's Sinn Féin in 1906, but both groups agreed on such key factors as: the extension of the city boundaries, the improvement of the living conditions of the poorer population, the expansion of technical education, and, with some disagreements, support for the "legitimate aspirations of labour".[7] Otherwise, an inordinate amount of members' time was taken up by political controversy. An occupational profile of the municipal council from 1899 to the start of the world war in 1914, manifests that the largest representative group, from 34 to 38 members, came from 'small merchants, publicans, wine merchants, and licensed grocers'. Others in small numbers, never more than ten, were builder/contractors, manufacturers, company directors/insurance managers, artisans, professional men, members of parliament, and some 'gentlemen'. Probably no group benefited more from municipal office than publicans and licensed grocers. In a city where they were frequently under attack from temperance organisations and others determined on curbing the abuse of alcohol through local ordinances or legislation, they availed of municipal office and political activity.[8]

Dublin Corporation, in the years after 1910, had 80 members. They were elected for a period of three years. An alderman, that is someone who topped the poll in the local election, was elected for six years. Membership was so constructed that one-third of the members retired each year. New elections were held every January. Meetings took place on a Monday on a regular basis at City Hall, Cork Hill. There were also quarterly meetings and special meetings as the need arose. To a newcomer to the corporation like Laurence O'Neill, the extent of its powers, duties, and areas of responsibilities must have been intimidating. The council derived its powers from municipal corporation acts, various local acts, and acts relating to public health and the housing of the poorer population. It was also empowered to levy "the Poor Rate" to meet the expenses of the boards of guardians that managed the workhouses of the North and South Dublin Unions. Although the council met in general session at frequent intervals, it conducted the main work of administration through smaller standing committees – responsible for finance and leases, improvements to roads etc., public health, waterworks, paving, cleansing, lighting and markets. These, in turn, supervised the work of the permanent staff of salaried employees serving the corresponding corporation departments. The number of staff at the turn of the century was around 100, but it increased with the expansion of engineering, electrical, and public health undertakings. By 1916, the number of non-manual, full-time employees exceeded 400 persons.

There were also a number of subsidiary committees, to which might be appointed private individuals and, on occasion, representatives of bodies such as the Dublin Trades Council. These sub-committees monitored such matters as the progress of technical education, and public libraries. Members of the corporation were also appointed to the boards of public and private institutions that received corporation grants, such as city hospitals and the Royal Irish Academy of Music, or levies in the case of the Port and Docks Board.[9]

The city council obtained its income mainly from poundage rates levied under the following headings: improvements, grand jury cess, district sewer, domestic water, and, after 1907, public libraries. The council also levied non-municipal rates to meet the costs of the chief commissioner of the Dublin Metropolitan Police, the Port and Docks Board, and the Poor Law Guardians. The Poor Rate levy was for the maintenance of the very poor in the city's two workhouses. The annual amount expended on the poor was generally in excess of £100,000. Belfast, by comparison, despite its larger population, spent less than half that amount. Additional sources of income included the considerable growing revenue from private and industrial electricity supply accounts, rents from corporation properties, proceeds from the sale of water for industrial purposes, and an annual sum of over £10,000 from the tramway company for way leaves. At no time, however, was the city council's income sufficient to meet current expenses. By 1916, expenses were running close to £900,000 a year, and the corporation's total indebtedness stood at £2.75 million.[10]

Dublin, like most municipalities, resorted to borrowing to find the revenue it dared not extort from resentful ratepayers. But there were statutory limits to the amount of debt the corporation might incur. Its margin for borrowing, under the Public Health Act of 1878,[11] was set at twice the city's rateable value, which, after 1900, was the smallest valuation of the large cities of Britain and Ireland. This was mainly because Dublin, as seen earlier, was denied such extensions of boundaries as brought increased population and revenue to other cities.

Despite its problems and limitations, the corporation in the 19th century cleared many slum areas in the interest of public health, and into the twentieth century hosted two successful international exhibitions as well as royal visits. The urban centre, moreover was a focus of business and commerce with elegant shopping streets. On the other hand, preoccupation with politics, and self-interest on the part of a number of members, resulted in an absence of urgency about social problems[12], and about Dublin's notorious red-light district overflowing on to the main streets of the city. In this last case, it took a public lecture by a well-known clergyman, Rev. John Gwynn, S.J., to evoke some acknowledgement of the problem from the municipal council. In 1910, the year Laurence O'Neill was elected, Gwynn declared that 'he could speak from experience when he said that the principal streets of London, of Brussels, of the great cities of Germany and France had by no means the air of… looseness and depravity which invaded our main thoroughfares with the fall of the night'. Following the publicity generated by the address, the city council, under the acting chairmanship of Alderman Dr McWalter, was moved to pass his feeble motion – 'That the attention of the police authorities be directed to an excerpt from an address delivered in Dublin this week by a clergyman'.[13]

Despite the anaemic response, medical doctor, Alderman James C. McWalter, B.L., was a highly respected and reforming figure in the municipal council. Laurence O'Neill was soon impressed by him and, in his first year on the council, wisely associated himself with many of McWalter's proposals.

In the succeeding chapters the terms City Council and Corporation seem interchangeable at times. From 1841-2001, the term City Council was applied to the elected representatives who formed the local government of the city; while Corporation, in practice, was applied to the elected representatives and the unelected officials working together.

Notes

1   The unionist representation including leading business families such as Guinness, D'Arcy, Jameson, Fry, and Pim. See Mary Daly. "Dublin Life" in T. Kennedy (ed.) *Victorian Dublin*, p. 86

2   Ruth McManus. *Dublin 1910-1940. Shaping the City and the Suburbs* (Dublin 2002), p. 13

3   Mary Daly, art. cit., op. cit. p.8; R. McManus op. cit. p. 13

4   R. McManus. Op. cit.

5   The office of alderman conveyed no special authority, but the holder enjoyed a six-year term (compared to the councillor's three years). He had the privilege of wearing scarlet robes on ceremonial occasions.

6   J.V. O'Brien. *"Dear Dirty Dublin", a City in Distress, 1899-1916* (London 1982), pp. 78-9

7   Idem, p. 78

8   Idem, p. 80

9   Idem

10   Idem, pp. 75-6

11   Idem, pp. 76-7. Section 238 (2) of the Health Act

12   R. McManus. Op.cit. pp. 14-15

13   Dublin City Archives (DCA) Mins. Municipal Council, 19 Oct. 1910, p. 483

Laurence O'Neill, 1864-1943
Lord Mayor of Dublin, 1917-1924
Patriot and Man of Peace

4.

Making Progress in the Corporation, 1910-1912

O'Neill was elected to the municipal council for the Rotunda Ward, a peculiar shaped area running from the Royal Canal to the north to Great Britain Street to the south, and bounded by Capel Street and Dorset Street to the west, and Mountjoy Ward to the east. It contained the Rotunda Hospital, but also Kings Inn Street and places where he was well known.

His name first appears in the list of corporation members on Monday, 17 January, 1910.[1] He was one of 43 councillors and 15 aldermen. Among the councillors were figures already well known or destined to become so: Joseph P. Nannetti, M.P., J.P., Ernest Bewley, Lorcan G. Sherlock, Michael Doyle, High Sheriff, Alderman Tom Kelly, and William T. Cosgrave. The meetings of the corporation took place in the council chamber, City Hall, Cork Hill. At his first two meetings, O'Neill was not recorded as voting. He was evidently observing and learning. On 23 January, however, he participated in the election for the office of High Sheriff. He voted for Ald. Farrell, who was the first choice of the three candidates presented to the Lord Lieutenant for appointment.[2]

When the Town Clerk submitted the list of the standing committees for the year ending 23 January 1913, Clr. O'Neill found himself on the Lighting Committee, one of eleven members.[3] The committee had 'charge of all matters pertaining to gas and electric lighting within the city, except those in charge of the Electricity Supply Committee'.[4] The matters to be covered included payment of staff, rates of same, sanctioning of wages and bonuses, as well the laying of thousands of yards of cable and the tenders for such work, meeting the growing demand for electric lighting, gauging and deciding a lighting time for different areas and special occasions, and dealing with telephone extensions.[5] On 23 February, O'Neill proposed his first motion, which protested at the action of the Lord Lieutenant in passing over Ald. Farrell, the first choice of the municipal council for High Sheriff, in favour of Clr. Robert Bradley, J.P. The motion, with a minor amendment, was carried.[6] Farrell was on the Lighting Committee with O'Neill. The latter's work on the Lighting Committee was recognised on 8 April by his appointment, with Ald. McWalter and Clr. Sherlock, to attend the convention of the Municipal Electoral Association to be held in Glasgow from 14-17 June.[7] In the event, as expenses were not allowed, the three delegates did not attend the convention.[8]

Supporting reform

It is perceptible from the minutes of the municipal council that Laurence O'Neill, in his first year on the council, admired and felt an affinity with the active and socially conscious Dr Ald. McWalter. Again and again, he seconded the latter's motions, which were usually concerned with alleviating the conditions of the poorer section of the population or improving the efficiency of the corporation.[9]

On 3 October, when McWalter was acting lord mayor, O'Neill seconded yet another of his reforming proposals. This time he took issue with 'the custom of promoting pecuniary or other testimonials for the benefit of members of the council, towards which the employees of the council feel themselves constrained to contribute', and he moved 'that no subscriptions should be accepted from employees of the council for such testimonials.'[10]

Other matters

A pleasing tradition in the corporation was to extend sympathy to bereaved families of public figures, irrespective of political or religious persuasion. On 12 May, the council expressed sincere sympathy and condolence to the Royal Family on the death of his Majesty King Edward VII.[11] Three months later, the Rt. Hon. Winston Churchill, Home Secretary, conveyed the thanks of the King (George V) and Queen to Dublin Corporation for their resolution.[12]

O'Neill had a high attendance record during his first year on the council. He was at ease in his new surroundings, and was well respected. Moreover, his time and prominence in the Lighting Committee may have been of benefit to his business and to adjoining areas. The report of that committee for the quarter ending 31 March 1910, noted that among the extensions of the mains in the previous three months was an extension 'from the Haymarket substation along Smithfield to supply the premises of Messrs. John O'Neill and Sons', and that 'the committee decided in connection with this supply to continue the main to the end of Smithfield, so as to link in the North King street and North Brunswick street mains';[13] a development likely to promote his popularity locally and to strengthen his vote in the Rotunda Ward.

A troubled New Year

The year 1911 was marked by upheaval and disagreement, especially in the Dublin region. There was a haemorrhage of strikes as James Larkin expanded his union amongst transport and general workers; there was excitement and disagreement arising from the royal visit by the new monarch, George V; women's agitation for political franchise generated mixed feelings; and there was a defiant assertion by the corporation in the form of a majestic statue of Parnell, at the northern end of the city's main thoroughfare, the unveiling of which was attended by the members in full regalia. The maelstrom of events, against a background of grinding poverty, unemployment, and a seemingly heedless government, evoked uncertainty about the future.

Reform and the poorer classes

The extent and depth of poverty weighed heavily on O'Neill and McWalter. Although O'Neill's attendance at meetings in 1911 was not as regular as in the previous year, he was active, in conjunction with McWalter and others, in seconding and even proposing motions. He shared McWalter's view that as there had been an 'enormous increase in the salaries and wage lists' of the corporation in recent years, it was appropriate, in the light of the poverty and unemployment in the city, that all excessive expenditure in the corporation's areas of responsibility be avoided, while everything possible be done to alleviate the condition of the poorer classes.[14] Some successful amendments were put forward also against proposals seeking a rise in wages, and both men made several unsuccessful attempts to have the lord mayor's salary reduced.

A number of forward-looking proposals benefiting the poorer classes were proposed by McWalter and seconded by O'Neill. Among them was the motion that the corporation requests the government to pass a bill providing 'insurance against sickness and invalidism...for the poorer classes', and that the government bring in as soon as possible 'a Provision for the Unemployed Bill, whereby persons willing to work may be kept from starvation or the workhouse by state aid'.[15] Both men also continued their quest for greater efficiency and accountability. They sought an account of how the duties of the office of High Sheriff had been discharged,[16] and moved successfully that it was 'not in the best interests of the city' to have 'a certain set of members' elected indefinitely to the Port and Docks Board, and that the system be changed so that other members might be elected in rotation.[17]

A particular abuse in the procedures for advancement in the corporation, led to a change in rotation between McWalter and O'Neill. The latter moved and McWalter seconded that the practice by corporation officials of seeking salary increases and promotion by 'personal and indirect canvassing' of members of the municipal council had 'a tendency to humiliate the employee and to interfere with the impartial conduct of public affairs by the representatives of the people' and that consequently 'all employees' were 'instructed to refrain from such practices under pain of dismissal from the service of the corporation', and that henceforth employees seeking higher position or increases of salary should 'make formal application for same in writing only to their respective committees or to this council'.[18]

Unemployment and major railway dispute

Unemployment was a very serious issue for the municipal council. The members' concern was greatly heightened by the fever of industrial unrest during the year, and especially by the declaration of an all-Ireland strike in September 1911 against the Great Southern and Western Railway. By early October the situation was at its most critical stage. The immediate occasion of the dispute was a walk-out by the workers when the company insisted on their handling "tainted" goods because of the company's carrier obligations. The all-Ireland withdrawal of labour, which threatened to paralyse the trade of the country, met with a steely response from the directors of the G.S.W.R. They brought in workers and drivers from England to keep the trains running. On 28 September, the company informed the strikers' representatives that before workers could be reinstated each would have to sign an undertaking to accept all traffic offered, and even then the company reserved the right to re-employ. The uncompromising chairman, Sir William Goulding, made clear that the directors were 'determined at any cost to re-man the system'.[19]

On 2 October, the corporation decided to intervene 'in the interests of Ireland and Dublin'. It passed a resolution requesting 'the Directors of Irish Railways to re-instate all the employees' and asking that the Directors would receive a deputation from the municipal council 'in reference to this resolution'. On the suggestion of Ald. Thomas Kelly, it was agreed that the members of the deputation should also act as 'a Conciliation Board for all disputes now existing', and that the following should be the members of the deputation: 'Aldermen Bergin, Corrigan, Bewley, and Flanagan, and Councillors Ireland, Laurence O'Neill, and Sherlock'.[20]

The approval of a conciliation board by the corporation was an important step forward, but it is unlikely that the deputation met the directors. Two days later, on 4 October, the workers' representatives accepted the company's terms. The united, unyielding stance of the directors served as a template for William Martin Murphy and other employers in the great strike/lock out of 1913.

Previous to the approval of a conciliation board, the municipal council had been requested by the secretary of the Dublin Industrial Development Association to appoint six delegates to attend the seventh All-Ireland Industrial Conference. In response, the council appointed six members, three of whom – Clrs. Sherlock, Laurence O'Neill, and Ald. Corrigan,[21] were subsequently named, as above, for the conciliation board, suggesting, perhaps, a perceived ability on their part for conciliation and arbitration. Certainly, O'Neill was particularly gifted in this respect as was to become evident on numerous occasions during his terms as Lord Mayor.

Supporting women's franchise

At a more political level, McWalter and O'Neill supported the Women's Franchise League, headed by Mrs J.H. Cousins, Mrs Hanna Sheehy Skeffington, M.A., and Mrs W. Palmer.[22] The excitement generated on occasion by the franchise issue was conveyed in the *Dublin Saturday Post's* report on the corporation meeting of 8 April 1911. Clr. Quaid put forward the motion that the corporation should support the forthcoming Women's Suffrage Bill, currently before parliament, and that the lord mayor and some members of the municipal council and civic officers should present a supporting petition at the Bar of the House of Commons. A lively discussion followed, with interjections from the gallery. The newspaper reporter observed that when Dr McWalter was supporting the motion 'the female occupants of the gallery were now beside themselves with enthusiasm and seemed to be vying with each other in suggesting fresh points to Dr McWalter to enlarge upon'. When Ald Kelly moved a contrary amendment he was greeted with hisses and cries of 'Get Out' from the gallery. O'Neill voted for the motion, which was carried by 22 votes to 9. Subsequently, the executive committee of the National Union of Women's Suffrage Societies passed a resolution thanking the corporation 'for their decision to present a petition for women's suffrage at the Bar of the House of Commons'.[23]

At the same corporation meeting of 8 April, there were further "lively scenes" when Clr. William Ireland proposed that the corporation present an address of welcome to His Majesty, King George V, on the occasion of his visit to Dublin. The *Dublin Saturday Post* reported that the public gallery was crowded, and among the large attendance were ladies connected with the Daughters of Erin and prominent members of the Irish Women's Franchise League. Laurence O'Neill voted for an amendment moved by Clr. Briscoe that as Ireland was still deprived of its parliament, the council should proceed with the next business. The amendment was carried by 42 votes to 9, and 'the result was received with loud cheers in the gallery, the ladies being most demonstrative'.

Welcome and honours

Despite such dissident reactions to the royal visit, George V received an enthusiastic public welcome when he visited Dublin and its neighbourhood from 7-12 July. The political state of mind was far from consensus, a virtual mosaic of views and allegiances. Responding to the public welcome, the lord mayor, John J. Farrell, made the case on 8 July, that as His Majesty's father, Edward VII, had expunged from the coronation oath the words critical of the Mass, which had given so much offence to Catholics, it was fitting that a civic welcome be given to his son, George V, by Dublin Corporation. Even this appeal to religion left the municipal council unmoved.

Before the end of the month, on the other hand, the council agreed to honour two Irish language scholars with the freedom of the city: Dr Kuno Meyer, founder and director of the School of Irish Learning, and Rev. Peter Canon O'Leary, P.P., author, and vice-president of the Gaelic League. Laurence O'Neill was named among the members appointed to make the required preparations for the bestowal of the Freedom of Dublin on the two men. [24]

Ordinary business in the New Year

At the beginning of the year, O'Neill was appointed to the markets committee in addition to the lighting committee.[25] The former dealt with the requirements of the cattle, sheep, and wholesale food markets, along with issues such as the granting of petroleum and carbide licences, including the approval of plans submitted by Messrs A. Guinness and Company for the storage of petroleum in tanks.[26] It was an appropriate committee for Laurence O'Neill to be engaged with, given his father's expanding business. *Thom's Directory* for 1911 reported that John O'Neill was a corn, hay and potato factor with bruising and grinding mills at 45 Smithfield. His son was described as a city councillor, at the same address but also at Riverside, Portmarnock, County Dublin.

Public and corporation politics in 1912

The introduction of the Home Rule Bill in the House of Commons, in April 1912, added to the grip of the nationalists on Irish politics, through the agency of the United Irish League (U.I.L), the party machine supporting the Irish Parliamentary Party. In municipal politics in 1912, the nationalists continued to be the controlling element. They held a large majority in members, reserved to themselves the lord mayoralty, and dominated those committees which determined the nature and extent of the annual expenditure of city revenue. Fortunately, most of the corporation's business was free of party issues, and the nationalist majority did not always operate as a solid front against their political opponents, the few Sinn Féin and labour members. Nationalist ranks could divide on such issues as labour's concern for workers' rights, or Sinn Féin's regard for the use of the Irish language.

The January municipal elections of 1912, besides, brought harbingers of political change. Despite the powerful party machine, the nationalists found themselves seriously under attack in certain wards. They were challenged and defeated in places where they had reigned supreme. The new challengers were James Larkin and his supporters. They were successful in five wards. By-elections during 1912, and municipal elections the following January, would bring the labour voice up to nine, though these, in alliance with Sinn Féin, could muster no more than thirteen votes against the nationalists' fifty-five. Nevertheless, the passion of Larkin and his adherents for the cause of the workers and on social justice issues succeeded, from time to time, in winning to their side nationalists like Laurence O'Neill.

On 22 January 1912, following Larkin's election to the municipal council, Clr. O'Neill seconded a successful motion by Clr. Alfred Byrne, in support of Larkin's highly controversial newspaper: 'that a portion of the advertising of each committee (of the corporation) be given for insertion in the *Irish Worker* at the usual rates'.[27] Some eight months later, when the council came to fill the vacancy resulting from Larkin's arrest and disqualification arising out of a labour dispute in Cork, O'Neill seconded an amendment by Ald. Thomas Kelly, Sinn Féin, conveying the council's regrets at 'the means taken to prevent Mr Larkin from remaining a member of this council'. The motion and the amendment were carried, although such prominent members as the Lord Mayor Clr Sherlock, Ald. McWalter, and Clrs. Byrne and Beattie, voted against it.[28]

Supporting the first woman councillor

Early in the year, on 22 January, at the same meeting in which advertising space was given to the *Irish Worker*, the first woman to be elected to the corporation, Miss Sarah Harrison, was present. She was well-known as a portrait painter, as a supporter of the distressed and unemployed, and a promoter of a municipal art gallery. She was also the sister of Henry Harrison, secretary to Charles Stewart Parnell; and she was elected to the corporation as an Independent (Parnellite) Nationalist.[29] During 1912 she served with O'Neill on the markets committee, and he appears to have made a particular effort to encourage and champion her work and status. On 15 April, when an invitation to send delegates to a national convention in the Mansion House to discuss the Home Rule Bill was being considered, O'Neill moved that Clr. Harrison be one of the delegates. She was one of the eight appointed.[30] He also seconded an amendment by Miss Harrison calling for a sworn inquiry into the administration of the Unemployed Workman's Act by the Dublin District Committee. She undertook to supply the town clerk with specific information in writing on the points requiring investigation. The amendment was carried by eighteen votes to five, but the demand for a sworn inquiry fell on deaf ears, despite it being repeated in the corporation on 10 June, 10 July, and at a special meeting on 2 August.

An act of political discrimination against Clr Harrison in October, led O'Neill to angrily propose, with strong backing from the council, that the corporation 'wished to place on record their strong condemnation of the attempt that has been made by the secretary of the Wood Quay branch of the U.I.L. to deprive Miss Harrison of her vote in the Rotunda Ward'. The motion was put, and Lord Mayor Sherlock, seconded by Ald. Coffey, moved a pointed addendum: 'And that the council notes that the president of the United Irish League (U.I.L.) and Councillor Swaine approve of the action of the council in this matter'. The addendum was accepted by O'Neill, and the motion, as adjusted, was put and carried.[31]

A more independent councillor

From the minutes of the municipal council for 1912, it is evident that Clr. Laurence O'Neill had become an increasingly independent but pragmatic voice in the council. He was one of ten members appointed to the electricity supply committee and, although he continued to move or support amendments deferring remuneration recommended by other committees,[32] he was careful to support remuneration recommended by his two areas of direct interest, the markets and electricity supply committees! Nevertheless, at a meeting on 6 May, he moved an unpopular amendment that further consideration of the report of the electric supply committee 'be postponed for two years'; an amendment that was roundly defeated by 39 votes to 12.[33] Nothing daunted, on 3 June he successfully opposed the report of the markets committee in its recommendation that that the pig market be moved to another site;[34] and later, on 2 September, moved that the report be adopted. His motion, which was carried, was seconded by Ald. McWalter.[35]

O'Neill still moved in tandem with McWalter, but not as much as previously. On matters of social relief, Clr. O'Neill continued to support proposals he considered important. Thus, in April he seconded a motion calling on School Attendance Officers to exercise greater care regarding the home conditions of children absent from school, before initiating prosecution[36]; and also a motion by the lord mayor supporting a proposal from the Ladies School Dinner Committee calling on Irish members of parliament to have the Free Meals Aid extended to Ireland.[37]

Various pressure groups

The corporation in those years was beset by a variety of pressure groups, political and non-political. The Gaelic League harried the city council on behalf of the Irish language movement; temperance groups decried the number of councillors associated with drink traffic; the Irish Women's Franchise League, which, apart from its political interests, championed certain social issues such as free meals for necessitous children; the Dublin Citizens Association, supported by big business establishments, which had as its chief targets fiscal irresponsibility and high rates, while also campaigning for municipal reform through the election of 'men of substance'; and the Dublin Trades Council, which raised various social issues. One intervention from the secretary of the Trades Council evoked what was, in retrospect, an egregious reaction from the lord mayor and council. The secretary transmitted a resolution from the Trades Council which urged the necessity of 'a housing scheme commensurate with the needs of the city to be erected on new ground, thus avoiding ruinously expensive slum clearances'. Responding at the council meeting on 12 August, Lord Mayor Sherlock proposed and Ald. Kerrigan seconded, 'that the Dublin United Trades Council be informed that the Corporation has initiated in the last three months schemes that will considerably tend to the settling of the Housing question'. The motion was carried.[38] The 'housing question' was to remain unsettled under British administration and well into that of an Irish government. It outlasted the corporation of which Sherlock and O'Neill were members.

Among events evoking motions of sympathy from the municipal council during 1912 were the disaster to the White Star liner, Titanic, and the suffering caused to so many people,[39] but also, perhaps unexpectedly, the death of the Jesuit priest, Matthew Russell, the benign editor of the *Irish Monthly* and sponsor of many young poets and prose writers, which the council regretted 'and the loss which the country' had 'sustained by his demise'.[40]

Wider events of significance

As O'Neill and other nationalists were celebrating in public demonstrations the prospect of Home Rule, the seeds of radical political upheaval were sown in Ulster. Unionists, strongly supported by the British Conservative Party, were prepared to defy Home Rule in arms and to contemplate partition rather than accept it. In response, there was a rising anger among the majority population at the unionist response and, especially, at the prospect of partition. A stranger reading the minutes of the Dublin Municipal Council for 1912, however, would receive little or no information on such critical developments. Like most of their contemporaries, the councillors did not grasp the significance of the present. It was not dissimilar with respect to the forthcoming social rebellion. Councillors, such as Laurence O'Neill, might empathise with James Larkin and denounce his removal from Dublin Corporation, but they little thought that, debarred from a political forum, Larkin would expend his anger and great energies so soon in a social upheaval that would have a devastating effect on the business and working population of the capital city.

Notes

1   DCA. Mins. of Municipal Council, vol. 352/04183, p. 23

2   Idem, p. 74

3   Idem, p. 76

4   Idem, p. 164

5   DCA. *Dublin Corporation Reports,* vol. 1/1910, 352/04183. Lighting Committee Report, p. 259

6   Mins. Municipal Council, no. 156, p. 92

7   Mins. no. 319

8   Mins. 19 Sept. Report of Lighting Committee, no. 163, re attendance at Electrical Conference – Report, vol.2, 1910, p. 657

9   Mins. Municipal Council (MC) pp.357, 268-9, 453, n. 381-3, 715

10   Mins. 3 Oct. n.715, p.453

11   Idem, 12 May, p. 357

12   Idem, Aug. 1910, p. 594, p

13   Report of Lighting Committee 1910, vol.2, p. 127

14   Mins. M.C. 1911, p.22

15   Idem, n.153, p.111

16   Idem, n.164, p.115

17   Idem, n.167, p.116

18   Idem, n. 331, p.246

19   Company Mins. of GSWR company, 27 Sept. 1911, cit. Peter Rigney in "Trade Unionism and the Great Southern & Western Railway, 1890-1911" (B.A. thesis, TCD), p.53

20   Mins. 2 Oct. 1911, n.672, pp. 453-4. "Laurence O'Neill", using the Christian name, was to differentiate him from another member, John O'Neill.

21   Mins. M.C. n.348, p.253. The other three members were Clrs. Beattie, Cosgrave, and Mahon

22   Idem, p. 58

23   Mins. 1911, p.301

24   *Dublin Saturday Evening Post*, 8, 22 July 1911

25   Mins. 23 Jan. 1911, pp. 46,49

26   Report of Markets Committee, vol.2, p. 507

27   Mins. M.C. 1912. Meeting of 22 Jan. n.51, p.32

28   Mins. meeting of 2 Aug. 1912, n.743, p.530. Larkin had spent time in prison, following a labour dispute in Cork. His opponents argued that a convicted felon had no place in Dublin Corporation. See Emmet Larkin. *James Larkin, Irish Labour Leader, 1876-1947* (London 1989 ed.), pp. 102-3.

29   Padraig Yeates. *A City in Wartime. Dublin 1914-1918*, p.181

30   Mins. 15 April, n.357, p. 262f

31   Mins. n.795, p. 571

32   Estates & Finance, Paving, and Improvements committees. Mins. n.31, pp.12, 16

33   Mins. n.38, p.24

34   Report of Markets Committee, 1912, vol.1, n.77, p. 791

35   Mins. meeting 2 Sept., n. 701, p.507: Report of Markets Committee, vol 2,, n.163, p.427

36   Mins. n.363, p.266

37   Mins. n. 986, p.686

38   Mins. 12 Aug., n.683, pp.494-5

39   Meeting 26 April 1912, pp. 301ff

40   Mins. p. 520

Laurence O'Neill, 1864-1943
Lord Mayor of Dublin, 1917-1924
Patriot and Man of Peace

5.
From Social Upheaval
to a World War, 1913-1914

The minutes of the Dublin Municipal Council for 1913 focussed, as usual, on the work and reports of the committees, and on notable issues that impinged on the city's interests. These, during 1913, were mainly three: a controversy over an art gallery to accommodate the paintings of Sir Hugh Lane; the great strike/lock out; and the operation and report of the departmental committee, established by the Local Government Board, to inquire into the housing conditions of the working classes in the city of Dublin.

Laurence O'Neill's year was a very busy one, and, as will appear later, not without public embarrassment. He devoted additional time and energy to the workings of the corporation. He chaired the markets committee, served on the paving committee,[1] was nominated once again for the electricity supply body but withdrew his name, was appointed to the Dublin Distress Committee,[2] and to a committee of inquiry into the whole system of expenditure of the Borough Council of Dublin.[3] In addition, subsequent to seconding William Partridge's motion that 'graving docks be constructed in Dublin', he was appointed to a committee to examine the matter[4]. His support for the Irish language[5] and for equality of treatment for women was again manifest. On the matter of equality, he seconded a motion by Miss Harrison 'that seeing that the women sanitary inspectors' had the same examinations, hours, starting salary, and equally onerous hours as the men, 'the Council agree to give them equal remuneration, subject to the approval of the Local Government Board'. The motion was narrowly carried, 17 votes to 14. Its advanced nature for the time was indicated by the opposition of prominent, usually supportive figures, such as Ald. McWalter, and Lord Mayor Lorcan Sherlock[6]. On the three major issues mentioned above, O'Neill was actively concerned.

Approving an art gallery

The question of the art gallery came before the corporation as a result of the promise of Sir Hugh Lane to donate his valuable and extensive collection of paintings to the city of Dublin, provided the corporation supplied a suitable gallery to house the collection. The promise occasioned widespread interest among the more educated members of the population. A special body, the Mansion House Committee, was established to make provision for a permanent municipal art gallery. A deputation from this committee addressed the corporation to considerable effect. The lord mayor moved, and Clr. O'Neill seconded, that the council agree 'to apply £22,000 to the erection of such a gallery' on condition that the Mansion House Committee, known as 'the Citizens' Provisional Committee', provide a site free of cost and a further £3,000 towards the erection of the gallery. Ald. Vance advanced an addendum, that the foregoing was provisional on Sir Hugh Lane 'binding himself, his heirs executors, and administrators, to make an absolute gift of the paintings ... immediately the Municipal Council takes over the new municipal art gallery from the contractors'. The motion, with the addendum, was put and was passed enthusiastically by 29 votes to 2.

The council envisaged a competition for the design of the gallery that would be open to Irish architects. Many members, as a result, were taken aback when Sir Hugh Lane insisted on a celebrated British architect, Edwin L. Lutyens, undertaking the design. Lutyens recommended a bridge-gallery built over the River Liffey, replacing the well-known Hapenny-footbridge. On 23 June, 1913, the Mansion House Committee presented to the corporation a report recommending the Lutyens design. Clr. John S. Kelly proposed the adoption of the report and Clr Laurence O'Neill seconded it. The design, however, evoked strong criticism from many quarters, including disapproving deputations from the Dublin Central Highway Committee and the River Liffey Protection Association. Prominent citizens, such as Lord Ardilaun (Arthur Edward Guinness) and William Martin Murphy, who were expected to contribute towards the project, withdrew their support. The design was represented as impractical on a number of counts, including the prospect of damage to the paintings from the damp rising from the river.

Nevertheless, a vigorous campaign was waged on behalf of the Lutyens conception. W.B. Yeats and Lady Gregory were among its protagonists. At a special meeting in City Hall, on 5 September, the council rejected the bridge site by 23 votes to 21. Laurence O'Neill voted for the project. An angry Yeats published in the *Irish Times* the poem *September 1913*, an attack on what he perceived as the philistinism of the opponents of the design, who 'add the halfpence to the pence' and 'dried the marrow from the bone'.

A final effort to save the Lutyens project was made by Clr. Miss Harrison at a corporation meeting on 19 December. The original estimate for £22,000 had risen to £45,000 with the Lutyens design. She proposed that the council approve of the erection of an art gallery on a site over the Liffey, near the Metal Bridge, and the Mansion House Committee would guarantee a sum equal to the difference between £22,000 and £45,000; moreover, if they further agreed to the Lutyens design, Sir Hugh Lane would guarantee any sum over £45,000 as well as the architect's fees[7]. When the motion was put, a decisive amendment was moved by Clr. Ireland, and seconded by Clr. William Cosgrave, that the council, while being grateful to Sir Hugh Lane for his most generous offer, 'is strongly of the opinion that the Bridge Site… is not the most suitable – it being expensive, unpopular, and highly impractical' – and 'hereby requests Sir Hugh Lane not to insist on the Bridge Site, but to leave the selection of site and the inviting of designs for the building to the discretion of the Council'. The amendment received 32 votes to 25 against. On the amendment being put as a substantive motion, it was carried by a similar margin. O'Neill, McWalter, and Lord Mayor Sherlock, who had been supportive from the start, voted against the amendment[8].

Yeats's public criticism did not help the cause of the gallery. By September, besides, a far more weighty matter than an expensive art gallery was occupying the attention of the councillors. The city was in the throes of economic chaos and bitter division.

The great strike and lock out

The great Dublin strike began on 26 August 1913, when tramway men belonging to Jim Larkin's Transport and General Workers' Union abandoned their vehicles in the centre of the city. In quick succession, from 30 August to 1 September, there were manifestations of labour unrest and a series of police baton-charges. On 2 September there was shock at the collapse of tenement houses in Church Street killing seven people. It was a further testimony to landlord neglect and the dire poverty of much of the population. The following day, the members of the Dublin Employers' Federation made a fateful decision. They decided to require of their employees a pledge not to belong to the Irish Transport and General Workers Union. This violation of a worker's right to choose his union, brought support for the strikers from British unions, and the prolongation of the dispute. The strike, which had become a lock out, engendered hardship and suffering for the workers and their families, and fear and hostility among large sections of the middle class citizens. The bitterness of the conflict was heightened, if not generated, by a clash of personalities: Larkin virulently determined to unionise the companies of Dublin's largest employer, William Martin Murphy; and the latter determined to rally employers to put a stop to Larkin's dominance of the commercial life of the city.

Much of the public press was highly critical of the workers, who were depicted as being led by anarchists and communists hostile to religion and to private ownership. The municipal council was divided on the conflict. The nationalist majority and Arthur Griffith's Sinn Féin were opposed to the strike, which they saw as destructive of city business and as undermining Ireland's claimed capacity to manage its own affairs. Among the nationalists in the corporation, nevertheless, there were some, like Laurence

O'Neill, with strong labour sympathies; indeed, although there is no mention in the minutes of the council, O'Neill at some stage spoke out strongly and openly in support of the workers. More than a decade later, the secretary of the ITGWU, William O'Brien, would assure him that the union would never forget his support for them when they were in great trouble and had very few friends.[9]

On 31 August, one of the most publicised events during the lock out took place. Following the dramatic appearance of Larkin in O'Connell Street, and his subsequent arrest, the police overreacted and baton-charged the numerous bystanders and others in the vicinity. The day became remembered as 'Bloody Sunday'. The *Dublin Saturday Post* of 6 September reported that the municipal council meeting on 1 September was long and stormy, with some members blaming the police and the Government for the excessive use of batons, while others defended the police and blamed Larkin. Ald. Dr McWalter brought a down-to-earth realism to the debate, pointing out that he was in his surgery on 31 August 'and it was crowded with absolutely harmless, inoffensive citizens, returning from devotions, who had been batoned. They made the grave complaint that many of the constabulary were drunk'. The fact that over 400 fellow-citizens had to be treated for injuries, induced Lord Mayor Sherlock to move 'that this Council... demands an immediate public inquiry into the general conduct of the police..., and into the question of instructions given by those responsible to the Executive Authorities. And that a copy of the resolution be forwarded to the Lord Lieutenant, the Chief Secretary for Ireland, and Chief Commissioner of Police'.[10] The motion, which was supported by Clr. O'Neill, was carried. Subsequently, the council formed a committee of ten members to examine the 'present condition of affairs in the city with a view to having peace and order restored'[11]. The ten included O'Neill. The meeting further proposed that the Archbishops of Dublin, Drs Walsh and Peacock, be requested to invite a conference between the tramway directors and Clr. Partridge and four of the tramway men on strike. Two days later, on 3 September, O'Neill and the other members of the corporation were among the great concourse of people who attended the funeral of James Nolan, a labouring man, who had been critically injured by the police the previous Saturday night. A painful sight 'was the number of men and women and even children who had bandaged heads'.[12]

In the course of his impassioned address to the council on 1 September, Lord Mayor Lorcan Sherlock had threatened that if the authorities refused to hold a public inquiry into the events on 31 August, he, as lord mayor, would hold a public inquiry 'in the most public manner'[13]. The Chief Secretary appeared to respond positively to the demand for an inquiry, but no government action followed. On 19 December, at a special meeting of the council, O'Neill seconded a motion by McWalter, that the council desired 'to press upon the Government the necessity of fulfilling the promise of the Chief Secretary of a public inquiry into the conduct of the police on the 30th and 31st August last'[14]. The motion was carried but had no further effect, and the lord mayor did not fulfil his threat.

In the meantime, on 29 September, the Government announced an inquiry into the dispute under the aegis of the Board of Trade. The inquiry was chaired by a man with a reputation in industrial relations, George Asquith, and it became known as the Asquith Inquiry. Major figures on both sides, as well as other witnesses, were interviewed, and recommendations were made, but, in the end, the efforts of the inquiry, like those of the two archbishops, were frustrated by the intransigence of the employers.

An effect on himself

The strike fever in Dublin came to impinge personally on Laurence O'Neill, as proctor or merchant, before the end of the year. The ITGWU's withdrawal of labour extended to farm hands in County Dublin. He found himself caught between two affinities. He empathised with the stance of labour, but many of the farmers were both his customers and fellow nationalists. One of the most prominent of the farmers and nationalists was P.J. Kettle, with whom, and with John Dillon, M.P., O'Neill had shared a platform at a large Home Rule demonstration, in Swords,[15] County Dublin, on 26 April.

At the beginning of November 1913, P.J. Kettle consigned to him at the market two loads of vegetables. Kettle's men were on strike. Employees at the market, who were members of the Irish Transport and General Workers' Union, immediately raised the cry "tainted goods". It took O'Neill's gifts of persuasion, and his known labour sympathies, to calm a difficult situation. The newspaper report of the incident merely noted that 'after a short while the vegetables were put up for sale by Mr O'Neill and disposed of'.[16]

Accused as a 'slum landlord'

If his reputation remained largely untarnished with his labour colleagues on this market issue, O'Neill's over all standing was seriously threatened by the proceedings of the Housing Inquiry appointed by the Local Government Board for Ireland. The proceedings received extensive publicity, and he was named, together with some other members of the corporation, as a slum landlord of tenement buildings which housed families in unhygienic and poor structural conditions. The Inquiry identified three types of tenements: 'First class property' – a tenement house that was structurally sound and, if not in good repair, was capable of being put in good condition; 'Second class'- houses on the border line of being fit for human habitation; 'Third class' – 'houses unfit for human habitation and incapable of being rendered fit'. Three members of the municipal council, Ald. G. O'Reilly, Ald. Corrigan, and Clr. Crozier, were drawing rent from 9 to 18 houses described as 'third class', unfit for human habitation. Ten other members owned or were interested in one to three tenement houses. Laurence O'Neill was one of these, and was subjected to intense criticism in the public press. His name was cleared during the course of the inquiry, but not before much pain and embarrassment had been caused to him and his family by press reports. His anxiety to clear his name was very evident in his interview before the housing inspector, Mr O'Connor, who conducted the inquiry.

He heard his houses, 44 and 43 Smithfield, accommodating four families in each, described as 'first-class tenements' houses in a 'good structural and sanitary state'. He explained how he had come by the buildings. When his father died, he was looking for a place to extend his family business. He found a location at Smithfield that was owned by his uncle. They purchased nos. 45. 44, and 43, 'not as a speculation in tenement property, I assure you, but merely to extend our business'. The houses were not in 'thorough repair'. He spent about £500 on no. 45, where he and his family resided, and on the out-offices of no. 44. At that time, ten years ago (1903), he considered no.43 an eye-sore and he approached his landlord, Colonel Arthur Hortley, of Clonsilla, to take 44 and 43 off his hands and give him a separate letting for no. 45. He refused, but they came to terms. Hortley extended the lease and O'Neill promised to rebuild no.43. He did this at a cost of £537. He did not want tenement property. He had nos. 44 and 43 examined by architects, whose reports described them as in excellent order, and in 'good structural and sanitary state'.

At this point, Mr O'Connor intervened: 'So, I think you have nothing to be ashamed of'. A relieved O'Neill responded: 'I am very much obliged to you for that expression of opinion. Like my friend Cummins, I have been pilloried by the press as a slum owner, and certainly for that expression of opinion, I am very grateful to you.' He went on to explain that in rebuilding no.43 he had in mind a place for his own employees. The rents were very reasonable. He had some of the rooms let at 2 shillings, and the highest was 2 shilling and six pence (2/6d). When he first went there, the rent from no.43, a big and old house, amounted to 25 shillings a week, now the rent he was receiving, 'after spending £537 building this new house, is only 14 shillings a week'[17].

From his evidence, it seems indicated that Laurence O'Neill inherited a thriving business from his father and then extended it by moving to Smithfield, where he spent considerable sums of money on property which brought a small return. He had the reputation of being a successful businessman among his colleagues on the corporation, but already, the indications were that far from adding 'the half-pence to the pence' he was over-free in his disposal of cash and property.

At odds with the Farmers' Association

During 1913, O'Neill and his business in Smithfield suffered not only from pillorying by the press, and short-lived attacks by trade union members, but also from severe attacks by angry farmers. The occasion of this last, was the decision in April by the municipal council to change the day for the sale of hay and straw at Smithfield Market from Saturday to Friday, despite opposition from many farmers. Clr. Richardson proposed the motion, which was seconded by Clr. O'Neill. Richardson declared that holding the market on Saturday deprived many of the half-day to which they were entitled, and that both employers and employees were united on the question. O'Neill announced 'that, as one closely identified with Smithfield Market, he was altogether in favour of the proposed change, which had been sanctioned by the Markets Committee'. He went on, unnecessarily, to venture criticism of the main opposition, the County Dublin Farmers' Association:

> No doubt any suggestion to change a custom that had been in vogue
> for a century or over was regarded by farmers as a bit revolutionary,
> and that was not strange in the case of a body about whom it had been
> suggested that they were imbued with a great deal of conservative
> ideas… The only solid reason they were against it was because they
> feared that if employees in Smithfield got a half-holiday, they would
> have to do the same in the country.

In his view, 'the sooner the half-holiday on Saturday became universal the better. It would do nobody any harm to make this change'[18].

O'Neill's words evoked an angry reaction from the North Dublin District Council of the Farmers' Association. A choleric and influential member, Mr Tighe, described the corporation's decision as the work of 'a clique', 'a couple of factors in the corporation got their friends to rush things through' without consulting the farmers. He moved that 'farmers should give their produce to the factors who took no part in having the change made'. The resolution was unanimously adopted[19].

Conscious of the dependence of his business on farmers, O'Neill made a special effort to win back good will. At the end of July, when the Farmers Association complained that the introduction of a market on Mondays was in contradiction of an agreement between farmers and proctors, and also expressed concern at the corporation taking over the potato market, O'Neill made it clear that his sympathies were with the farmers. He, as a factor, had been loyal to the former arrangement, and he believed that 'from both the factors and the farmers point of view the resumption of the Monday market was the greatest mistake that could be made, and that the Association had taken the right course in protesting against it and in asking their members not to send in potatoes that day'. 'With regard to the potato market proper', he added reassuringly, the deputation from the Farmers' Association to the Market Committee had clearly expressed the farmers' case. He could say that the corporation was carefully examining the matter, 'and he did not think there would be any raising of tolls as some of them seemed to fear'. After further discussions, a resolution of support for the corporation 'buying or acquiring the rights of the present potato market' was unanimously adopted.[20]

Looking back on 1913, it had been a busy and challenging year for O'Neill as a member of the corporation. It had also brought pressure on his business and, above all, occasioned humiliation for himself and his family in his being publicly termed a slum landlord.

The New Year started on a high note. He topped the poll in the local elections and became alderman for the Rotunda Ward. Soon, however, a more depressed climate took over. The great strike was on its last legs, and workers not taking the pledge against the union were faced with unemployment or emigration. The Transport Union was depleted in numbers, almost bankrupt, and its leader's health had broken down. He was soon to leave the country. And then there was the publication of the Report on Working Class Housing, which proved even more devastating than the corporation had feared.

The Housing Report and a vigorous response, 1914

The published report caused a major stir. Accompanied by detailed photographs, it presented a horrific picture of tenement life. The corporation was accused of inadequate administration leading to over-crowding and conditions hazardous to health. Seventy-eight per cent of lettings were one room lettings, a higher percentage, with a higher rate of occupancy, than in any city in Britain.

Ald. O'Neill felt personally implicated as a landlord, while corporately sharing the municipal council's sense of outrage and frustration at being unable to respond to the attacks. The council's frustration was occasioned by the fact that the evidence on which the report was based was not published until two months later, while a favourable minority report by J.F. McCabe, signed 7 February 1914, received no publicity. McCabe disagreed that the corporation was responsible for the prevailing housing conditions:

'What the Corporation (during the short time it had powers to act) has done is to reduce by thousands the number of tenement houses' and it reduced enormously the death-rate from acute infectious maladies. 'What the Corporation has left undone is…beyond its power to effect in practice'.

The municipal council set up a sub-committee to respond to the report. Its resolute reply[21] pointed out that the corporation had protested from the start that only one member of the committee conducting the inquiry had had contact 'with the housing, sanitary and general work of the city', and, while not wishing to justify the preponderance of one-room accommodation, the report's comparison with cities in Britain should have mentioned that most of the rooms in Dublin were in old mansions, which had greater cubical capacity and air space than tenements in British cities. 'The housing problem in Dublin to-day'[22], the response continued, was 'the out-crop of generations of vicissitude in the political, manufacturing and social conditions of our people.' The report's narrow treatment of the housing problem and its unfair comparisons confused the public mind and encouraged 'the growth of a species of housing-quack which seems to flourish and luxuriate in the public press'. The sub-committee drew attention to the neglect by the press of McCabe' minority report[23], and also to the significance of paragraph 34 in the Report, which acknowledged that the corporation, since the Acts in 1890, had 'taken advantage of the powers given them to increase their borrowing and their rating powers', and that the municipal council, 'in proportion to their responsibilities, have done more for the housing of the working class than any other city in the United Kingdom.[24]' Rounding off its vigorous presentation, the municipal council's sub-committee protested that the greater part of the report was a general attack on the Corporation of Dublin in its public health administration which was proved to be without foundation by witness after witness[25].

The response came too late to gain attention. By comparison, the gruesome details of the report, trumpeted by the press, had an immediate public impact. Even the Chief Secretary for Ireland and president of the Local Government Board, Augustine Birrell, was moved to comment 'that this report cannot be allowed to rest, as so many other reports have done, in the pigeon holes of offices'[26].

Despite such an official reaction, the Government in Westminster refused to provide the preferential interest rates that would have enabled the local authorities to build working class housing in Irish urban areas. The Government feared, perhaps, that such special arrangements would give rise to demands for similar treatment in English cities. In the event, increasingly urgent appeals to the Government were ignored. The outbreak of war in August 1914 relegated local concerns to a low place in the Government's agenda.

Work in the council

Returning more immediately to Laurence O'Neill, now Alderman O'Neill, he seems to have cut back on his work in committee. He was nominated to only one committee in 1914, the standing committee for lighting. His name was put forward, however, for the office of High Sheriff, but received little support. On 10 August, six days after Britain declared war on Germany, he was elected to a special committee that would adjust the prices of food in the city for the duration of the conflict[27]. In the routine business of the council, he manifested concern for electoral reform. The number of bogus voters in the Rotunda Ward led him to introduce a proposal to rectify the situation, only to have it ruled out of order[28]. He subsequently seconded a successful motion by Clr. Richardson that was critical of a voting register stuffed with bogus votes and requested that the Finance Committee place £500 at the disposal of the town clerk to purify the list of voters.[29] Continuing his social, higher-standards campaign with Ald. McWalter, he seconded the latter's motions that no member of the corporation be allowed to utilise his public position for his private benefit, and requesting the commissioner of police, if he has power to do so, to prohibit from Dublin's streets vehicles carrying five tons or more because of the vibration caused and the danger to the city's mains and houses.[30]

Political developments

On the political scene, 1914 started quietly in Ireland. O'Neill left no information on his political views or activities during the year. It seems fair to assume that he shared many of the views of fellow nationalist supporters of the Irish parliamentary party, and that he would have been concerned in April when the Ulster Volunteers landed guns at Larne without any interference from police, and in June at the Government's 'temporary exclusion' of Ulster from the Home Rule Act. He would have shared the growing distrust of the Government, and been aware of the impetus towards a militant solution to the Irish question. Dublin was a relatively small city in 1914. O'Neill had acquaintances in the Irish Volunteers as well as in the labour and nationalist movements, and, following the example of the Ulster Volunteers, would not have been surprised at the Irish Volunteers importing arms. When they did so at Howth on 26 July, they, unlike their Ulster counterparts, found police and army waiting to disarm them as they returned to Dublin. An incensed crowd jeered and obstructed the police, and some of the soldiers opened fire, killing four people and wounding thirty. O'Neill, like the majority of the population, was shocked and angry. The Lord Mayor, Lorcan G. Sherlock, set up a fund to provide assistance for the families of the bereaved and of the wounded.

At the next meeting of the municipal council, on 10 August, there was an unreserved condemnation of 'the savage crime of Sunday, 26 July' and a call for 'the dismissal of the permanent officials of Dublin Castle who were responsible, either by direct action or by negligence, for the calling out of the military'[31]. An outraged Ald. McWalter moved 'that the officers and soldiers involved be charged with murder', a proposal later put aside.[32]

By that date, however, the public mood had begun to change. Germany had declared war on France on 3 August, and the British propaganda projecting Germany as a power-hungry aggressor had already taken hold. John Redmond, in the House of Commons, pledged Ireland's support in the event of Britain entering the war. Britain's entry into the war on 4 August, met with mixed approval in Ireland. In September, O'Neill rejoiced with most other nationalists when the Government of Ireland Act (legislating for Home Rule) was carried, even though its operation was suspended until after the war. The war rhetoric was such by 20 September that Redmond called on the Volunteers to serve 'wherever the firing line extends, in defence of right, of freedom and religion in this war'[33], and in the corporation, according to Clr. William Partridge, an amendment, postponing a motion of congratulations to Mr Redmond, was met with a criticism from Lord Mayor Sherlock that implied German money was involved, and that such money was 'being circulated throughout the country'[34]. In the war hysteria that looked to a quick allied victory, recruiting agents found a ready response among Dublin's working class. The benefit to men's wives and families of separation allowances added to the attraction. The farming community was also set to benefit, as shortage of foodstuffs increased prices.

There is no definite evidence that Laurence O'Neill, at this stage, viewed the war any differently from most of his nationalist colleagues. His tendency to act independently, and his close links with labour and across party lines, might suggest, nevertheless, a certain distance from the prevailing mood of loyal unity. That such 'distance' was present in the corporation was made evident on 14 December, when the council expressed its sense of loss at the departure from the viceroyalty of Earl Aberdeen, and appropriately praised his work and that of his wife for the health and well-being of the Irish people. Despite that, the lord mayor felt it necessary to urge a large turn out of councillors at the Mansion House to bid farewell to them.[35] Indeed, by December there was sufficient criticism of the war, and protests that the Volunteers ought to stay at home to defend their own country rather than fight Britain's battles, that the police were instructed to suppress three Irish newspapers – *Sinn Féin, Irish Freedom*, and the *Irish Worker*. Still, it would be well into 1915 before the mounting toll of deaths, and no sign of a resolution, resulted in a sharp decline in the surge of recruits and a waning in the popular enthusiasm for war. By then, Laurence O'Neill had acquired a notably high-standing among his colleagues in the corporation.

Notes

1   Mins. M.C. 23 Jan. meeting

2   Idem, 24 Feb. pp. 131-2

3   Idem, 16 June, no. 488, p. 334

4   Idem, 10 March, p. 158

5   Idem, no. 246

6   Idem, 7 April, pp. 233-4

7   Idem, 19 Sept., no. 723, p. 462

8   Idem, pp. 462-4. See, too, Thomas J. Morrissey. *William Martin Murphy* (Dublin 1911 ed.),pp.42-45

9   National Library of Ireland (NLI), O'Neill papers, Wm O'Brien- Ld Mayor L. O'Neill, 29 Jan. 1924, Ms 15,294/15

10   DCC. Mins. no, 683, p. 441

11   Idem, p. 441

12   *Dublin Sat. Post*, 6 Sept. 1913

13   Idem

14   Mins. M.C., no. 928, p. 584

15   *Dublin Sat. Post*, 3 May 1913

16   Idem, 8 Nov. 1913

17   *Report on Working Class Housing, 1913,* by departmental committee appointed by the Local Government Board, published 1914, nos.7241-7245A, p. 282; and see *Dublin Sat. Post*, 27 Dec. 1913

18   *Dublin Sat. Post*, 12 April 1913, under the heading "Dublin Markets. Important Changes by Corporation. Opposition by Farmers."

19   *Dublin Sat.Post, 3 May 1913*

20   Idem, 2 Aug. 1913

21   Dublin Corporation Report, vol.2, 1914, no. 120, pp.155ff

22   Idem, p. 158

23   Idem, p. 167

24   Idem, p. 162

25   Idem, p. 178

26   A. Birrel cit. in Report 35/1916, p. 349, cit. R.McManus. *Dublin 1910-1923* (Dublin 2002), p. 23

27   Mins. M.C., no. 578, p. 358

28   Idem, no. 354, pp. 174-5

29   Idem, no, 532, p. 334

30   Idem, no. 253, p. 178

31   Idem, no. 579, p. 358

32   Idem, no. 604, p. 369

33   T.W. Moody, F.X.Martin, F.J. Byrne. *A New History of Ireland,* (Oxford 1982) viii, p. 388

34   Mins. M.C., Letter of Clr. W. Partridge, p. 508

35   Idem, no. 863, p. 498

6.
The Pivotal Years, 1915-1916

The range of political aspirations in the country created an atmosphere of transition during 1915. This was eloquently conveyed by T.P. Gill, M.P., J.P., secretary to the Department of Agriculture and Technical Instruction, when he praised the choice of Ald. John Clancy as Lord Mayor of Dublin on 23 January 1915. Gill saw Clancy, a former Fenian and member of parliament, as 'a benign influence upon our transitional period, helping to reconcile the apparently irreconcilable …Democracy, Conservatism, Nationality, the ideal of Imperial Comity' which have 'got to be welded somehow into the compost of the new-old nation'[1]. Unfortunately, the elderly Ald. Clancy died a week later. At this, many members urged Ald. Laurence O'Neill to put his name forward, but he declined[2], preferring to give his support to Ald. Tom Kelly, a highly respected member of the corporation, a founder of the Old Dublin Society, and a member of the Sinn Féin organisation from its beginning. Kelly, however, was defeated by Clr. James M. Gallagher, J.P., whom O'Neill believed he would have defeated had he allowed his name go forward.

Effects of war

The emotions of war revealed a strong anti-German bias among unionist and most nationalist members of the corporation. This was manifested on 1 March 1915, when Ald. Quaid proposed, and Clr. O'Hara seconded, that the name of Kuno Meyer, be expunged from the roll of Freeman of the city. William Cosgrave protested that the proposal was made 'at a time when passions and prejudice cloud the better qualities of the human mind', and he appealed to the council 'not to degrade a scholar who loved our country and served her soul'[3]. Laurence O'Neill, to his credit, put forward a forthright amendment, seconded by Clr. John (Sean) T. O'Kelly, 'that a further consideration of Ald. Quaid's motion be postponed until after the war, and that the council begs to place on record its strong condemnation of Ald. Quaid's action in bringing forward contentious matter of a political nature at this crisis of our history'. The "contentious matter" referred to reports that Kuno Meyer, while lecturing in the United States, had urged Ireland to assist Germany in its war effort. O'Neill's amendment was defeated by 30 votes to 22, and Quaid's motion was passed.[4]

Some six weeks later, however, O'Neill had the pleasure of obtaining overwhelming approval for a motion which he had seconded. The motion, put forward by his friend Ald. Alfred Byrne, responding to food shortages and increased prices, requested the assistance of the Irish Parliamentary Party in obtaining an increase in the old-age pension from 5 to 7 shillings a week.[5]

Such proposals and debates were pursued against the sombre background of daily bulletins of death at the war fronts. The death-rate in France and at Gallipoli was such as to move Hanna Sheehy Skeffington, and some other prominent women, to organise a mass meeting calling for peace. On 9 May, O'Neill wrote to her regretting his inability to attend the meeting as he had made arrangements 'to go down the country on the day'. He assured Mrs Skeffington, however, 'nothing would give me greater pleasure than to attend and render you any assistance that may be in my power'[6]. The projected meeting was refused permission by the Government and did not take place.[7]

Independence from party

O'Neill's movement away from the nationalist majority in the municipal council became evident from June 1915, when the corporation extended a 'sincere welcome' to the new viceroy, Lord Wimborne, and assured him of its 'loyalty to the throne and person of his Majesty the King'[8]. The motion was passed by 20 votes to 3. The objectors were Alds. Laurence O'Neill, Thomas Kelly, and Dr William McWalter. At a special meeting on 14 July, when the council approved an amendment that the Home Rule Act 'recognised the national right of Ireland' and congratulated Mr John Redmond and the Irish party on their success, O'Neill joined with Sinn Féin and Labour colleagues – Tom Kelly and William Cosgrave, and William Partridge and P. T. Daly – in voting against the amendment.

First reports of conscription

Six days later a more significant prospect occupied O'Neill's attention. There were reports of conscription being imposed in Ireland. He chaired a conference against conscription, which was attended by representatives from the principal national, industrial, and labour bodies. 'Resolutions against conscription and in favour of forming a national committee were unanimously adopted' after hearing speeches by some of the leading citizens. Ald. Tom Kelly, acting as secretary, wrote to various organisations, including Dublin Corporation, asking them to endorse the resolution against conscription and to nominate a delegate to the national committee. 'There is no use in shutting our eyes', he warned, '… we are faced with the attempt to exterminate the remnant of our young and vigorous manhood, and we must resist it.'[9] The corporation passed resolutions against conscription and in favour of a national committee, and, on the motion of Clr. Cosgrave, seconded by Ald. Alfred Byrne, Ald. Laurence O'Neill was appointed as the delegate of Dublin Corporation to the national conference.[10] This was to place him in a central position two years later, when conscription became an immediate issue.

Grievances against the military

The changing attitude towards the European conflict was hastened by the heavy-handed action of the military authorities in Ireland against public criticism or protest. In August, the municipal council, in response to a resolution from Limerick corporation, and claiming to represent 'every shade of opinion in Dublin', entered 'an emphatic protest against the unjust treatment of our fellow countrymen … who have been sentenced to terms of imprisonment without satisfactory reasons being given'. The council demanded 'their immediate release', and also wished to draw the attention of Irish Parliamentary Party representatives 'to the unequal administration of the law as regards public utterances and writings in Ireland and in England'. They insisted that 'the same privileges be extended to Irishmen' as had 'been given to Lord Northcliffe and the English press presently opposed to the British Government'. The motion was carried by a decisive 30 to one.[11] It evoked letters of support from various public bodies throughout Ireland[12].

The local constraints of war also added to the grievances against the military and the Government. In September, the council moved that 'the commandeering by the military authorities of hay in the immediate vicinity of Dublin' was 'certain to create a milk famine in the near future, because it' would 'leave very little fodder for dairy proprietors, thereby increasing enormously the price of milk and compelling the poor to do without it to a great extent'. Speaking 'as the Public Health Authority', they suggested 'that hay should not be commandeered within a radius of 25 miles of Dublin'. Copies were to be sent to the Government, John Redmond, and the Dublin members of parliament. Ald. Laurence O'Neill, not without self-interest, proposed an addendum, which was accepted, that the Lord Mayor, Ald. Farrell, Clr. Sherlock, and Ald. O'Neill 'be appointed to wait on the military authorities on the question of the sale of hay in this country during the war'. The motion, with the addendum, was put and carried.[13]

The aura of dissatisfaction with the Government was intensified among the members of the municipal council during October, when the Local Government Board refused to support the corporation's plea for financial assistance under the Housing Act. An angry Clr. Cosgrave recalled the Board's inquiry into working class housing, 'which had been utilised for slandering the administration of Dublin', yet now when the corporation put before it 'the absolute necessity of granting the loans for working class dwellings, which the public health of Dublin' required, the Board refused to recommend their request to the Treasury.[14]

Work and sorrow

During 1915, Ald. O'Neill served on the markets committee and on the joint committee of management of the Richmond District Lunatic Asylum. In October he was appointed to a committee representing the corporation in a dispute with the Dublin Port and Docks Board regarding 'the ownership and control of the highways adjoining the river on both sides, to the east side of O'Connell Bridge[15]. After four meetings, into November, a compromise agreement was reached[16]. Before that, however, Laurence O'Neill experienced a painful bereavement. His colleagues in the municipal council acknowledged it in a motion by the High Sheriff, Clr. Shortall, seconded by sub-Sheriff, Clr. Sherlock, tendering the council's sincere sympathy in the sad loss which he had sustained in the death of his mother[17]. With her passing, it was as if a section of his life had come to an end and a new era awaited him.

Nominated for Lord Mayor. An impressive speech

By the close of 1915 it was clear to many of his colleagues that, as well as having considerable ability, Ald O'Neill was independent and politically neutral when it came to the needs of the city. This was reflected at the mayoralty election on 24 January 1916. He was nominated for lord mayor and, though defeated, he received 29 votes. The incumbent lord mayor, Clr. Michael Gallagher, was re-elected. O'Neill was proposed by Ald McWalter as 'a nationalist of very considerable means', of 'unspotted character and high ability', an 'advanced nationalist with labour sympathies'[18]. O'Neill, however, decided to speak for himself. Knowing that some of his supporters had changed their allegiance, he at first 'fingered nervously a bundle of notes' but, as the columnist for the *Daily Express* observed, 'when his speech came it carried every sign of thought and preparation'. 'Seldom', the columnist pronounced, 'have I heard a more successful speech. To some of his intimate friends it was a revelation of the strength of his personality and his power as an orator. Polished in form, it was delivered with extraordinary passion and point – even the snap of his fingers being struck with the proper emphasis at the right moment.'[19]

The speech manifesto

O'Neill's long speech, reported in the *Daily Express*, revealed much about his political views and principles. It opened with the disclosure that on the occasion of Clr. Gallagher's first election as lord mayor he had refused to let his name go forward. 'At the time', he was 'the white-haired boy' of the corporation, and the present lord mayor made the startling statement that 'only for Larry O'Neill he would never have been Lord Mayor of Dublin'. 'But twelve months make a change', O'Neill continued, 'and to-day the fulsome flatterers are put to the test…There was nothing left for him but to blow his own trumpet. He believed that any man who went for the proud position of Lord Mayor of Dublin should be prepared to face all issues, and to put all his cards on the table.' He explained that he was not pro-German, nor was he "a Liberty Hall man" (a Larkinite) or a Sinn Féiner – though he was careful to make a kindly reference to 'his friends the Sinn Féiners', and he had 'a glowing sentence about his zeal for the toiling masses, which was cheered by Mr Daly, and the other Liberty Hall gentlemen'. He said a good deal about the war and recruiting, but 'forbore to utter one syllable of personal sympathy with the cause of the Allies, or commendation of the Irish soldiers for anything but their bravery'. He made a distinction between compulsory conscription, and Irishmen who considered it their duty to fight for England, France, or America, which was a matter 'entirely for themselves'.

'He had been accused', he continued, 'of not being an up-to-date nationalist; he had been called a nationalist whom the common people regarded as having a mind of his own, but who was regarded by the aristocratic politicians as a crank. On looking through some old papers, he found that on 19 December 1880 (when he was sixteen years) he joined the Land League at a meeting at Baldoyle, at which Mr Sexton was chairman and Michael Davitt one of the principal speakers; and through the long years since then he had been a follower of Parnell's policy. He was always a consistent subscriber to nationalist funds. But at the same time – speaking with special emphasis – 'he would not pander to any man for his vote, and if any wished to vote for him they could do so, and if not he did not give a snap of his finger. But even if they were to elect him Lord Mayor of Dublin with a salary of £10,000, and with all the forces of the British Government at his back, it would not induce him to stultify his convictions, or to act otherwise than in accordance with the dictates of his conscience. Why would they not transact their business at the Council without any reference to politics? If they elected him that would be his motto. If they did not elect him, he would not, like a character in history, hang his harp on the village willow tree and go drown his grief in love or blood (laughter).'

The speech, a virtual manifesto, clearly sounded better than it reads. The impressed columnist concluded with the observation: 'He held the audience throughout, and at the close all, friends and opponents, not least the ladies, cheered him'[20].

Ordinary business

Earlier in January, O'Neill was one of six chosen delegates to a meeting in the Mansion House to protest against any reduction in funds for education in Ireland[21]. A week later, on 10 January, the municipal council endorsed the declaration by the Irish Parliamentary Party that 'compulsory military service' would meet with their 'vigorous resistance', and praised other parties opposing conscription[22]. In March, the deleterious effects of the war on the country were stoutly asserted. The increase in taxes to the imperial revenue had risen from £8 million in 1906 to £17 million in 1916. Moreover, 'Ireland's building and other chief industries' were 'practically dead owing to the war'; and Ireland had 'not received any return in munitions or other work *pro rata* with her contributions either in men or money'[23].

Aspects of the Easter Rising

Despite public marching and manoeuvres by the Irish Volunteers and the Irish Citizen Army in the early months of the year, the insurrection on 24 April took everyone by surprise. The city was paralysed for several days. The municipal council, as a result, did not meet until 10 May. The days from 24 to 29 April were days out of time for many people. 'None of us knew one day from another all that time', a middle-class friend wrote to Mary Spring-Rice. 'I wish you had seen Merrion Square and Fitzwilliam Place carrying home cabbages and loaves of bread and bartering dripping at the street corners! The night the rebels surrendered, men were rushing along shouting it on Donnybrook Road, and everyone was talking and gesticulating. It *was* queer.'[24]

The Rising resulted in some 3,000 casualties, including some 450 dead. Of these last, a number were from the poorer section of the population. The *Evening Herald* recounted unusual happenings that took place from 25 April to 3 May, some bizarre, but some sombre and distressing:

> One of the most pathetic spectacles of the streets for days past has been
> the solitary hearses unaccompanied by mourners proceeding
> towards the cemeteries. Only the hearses with the remains are permitted
> by the military.

From 3rd to 9th May, and again on 12th, all the main newspapers carried news of the insurgents executed each day. At the same time hundreds were arrested, many having little or no connection with the insurrection.

Among those arrested, to his surprise and shock, was Alderman Laurence O'Neill. He was imprisoned in Richmond Barracks with men who had been active participants. Writing of his experience years later, he mentioned that 'a thoughtful neighbour informed the authorities that I was out in the Rising'.

Imprisonment and humiliation

His account of his time in Richmond Barracks mentioned 'the filth and the stuffiness' and sleeping on bare boards with his boots for a pillow. He recalled how, finding sleep difficult, he got into an unusual conversation with a soldier on night-guard, who asked him for "beads". On being asked why, he replied:

> I have been with two firing squads in Kilmainham Jail. Your fellows came out with their beads in their hands, a smile on their faces, and they died like men. As I am under orders for the Front, I believe if I had a beads I would be safe.

O'Neill also recounted speaking up to and refusing to obey a bullying officer, whose soldiers spat on them, and who imposed very taxing exercises on the prisoners. As a result, he and Count Plunkett were left in suspense expecting to be shot.

The trial of de Valera

The main thrust of his recollection, however, concerned Eamon de Valera, a fellow prisoner in Richmond Barracks. He told how he and other prisoners passed the time and eased tension by taking part in a theatrical trial of de Valera for high treason. O'Neill and Sean T. O'Kelly appeared for the defence. After what appears to have been a hilarious drama, the prisoner was acquitted. Next morning, de Valera was taken out for his real trial. O'Neill had embedded in his memory how, 'after the Holy Rosary had been recited', de Valera handed over 'his little belongings to Paddy Mahon to be delivered to his wife', and 'standing in his blood-stained uniform of the Volunteers, with bravery and determination, no flinching, he saluted all and marched out between his military guards to what he and all of us believed to be his doom'.

O'Neill's admiration for de Valera shines through his account. 'Eamon de Valera', he acknowledged, 'may have made mistakes. History will deal with them, but no historian of the future can deal with a man's honesty and sincerity so well as those who came into close quarters with him in days of danger.' He was proud to regard de Valera as a friend for the rest of his life.

After twelve days in Richmond Barracks, O'Neill was released owing to the intervention of his son, William, a captain in the medical corps of the British army.[25] As public feeling swung strongly against the Government and towards those who were imprisoned, Laurence O'Neill's time in prison became a badge of distinction that helped his political career.

The corporation and the rising

In the aftermath of the insurrection, the municipal council applied successfully to the Local Government Board to allow relief to those experiencing exceptional distress. Extra relieving officers were appointed, and an extra eight shillings a week was given to necessitous households.[26] Otherwise, the initial response of the corporation to the events of Easter Week was limited to a vote of sympathy with the relatives of those who lost their lives. By mid-June, however, a change in the public mood was evident. William Martin Murphy informed Lloyd George that the 'public horror and universal condemnation' of the insurrection had so changed that the rebel leaders were 'being already canonised as martyrs to the cause of Irish freedom'.[27] Six days later, on 20 June, he warned that the process was being accelerated 'by your proposals for lopping-off one end of Ireland'[28]. A more immediate occasion of the change in public feeling was the large number of people imprisoned without charge. This was reflected in the meeting of the municipal council of 3 July, when the members protested at the 'hundreds of citizens, men, women and boys' who had been 'arrested upon suspicion in connection with the insurrection and were confined in detention camps'. Lord Mayor Gallagher reminded the Government that 'only the promptest action… in restoring to their homes people against whom there was not serious evidence, could allay the public resentment which had been occasioned'[29]. The resentment was further kindled by the continuance of martial law, and the killing by soldiers of 'unarmed and unoffending civilians'[30].

In October, the corporation moved that the time had come 'for the Irish nation to unite in demanding the release of our fellow countrymen and women interned in English prisons without trial, and amnesty for those who have been sentenced to terms of imprisonment'. Pending their release, they requested the Government 'to consider the advisability of treating them as political prisoners'. As if to underline how much its sympathies had changed, the municipal council proposed that twenty of its members be appointed to make arrangements 'in conjunction with the national and labour bodies of the country, for the holding of an all-Ireland conference for the purpose of establishing a Political Prisoners' Amnesty Association'. Invitations were sent to all public bodies, trades unions, trades councils, and national organisations 'inviting them to appoint delegates to the conference' with a view to joining in whatever steps the Association might think proper 'to obtain the release of all Irish Prisoners arrested and imprisoned in connection with the "Rising" of Easter Week 1916'. The initiative was to have a major country-wide influence. Twenty members were deputed 'to make the necessary arrangements for the holding of the all-Ireland conference'. First in the list of names appointed was Alderman Laurence O'Neill.[31]

At the same meeting he was also one of those appointed to a deputation to meet the Chief Secretary for the purpose of discussing the Report of the Commission on Housing, 1913, and the proposals to date of the corporation's housing committee.

From the Somme to happenings at home

The tragedies on a wider stage were brought home in a personal way to Laurence O'Neill by news of the death of Thomas Kettle, killed in action before Ginchy. Professor, poet, and politician, he had been an outstanding figure in the nationalist party to which O'Neill had belonged. All members of the corporation united in paying tribute to him as one of Ireland's 'most brilliant intellects', who 'gave his life for a cause that to him meant truth and justice and humanity, and no greater tribute can be laid on any man's grave'[32]. His death was just one in the thousands whose lives were being lost on the Western Front. The scale of the carnage led some British politicians and newspapers to call once more for conscription in Ireland. The municipal council responded vigorously on 9 October, describing such activity as 'callous recklessness' and an utter disregard for the effect of the application of conscription on peace in Ireland; and it repudiated 'the right of any authority other than an Irish parliament to impose compulsory military service on Ireland'[33]. Thus, lines for the future were drawn.

In the final months of 1916, a change was perceptible in Ald. O'Neill's attitude to salary increases in certain circumstances. Early in September he moved that a resolution in 1912 against an increase in salary to the city coroner for a period of five years, be rescinded[34]. The coroner obviously had been very busy during 1916! In November, in keeping with his appreciation of the importance of education, he seconded a motion in favour of the recommendation by the Drumcondra and Glasnevin School Attendance Committee that the salaries be increased of their inspector, Miss A. Campbell, and their secretary, Mr C.J. Moore.[35]

Concern for political prisoners

The issue of political prisoners was to remain an abiding issue with Dublin Corporation for years to come. On 4 December, the members learned the failure of their request to the American ambassador in London to visit the Frongoch internment camp to inspect conditions there.[36] Ald. Tom Kelly then proposed that three members of the corporation be appointed to visit Frongoch camp to provide a report 'on the conditions under which hundreds of our countrymen are interned there'. On this being carried, the visiting members were declared to be Alds. Thomas Kelly, Laurence O'Neill, and Clr. Sherlock. The Home Office, however, refused permission for their visit, pointing out that provision had already been made for the Dublin chief medical officer, Charles Cameron, to carry out an inspection.[37]

Empathy with the political prisoners and compassion for them was felt by O'Neill. Similar feelings led to his paying above the going-rate to some of the poorer workers in the market. This gave rise to a difficult period for him and his business. He was subjected to criticism, intimidation and boycotting from fellow factors and other interested parties. In the corporation, however, he remained highly respected and popular. He treated opponents almost invariably with respect and courtesy, and was admired for his independence and general integrity. As a consequence, it came as no surprise when, in January 1917, he was elected unanimously as Lord Mayor of Dublin.

Notes

1   Mins. M.C. 1915, no. 128, p. 57
2   See speech at 1916 election
3   Mins. 1 March 1915, p. 131
4   Idem, pp. 132-4
5   Mins. 19 April, no.373, p.214. Motion was carried 30 votes to 4.
6   L.O'Neill-Mrs Sheehy Skeffington, 9 May 1915, in (NLI) Letters to Hanna Sheehy Skeffington, Ms. 22,674
7   J.C.McWalter- Mrs Sheehy Skeffington, May (no further date), idem.
8   Mins. p. 277
9   Mins. 20 July, 1915, p. 416
10   Idem, pp.416-7
11   Mins. 20 August, pp. 382-3. The letter from Limerick was dated 28 July.
12   No. 745, p. 442
13   Mins. Sept., no. 724, pp. 435-6
14   Mins. 25 Oct., no. 780, p. 472
15   Letter 16 Oct., p. 474
16   Mins, Nov., no. 874, pp. 528-30
17   No. 872, p. 528
18   Mins. Jan. 1916, pp. 82-84
19   *Daily Express,* 25 Jan. 1916; columnist "The Man in the Gallery"
20   Idem
21   Meeting 3 Jan. 1916

22   Mins. 10 Jan 1916, no. 48, p. 30

23   Mins. 6 March 1916, no. 277, p. 145

24   Dora, 2 Woodstock Gardens, Dublin, 15 May 1916- Mary Spring Rice. *Italics* in text. NLI. Mary Spring Rice papers, Ms 43,334/5

25   ONFP. Typed pages: "Eamon de Valera (Richmond Prison, Easter Week)".

26   Marie O'Neill. "Dublin Corporation in Troubled Times, 1914-1924" in *Dublin Historical Record,* vol. 47, no. 1, 1944. Also Mins. DMC, 16 May 1916 for response of Local Govt. Board.

27   W.M. Murphy- Lloyd George, 14 June 1916 in NLI. William O'Brien papers, Ms. 8557/9, Pos 8425.

28   Idem, 20 June 1916

29   Mins. 3 July 1916, no.478, pp. 300-301

30   Mins. 2 Aug. 1916, pp. 345-7

31   Mins. 9 Oct. 1916, no. 726, pp. 447-8

32   Mins. 2 Oct., no. 682

33   Mins. 9 Oct. 1916, no. 725, p. 447

34   Mins. 4 Sept. no. 645, p. 390

35   Mins. 6 Nov.

36   Mins. 4 Dec. 1916, no. 877

37   Idem, no. 868, p. 348. See, too, Marie O'Neill, op. cit. art. cit., p. 61

Laurence O'Neill, 1864-1943
Lord Mayor of Dublin, 1917-1924
Patriot and Man of Peace

PART II

The Mayoralty, 1917-1924

There is no man, in my opinion, to whom Irishmen and Ireland,
no matter what their politics or opinions, owe a greater debt of
gratitude than to yourself …

[General Bryan Mahon – Lord Mayor O'Neill,
8 December 1921]

Laurence O'Neill, 1864-1943
Lord Mayor of Dublin, 1917-1924
Patriot and Man of Peace

7.

Lord Mayor of Dublin, 1917:
Orator, Thomas Ashe and hunger strike

The year 1917 was of special significance for Laurence O'Neill. On his performance as lord mayor during this difficult year depended his run of successful re-elections.

I

From Mayoral Election
to the National Convention
January to September 1917

On 23 January 1917, Ald. Patrick Corrigan, proposed Ald. Laurence O'Neill for mayor, describing him as 'a man of the highest integrity, who, at all times, and on all occasions, had put the public good against private gain. He hoped it would be the great privilege of Ald. O'Neill, while occupying the civic chair, to give a worthy reception to their countrymen who were suffering in the penal settlements of their sister country (Hear, hear).'[1] Clr. John MacAvin, seconding the proposal, spoke of Ald. O'Neill as a man of strong administrative capacity and emphasised that his selection by the council 'had behind it the enthusiastic support of Dublin citizens of every class and creed (Hear, hear).' [2]

Other speakers noted that he had won 'without canvassing, wire-pulling, and without promises'. Clr. Sherlock, a former lord mayor, observed soberly that he 'doubted if anyone had been elected to the civic chair of Dublin in times of greater difficulty and uncertainty than those they were now passing through. In his year of office, Ald. O'Neill would have the loyal support of his colleagues in the council (applause)[3].

The proposal was carried unanimously. 'It was a good many years', the *Dublin Saturday Post* commented, 'since a lord mayor of Dublin was elected unanimously'. The meeting was attended by 'a very large number of members and a good representation of the public', who greeted the result 'with ringing cheers, which were again renewed when Ald. O'Neill rose to return thanks.[4]

Confident of his election, he had prepared his address with special care – availing of the opportunity to counter former occasions of public obloquy and humiliation, before going on to express his political views and how he considered his role as Lord Mayor and Chief Magistrate of the capital city. In time, he was to become increasingly conscious that, in the absence of an Irish parliament sitting in Dublin, the city's lord mayor had a pre-eminence extending far beyond the Dublin region.

His lengthy vote of thanks became what the *Evening Herald* termed, 'a remarkable speech'. It was, in part, an exercise in self-promotion conveyed in a personal, spontaneous style. Its style, even in the written text, suggests why he was such a popular figure. The following account is mainly compiled from reports in the *Evening Herald* of 23 January 1917 and the *Dublin Saturday Post* of 27 January.

O'Neill began by thanking all the members of the council for their kindness and good-will towards him. This was a red-letter day in his life, conscious as he was of the distinguished men who had gone before him, from the mighty O'Connell downwards. He then moved into the body of the address by recalling certain unpleasant, personal experiences and vindicating his reputation.

Detractors and the Poor

'Few could believe', he declared, 'the amount of deceit and intimidation with which he had to contend because he took a little interest in the uplifting of the poorer class of workers in the city and county of Dublin.'

'I have seen these poor people, with whom I have lived and moved all my life, these poor worn-out men and women around the markets in the morning. I have seen them going through the fields in the country districts of Dublin, and in the distance you would not know whether they were scarecrows or human beings. I have seen women, within a few days of child-birth, carrying heavy loads from one field to another for a wretched pittance of eight pence, ten pence, or a shilling a day. I have seen men leaving their homes in early morning, going six, seven or ten miles to markets, and arriving home late at night with the noble sum of 10 shillings, 11 shillings, or twelve shillings a week, with a few perquisites thrown in.'

'Because he took an interest in these poor people, he was to be destroyed in public life, his home was to be destroyed, and a company was actually organised to boycott him and his little business. He did not mention these things to excite sympathy for himself, or to cause pain to anyone, but to demonstrate that his election as lord mayor signalled the dawning of a new era in the public life of Dublin, and that the day of cant, hypocrisy and political thimble-rigging was over.'

Prison experience. The Irony

Then, referring to a few things on his mind, which he wished to get rid of forever, he spoke of himself in the third-person. He knew a man, who, only a short time ago, was despised and degraded. At the instigation of someone, he was torn away from his family, marched ignominiously between a company of soldiers with fixed bayonets, jeered at and actually spat upon by English soldiers, and incarcerated in a filthy and unsanitary prison not knowing what fate awaited him. He would not shock his hearers' sense of decency by enumerating the many indignities he and others suffered in Richmond Barracks for the first fourteen days after Easter Week. The greatest of all indignities, however, was when one who was near and dear to him, and a British officer,[his son, William], demanded fair play for his father. 'Without any charge whatever being brought against him, or without being brought before any tribunal whatever, that man was insolently told, in the dark of a summer's evening, to get out and go home, not knowing whether he had a home to go to or a friend left to receive him. But, such is fate. Today that man stands before you. (applause)' He stood before them in the unique position of being lord mayor of his native city.

He did not mention these things to stir up ill-feeling between the civic and military authorities, but to show that it was one of those little episodes which were found scattered here and there throughout the history of Ireland. 'One day a political convict, the next placed in the highest position of trust which his fellow citizens can bestow upon him; thus carrying out the old maxim that the lower the degradation by English methods, the higher the elevation in the esteem of the Irish people' (Hear, hear).

At this point, he trusted that the members would excuse him for indulging in personal romance, but it was seldom a man was elected Lord Mayor (laughter).

A Man of no Party

'Seven years ago,' O'Neill continued, 'I was sent here by the electors of the Rotunda Ward to represent them, as the child of no party. I understand that I am generally looked upon as a sort of nondescript in this house. But I must frankly own that I have never received anything but the greatest kindness, greatest consideration, and the greatest courtesy from both the members and the officials. It has been mentioned very often by the citizens outside that the man elected as lord mayor was not the free choice of the council and had not the sympathy of the people outside.' But he thought that after the proceedings that day, few would have the temerity to suggest that the free choice of the Corporation had not been elected (Hear, hear). He trusted that he would have the sympathy of the citizens, as he had been elected free and unfettered, without giving any promises whatever as to how he would act or what he would do (Hear, hear). That was why he was so grateful and, in the main, why he felt so absolutely proud.

Political views. How he will Act

Turning to another possible hurdle, he commented with a mixture of humour and gravity: 'As one having such a variegated public career as I am supposed to have – pro-German, Larkinite, socialist, red-hot Redmondite, Sinn Féiner, and, above all, a hardened old crank (laughter) – with such a peculiar reputation gone before me, it is only natural that there should be a good deal of whispering as to how O'Neill will act when elected Mayor.' Such whispering had reached him as the "old-time wheeze" – 'Would he receive the King?' He wished to make his position clear once and for all. 'If any man comes to this country while I am Lord Mayor, or any body of men, or any regiment of men, let them be kings, commoners or peasants, to exploit the city for political reasons, as they have done in the past (Hear, hear), I will have nothing whatever to do with them (applause)'. But if any such came with a message of peace, hope and good will for the social and material benefit of Dublin, he would receive them with open arms, no matter whom he pleased or displeased (Hear, hear).

Another question which seemed to upset some people was – 'What are his politics?' To this, he responded graphically. 'I am not a politician in the accepted sense of the term. But I think that any man or woman in this country, who is not imbued with patriotic sentiments towards the uplifting of Ireland, is not worth his or her salt. I have my political leanings, it is true, and they are solely and entirely constitutional. I am a firm believer in the policy of Parnell (loud cheers)...I do not believe in standing under a banner with the inscription: "Open your mouth and shut your eyes and see what the British constitution will send you" (applause). I believe in standing under a banner having inscribed upon it the immortal words of Parnell:-

> No man has a right to fix the boundaries to the march of a nation,
> or say to his country 'This far and no farther'. We have
> never attempted to fix the *ne plus ultra* to the progress of
> Ireland's nationhood. And we never shall. (renewed applause)
> Gentlemen, these are my politics. Take them for what they are worth.'

As if in parenthesis, O'Neill remarked that some of his friends had raised a tender feeling in his heart when they referred to his old cycling days. He appreciated all that his friends had said. It was true, that once before he was placed in a great position of trust by his fellow-countrymen, 'having represented Ireland in the field of cycling sport in almost every country in Europe'. From this, he moved easily into

The Aim of his Life:

> 'My dream to-day – it may be utopian – is that I may be allowed to represent Dublin as I represented Ireland in the past, irrespective of creed, politics, or class. To represent Dublin and its people as a whole, is the aim and ambition of my life... Dublin, where I was born, where I was reared, where I mitched from school, where I have my being, and which, with one exception, I hold everything that in my life is most dear to me! Dublin, where I hope to husband out life's taper to the close! Dublin, my own, my all! I love you!'

He knew that the year before him would be difficult. He would have hesitated to have allowed his name go forward if he had not believed that he would have the sympathy and support of all his colleagues (Hear, hear).

Then, in straining diapason, he re-invoked the appeal of city and country, expressing the hope that everyone present would live to see Dublin rise phoenix-like from its ashes, to become a capital more than in name of Ireland a nation; 'not the palsied, dismantled, mutilated thing that some people want her to be, but ... a nation such as Parnell fought for, and such as poor Davis sighed for in the inspiring lines –

> For Freedom comes from God's right hand,
> A Nation once again! (Loud applause)'

Impact and Comment

Such oratory may ring somewhat hollow a century later, but it was greatly appreciated both by O'Neill's audience and members of the press. The most perceptive valuation, in terms of speaker, style, and occasion, came from the enthusiastic commentator on "Town Topics" in the unionist *Evening Mail* of 24 January. He had feared that the arts of the orator had fallen out of fashion, but he was reassured on hearing Alderman O'Neill 'make his tremulous and high-strung speech of thanks'. A city magnate, as a rule, fell considerably short of Demosthenes, but Alderman O'Neill rose to a higher plane. 'He has a mastery of thoughts that breathe and words that burn; and he has the courage of his convictions. Yesterday, I saw him shut his eyes, and clench his fists, and observe in tremulous parenthesis: "Dublin, O'God, O'God, how I love you".'

'It is a very daring author who can do things like this' and get away with them. 'The average corporator' (*sic*) would be shy of such dramatic asides. 'It requires great skill to carry them off successfully and without making anybody smile, because passion, if you suspect it to be overdone, appeals to the risible faculties." But nobody smiled, 'which is a great testimony to the esteem in which Alderman O'Neill is held, and to the genuine and unmistakeable sincerity of the man'.

The writer viewed the new Lord Mayor's allusion to Dublin as the place where he had mitched from school when a boy, as an example of the ease in with which he could move into the vernacular from 'the rarer atmosphere of the lofty and thaumaturgic *(sic)*'; and, as regards O'Neill's contrast of his arrest to his present exaltation, the columnist declared himself deeply touched 'at once by the pathos of the man and the art of the story-teller'.

Although there was very little about municipal affairs in Alderman O'Neill's 'tremulous allocution', the writer believed that he would make a very good lord mayor. It was evident that he had the respect and esteem of his colleagues, and had 'the reputation of being a straightforward and honourable man. A man of character and integrity'. The only matter on which the writer had any doubts was whether he could 'keep up the high standard of tremulous and passionate and vibrating eloquence which he set himself in his inaugural speech'.

The *Dublin Saturday Post* of 27 January recalled that though the lord mayor was Dublin born and reared, his father's people were the O'Neills of Portmarnock, who had been in that district for some two or three hundred years. It also recalled Ald. O'Neill's successes in the cycling world – 'winning many valuable trophies, which now adorn the magnificent drawing room of his city residence'-, and his time as a cycling legislator and as an international delegate at annual conferences in Copenhagen, Antwerp, Cologne, Berlin, Vienna, and Paris, from 1890-1898. In addition, he was 'president of the Irish Cyclist Association in its palmist days, and was also chairman of the Dublin Centre'. Rounding off its *miscellanea* about the new lord mayor, the paper noted that, much to Alderman O'Neill's regret, Alderman Captain Dr. McWalter was serving in the Mediterranean and was unable to be present at his election. McWalter had proposed him in 1916.

Formal installation

On 23 February, Laurence O'Neill was formally installed as Lord Mayor. His speech of acceptance , before a large attendance, was mainly about municipal affairs and lacked the personal drama of his earlier allocution. It was, nevertheless, an eloquent and vivid address.

With the world at war, Ireland in a confused state, and Dublin in a condition of sadness, poverty and dilapidation, he had no policy to place before the council or before the public. Many things needed attention, but he would endeavour to the best of his ability to find a satisfactory solution for the following city problems: 1. The rebuilding of the destroyed areas; 2. The housing of the workers; 3. The Land Cultivation Allotments Act; 4. Keeping down the rates.

Before speaking further on these issues, he referred to the members of the council still imprisoned: Clr. Partridge, whom O'Neill described as a man who uplifted those among whom he worked; and a revered friend, Clr. William Cosgrave, who was 'one of the brightest, keenest, and cleanest intellects that ever represented any constituency, the embodiment of everything that was gracious and good'. He also referred to Clr. O'Carroll, who was killed during Easter Week. Treading carefully, he made it clear that he was not going to say that the men involved in the Easter Rising were right or wrong. 'In the mellowness of time let posterity judge them by their motives and their actions.' He then went on to remind his audience that, in the aftermath of the War, there would be many maimed in body and mind to be looked after. Initially, they would be well cared for, but as time passed they might be left to their own resources. After the War, the old problems were likely to reassert themselves. All round, the working man and the corporation would be faced with a trying period. Where the country as a whole was concerned, Mr Asquith had admitted that Castle rule had failed. The country, in fact, was a pawn in imperial politics.

Addressing Dublin and its problems, he observed that the city's main street was as if it had been in the firing line in Flanders; in addition, there was poverty and distress amongst a large section of the working class, largely due to unemployment, but rendered more acute by the scarcity of foodstuffs, and the prevailing high prices which had been further inflated by wealthy hoarders of food. To deal with the problem, exceptional energy was required and generosity. True kindness was tested in adversity. With all the authority that his position bestowed, he entreated his fellow-citizens in every district to join in a combined determination to share with those less happily placed. All must help one another over the craggy paths of war.

Turning to the city's housing problem, he described the housing of Dublin's poor as 'the precursor of the evils of intemperance, tuberculosis, and moral decadence of every description'. No subject had received as much attention as Dublin housing, but little real progress had been achieved. The Corporation had spent half a million pounds in clearing insanitary areas and in building new dwellings, but the Corporation had not yet succeeded in providing housing for many thousand families. Over 100,000 people were housed in intolerable conditions. If the wealthy merchants and kind philanthropists of the city, with their brains and money, could stimulate private enterprise in the building of houses, the State would come to realise its obligations and provide the assistance it ought to give. When it did, that would be the beginning of the end of the housing problem.

On the Land Cultivation Allotments Act, O'Neill spoke of the pressing demand for allotments arising from the widespread food shortage,[5] and he outlined the plans that were underway to acquire extra land in the north of the city. He reminded his listeners, however, that, unlike in Britain, compulsory powers to acquire land directly were not granted to local authorities. On the Act that was to remedy the situation, the most that could be said was that negotiations were at an advanced stage.[6]

On the fourth civic problem, "keeping down the rates", he was forthright. There was little prospect of rates being lower this year. The demands on the city were much greater than last year; there was an increase in wages and war bonuses, and a loss of rates and of the electricity supply arising from the destruction of parts of the city.

In conclusion, he observed that under ordinary conditions the position of lord mayor was one of great difficulty, but, under the extraordinary conditions that prevailed all over the world, the present year would be one of supreme responsibility. He had a presentiment that many responsibilities and difficulties would arise during his year of office, but he was buoyed up by the knowledge of the support of his colleagues and the sympathy of the citizens. He finished with a valediction that expressed the hopes of many early in 1917: 'I hope that very soon the dark clouds of war, rebellion, dissatisfaction and bloodshed will have passed away, and that the silver lining of a brighter dawn will appear, bringing happier times to our dear old city, and to the world as a whole.'[7]

Following the inauguration, the Lord Mayor made the customary visit to the Catholic and Church of Ireland archbishops of Dublin. He viewed the meeting with Dr William Walsh, the Catholic archbishop, with some trepidation. The latter, though coming to the end of his life, remained a revered and widely influential figure, honoured for his long commitment to the social and political welfare of his people. O'Neill, feeling that his support for Jim Larkin might make him unwelcome, decided to break with convention and bring his wife with him – presumably with a view to diverting any censure from His Grace. When he and the Lady Mayoress arrived, accompanied by his Capuchin chaplain, Fr. Nicholas, and his private secretary, John Foley, the archbishop greeted him with a smile, saying – 'I see you have brought your wife! You are likely to be Lord Mayor for a number of years.' [8] Thereafter, they enjoyed a friendly relationship. There was also a gracious welcome from Most Rev. Dr. Bernard, the Church of Ireland archbishop, when O'Neill, accompanied by his private secretary, visited him at the episcopal palace, St. Stephen's Green.

In the weeks following the inauguration there were not enough hours in the day. In addition to moving his family into the Mansion House, and renovating and refurnishing it at his own expense,[9] and his many responsibilities as chairman of the City Council, he had a stream of callers and visitors to be made welcome, various deputations to the Chief Secretary that sought the lord mayor's presence, and the requirement to "be all things to all people" in accordance with his promise to be lord mayor for all the people, irrespective of class or creed. The expenses of office, according to a family tradition, were met out of his own pocket, as he magnanimously, if unwisely, refused to accept a salary because of the difficult economic condition of the city.[10]

Against this busy *mise-en-scène*, certain general needs stood out as requiring immediate attention, "the cruel, hard facts" of public housing, and hunger and poverty.

Constructive approach to public housing

On 3 March Lord Mayor O'Neill announced his intention of convening a representative conference to consider the question of Dublin Housing with a view to preparing a plan to be put into operation after the war. He requested the Corporation to nominate 12 delegates.[11] At the end of the month, six members of the Council were appointed, and six others were to be appointed by the Corporation's Housing Committee.[12] On 4 April, the *Freeman's Journal* reported that the Lord Mayor had an interview with Sir Henry Robinson, vice-president of the Local Government Board, on the housing problem, and had been assured that £100,000 had been sanctioned by the Treasury for housing. As Lord Mayor, Laurence O'Neill made a particular effort to establish a *rapport* with key figures of the establishment such as Robinson, H.E.Duke, the Chief Secretary, and Lieutenant-General, Sir Bryan Mahon, the commander-in-chief in Ireland.

Some years later he recalled that almost every day as Lord Mayor he was 'introducing deputations to Mr Duke at the Castle, for every conceivable object, increased supply of flour to bakers, increased supply of material for builders and so on, on all occasions finding him most obliging'. O'Neill raised the question of a loan for housing with him, and described the result. 'He accompanied me with two of my colleagues, Alderman Corrigan and Alderman Dr Sherlock, to visit many housing sites', where work was held up due to lack of funds, and shortage of material caused by the European war. 'The first time in the memory of the oldest citizen, a Lord Mayor and an English Chief Secretary were seen driving together through the streets of Dublin. Luncheon at the Shelbourne Hotel, return luncheon at the Chief Secretary's Lodge, consternation among my friends, comments free and frequent, "Oh Larry has gone the way of all flesh". My nationalist friends turning up the whites of their eyes in horror, my imperial friends (exclaiming) "He's a jolly good fellow".'

'My nationalism was not tainted, nor my imperialism strengthened' but a letter from the Chief Secretary on 19 April was the outcome. This announced that the Chancellor of the Exchequer had made arrangements 'with regard to the advances your Corporation will require for its proposed work during the current financial year upon its housing schemes on the following estates viz. Spitalfields and the MacCaffrey Estate, Fairbrothers Fields, James's Walk and Crabbe Lane. The Spitalfields operations to begin with as little delay as possible, and the others to be taken up in the order which your Housing Committee will arrange with Sir Henry Robinson.' He understood from Sir Henry, 'that £10,000 now, £10,000 on 16 July, and £80,000 between 2nd October and March 31st next, will probably cover the loans necessary in the current financial year...' The letter concluded 'I need hardly assure you of my hearty good wishes for the satisfactory progress of these undertakings of your Corporation'.[13]

Less than two months later, 11 June, Ald Tom Kelly commented at a special meeting of the Corporation that already at the MacCaffrey Estate 'it was proposed to build 205 artisans' houses from seven to eight shillings a week', and in 'St. James's Walk a number of cottages at from 4 shillings to 4 shilling and sixpence per week'. He congratulated the Lord Mayor on the keen interest he had taken in the scheme, and also paid tribute to the Corporation officials. His regret was that Willie Cosgrave was not with them, as he had worked most energetically on the housing business.[14]

The independence and dignity of office

O'Neill's friendship with the Chief Secretary in no way limited his independence in dealing with senior members of government. He preserved a deep sense of the dignity of his office. A case in point was his dealings with the Lord Lieutenant, Lord Winborne. He related that strenuous efforts were made to persuade him and his family to pay an official visit to the Vice-Regal Lodge. He resisted each time. Eventually, the Lord Lieutenant sent his secretary (a Mr Power) to press his invitation. O'Neill replied: 'If the Lord Lieutenant is so anxious to see me, he is welcome to call to the Mansion House any day. Mr Power seemed thoroughly shocked at my presumption and said "The Lord Lieutenant is a very big man," to which I retorted – "The Lord Mayor is a far bigger man in his own city".' The Lord Lieutenant did call to the Mansion House, and the Lord Mayor found him 'a thoroughly earnest man'[15]

Addressing poverty and food shortage

An even more immediate priority than housing was the prevalence of widespread poverty, shortage of foodstuffs, and the cold of winter. The budget for school meals in Dublin ran out at the end of February, to the detriment of thousands of children in the poorer districts. Starvation had become widespread among the poorer classes, a probation officer, Miss Gargan, informed the *Irish Independent*.[16] The dearth of concern for their plight, however, was evident among suppliers and many members of the public. The food shortage was accentuated by large farmers withholding stocks of potatoes, and by dairymen both increasing the price of milk and adulterating it.[17]

In this situation, Lord Mayor O'Neill sought and rallied support from better-off individuals and organisations across the community. He organised the bringing of food and other necessary supplies to people in need. Subsequently, in a letter in the press, he thanked the citizens generally for their support, adding: 'In particular, my grateful thanks are due to the Irish Automobile Club, whose Secretary, Mr Chayter, with his assistants, most courteously placed at my disposal numerous motor cars for the conveyance of food to the people, and for other purposes'.[18] It also seems likely that O'Neill's intercessory powers played a role in the unusual decision of the military authorities, at the end of March, to open some of their stores of potatoes and to set up a market at Amiens Street Station, where retailers were offered produce at the current official price. The action helped to put pressure on the large farmers to release stock before the plentiful summer supply became available.

Already, it would appear that the new Lord Mayor was manifesting the qualities that encouraged the historian of the Royal Irish Automobile Club to applaud him as 'a born diplomat with a gift for reconciling the opposing Unionist and Nationalist camps'.[19] It is important to keep in mind that at the outset of the war there were over 90,000 unionists in the Dublin region, that they held a dominant position in business and the professions, and that the unionist political party was the second largest party.[20]

The reference to the divergent camps, introduces the political issues with which Lord Mayor O'Neill was actively concerned during his first year in office; but before addressing these, it is instructive to observe something of the press coverage of his many activities in social, charitable, and sociable matters in the weeks and months following his inauguration.

Press reports on lord mayor's activity

There's a succession of events ranging from the opening of a fete to lessen the debt on schools in Little Denmark Street on 13 April,[21] to presiding at a conference in the Mansion House regarding the Lane pictures bequest, and bringing together, during May, workers and representatives of the shipping firms at Dublin Port and presiding over negotiations leading to a settlement. This last resulted in a number of newspaper tributes to the initiative, energy, and ability of the Lord Mayor. On behalf of the workers, Mr Tom Foran observed that the settlement 'opened up a new era in the relations between employers and employees when the representatives could sit down under the chairmanship of the Lord Mayor, discuss their differences, and reach a settlement. The satisfactory outcome of the proceedings was largely due to the tact and perseverance of the Lord Mayor, who was the means of bringing the parties together.' It was the first of many arbitration activities conducted by Lord Mayor O'Neill.

The public press, especially the *Evening Telegraph* and the *Freeman's Journal*, continued to report on other aspects of his work. A few days later, on Saturday 19 May, he chaired a major protest meeting in the Mansion House against the government's stoppage of horse racing. 'It was a pleasure and a privilege', he observed, 'to be allowed to preside over a meeting of men of different views and backgrounds, men coming from all parts of Ireland, standing together as one to take action against an act being put into operation which affected not only the material interests of the country, but the sentimental interests also.'(applause) The Lord Mayor had several interviews with Henry Duke, the Chief Secretary, who 'always adopted the line of least resistance'. The government gave way before the combined effort of unionists and nationalists, and horse racing was allowed to continue in all its glory[22]

The same Saturday that he chaired the major protest meeting in the Mansion House, O'Neill spoke eloquently at the opening of the 'Carmel' Fete in Terenure College Park. Two days later, he addressed a very different meeting, one dealing with a report by Dr. E.C. Bigger, medical commissioner to the local government board, on infant mortality and the economic conditions under which Dublin's poor lived. The *Freeman's Journal*, of 23 May, was of the opinion that the lord mayor 'voiced what might be regarded as the general nationalist view that only in the control by the people of Ireland of the affairs of Ireland will an effective remedy be found for the evils with which Dr Bigger's report deals'. He emphasised the importance of improved housing and higher wages in overcoming the evils. As a contribution towards easing the problem of infant mortality, he made the Mansion House available for a "Baby Week", which he opened on 3 July. The week was devoted to programmes and methods devoted to improving the health of mothers and infant children. The *Evening Herald* of that date pictured the Lord and Lady Mayoress among a group of medical doctors, nurses and other notable citizens who had gathered for the occasion.

Two aspects that captured much attention was his concern for the unemployed, and the hospitality of the Mansion House.

Acting for unemployed workers

Dublin's huge unemployment problem in 1917 gave rise to unrest. Processions were formed carrying black bannerettes with a skull and cross-bones. They came to the Mansion House and demanded that the Lord Mayor find work for them. He invited them into the Round Room, and the spokesman for the men informed him briefly: 'We want work, we don't want charity, and it is your duty as Chief Magistrate to get it for us'. O'Neill was equally brief, telling them that he would do his best and that they should come back in a few days. He called on Mr Duke, explained the situation and also made the case that the extent of unemployment in Dublin meant that Dublin workers were at a disadvantage compared to workers in other parts of the country. The Chief Secretary was alarmed by O'Neill's account. 'I never met a man so easily frightened as Mr Duke', O'Neill wrote, 'or a man who was so anxious to do the right thing'. On 26 June he was delighted to receive a favourable response. The Under-Secretary, W. P. Byrne, wrote on behalf of the Chief Secretary to inform him that Mr Duke had been in touch with the Ministers for Labour and Munitions, and he hoped that about 200 Dublin unemployed could be given work on the railway at Athy, County Kildare. He had also arranged that the Local Government Board would consult with the two Dublin Boards of Guardians to provide such relief by way of employment as would avoid the possibility of a large degree of destitution among able-bodied workers.[23]

The following day, an *Evening Telegraph* photograph depicted a large body of unemployed men forming outside the Mansion House, with the sub-script: 'The Lord Mayor of Dublin has been untiring in his efforts to solve the acute unemployment problem which at present exists in the city, and has had numerous conferences with the men'. On this occasion, he and his secretary, John Foley, received an enthusiastic reception from some 1500 men. He informed them of his meeting with Mr. Duke, and spoke of employment prospects. He asked them to form a committee to confer with him from day to day with regard to how matters were going along. He took it that all present were legitimate workers, and that there were no idlers (cries of 'Yes').

The hospitality of the Mansion House

Lord Mayor O'Neill had little in the way of funds at his disposal. For years there had been proposals at city council meetings on cutting back the lord mayor's salary and expenses. On 20 June 1917, the column "Gossip of the Day" in the *Evening Telegraph* noted that 'for good or ill the city council has made it impossible, by cutting down by £2,000 the yearly allowance to the Chief Magistrate, that there can be now any such display (as in the 19th century) of entertainment and hospitality at the Lord Mayor' official home in Dawson Street.. If it were otherwise… no person would fulfil this part of the duties of his office more worthily than the present worthy occupant…The Mansion House now has become a place of business meetings of citizens for all sorts and kinds of excellent purposes, and if music and dancing are heard there at all it may be taken for granted that the object is primarily for charitable purposes, the enjoyment of those present being a secondary consideration. The money saved by the civic economics was to be used for all sorts of civic improvements as well as the relief of the oppressed rate payers'.

The economic constraints on someone of O'Neill's expansive nature meant that he drew on his own financial resources to a considerable degree, a circumstance, which, as he continued in office over years, greatly reduced his business and his financial security. In June 1917, however, such gloomy prospects were well below the horizon, and he happily extended the hospitality of the Mansion House to old friends and rivals from his cycling days. He subsequently remembered the occasion as 'one of the brightest events in my occupancy of the Mansion House'[24]

Writing of the occasion, the *Irish Cyclist and Motor Cyclist*, of 13 June, provided an enthusiastic account of the day's cycling and its conclusion with a "smoking concert" at the Mansion House, where the cyclists were guests of 'Larry O'Neill, Lord Mayor of Dublin, who, in the eighties and nineties, was a leading light in the Irish Cyclists Association, and who quickly gained the reputation of being a man who had the courage of his convictions'. As Lord Mayor, he had fully demonstrated that he still possessed this valuable characteristic. The account described the arrangements exercised towards his guests by the lord mayor: an official was on duty to take charge of each bicycle and to give a voucher in exchange, thus putting the most nervous owners at ease; ample toiletry and cleaning accommodation was provided, so that all felt relaxed physically and sartorially after their dusty ride and ready to face the camera for a group photograph in the garden. In the same location, the more than 100 guests sat down 'at long tables, covered in dark green, on which dainty glassware shines and shimmers in the blaze of electric light'. At an end table many of the Old Timers assembled with the Lord Mayor, whose fine features were illuminated by a kindly smile and twinkling eyes. The meal was punctuated by singing, music and speeches. The attorney-general, James O'Connor, K.C., proposed the toast of "The Lord Mayor" and related several amusing incidents from the old days. In replying, the lord mayor 'made a feeling reference to two Old Timers no longer with us – E.J. O'Reilly, "the Scorcher", and "Crock" Kennedy. Indicative of the cycling fellowship, bridging political and religious differences, a telegram was sent from the gathering 'conveying fraternal greetings to the English Fellowship of Old Cycling Timers'.

In a country so divided politically, the sense of unity among his guests, many of whom he had not met for years and whose positions, business or professions were far removed from his own, made a lasting impression on Laurence O'Neill. 'That June evening in 1917, many of us who had ploughed a fairly hard furrow forgot everything, no barriers, no partitions of any sort. All one.' [25]

There were also, of course, more solemn, sad occasions that called for the First Citizen's attendance. In the same month of June, the condolence of the corporation was extended to John Redmond and the Redmond family on the death of the highly popular Major Willie Redmond, M.P., killed in action at Messines on 7 June. The lord mayor attended the Pontifical High Mass in the Pro-Cathedral on 22 June, and the funeral afterwards. The large cortege included people of all political persuasion paying tribute to the man as distinct from the Irish Parliamentary Party. His death left a vacancy in East Clare, the filling of which, on 10 July, was to highlight the marked change that had taken place in political feeling and outlook during the previous months.

Political issues and problems early in 1917

From early in the year, there was increased public concern for the welfare of prisoners in internment. The Corporation gave expression to this at a special meeting on 2 April. The first Russian revolution of 1917 had taken place. Lord Mayor O'Neill moved, and Ald. Byrne seconded, 'that this House sends to the Duma its fraternal greetings', and then, drawing attention to the proclamation by the Provisional Government of Russia ordering 'a general political amnesty', the motion continued – 'It is hereby resolved that this meeting of the Dublin Corporation, representing all shades of political opinion, ... demands that the British Government shall adopt a similar policy to that upon which they have congratulated the Provisional Government of Russia, and declare a general amnesty of Irish Political Prisoners, and a revocation of the recent order of deportation upon other Irishmen: And that a copy of this resolution be forwarded to the Prime Minister and Mr John Redmond, M.P.; to His Holiness the Pope; the Presidents of the United States and the French Republic; the Russian Duma; the Premiers of the Colonial Governments, and also (with a request for its endorsement) to the public bodies in Ireland.' The motion was put and carried unanimously.[26]

Hostility against the government had been further ignited on 7 March by Lloyd George's assertion that the Government of Ireland Act would exclude Ulster. Political support for Sinn Féin increased. The Commander-in-Chief, Sir Bryan Mahon, fearing disruption as the first anniversary of the Rising drew near, issued a proclamation banning public meetings and assemblies during Easter Week, with the exception of the procession of the Lord Mayor and civic members to the Pro-Cathedral on Easter Sunday, 8 April. The anniversary on the following day had its moments of tension, but overall passed quietly. One possible flash point was the congregation of large crowds in O'Connell Street following the erection during the night of a republican flag over the General Post Office. The crowd was in good humour, but there was tension in the air. The police were dispersed in numbers among the crowd. Seeing this, O'Neill, ever vigilant for occasions of trouble in the city, told the superintendent that he considered such dispersal unwise. The superintendent took his advice, and placed all his men together by the ruins of the Post Office. The police, in O'Neill's estimation, 'behaved with great patience, enduring the insults of many thoughtless boys and girls', with the result that a day that was feared passed off quietly.[27] Disaffection, however, ran deep countrywide, and sought opportunity for public expression.

The opportunity arrived ten days after the anniversary date. Lord Mayor O'Neill, in keeping with his promise that the Mansion House would be open to all, 'irrespective of creed, politics and class', made welcome to his mayoral residence, on 19 April, a conference convened by Count George Plunkett, father of the executed Joseph Mary Plunkett. It attracted more than a thousand representatives of organisations from different parts of the country. The assembled members observed a minute's silence for those who died in the Rising; issued a call for those still in custody to be treated as political prisoners; and, significantly, adopted resolutions asserting 'Ireland's right to freedom from all foreign control' and its right to representation at the post-war Peace Conference in Paris. Plunkett's convention proved a pivotal step towards a nation-wide movement.

The militant mood of the conference caused disquiet in government circles. Three days later, on 22 April, the Lord Mayor was informed by the Chief Commissioner of the

Dublin Metropolitan Police (DMP), W. Edgeworth-Johnstone, that 'in the interests of the peace of the city, it would be wise to postpone the holding of any further meetings in the Mansion House, until the end of the month at any rate'. 'The meetings' were 'likely to attract crowds, upon the outskirts of which undesirable elements collect with a view to creating disorder and looting.'[28] O'Neill chose to interpret the Commissioner's letter as referring only to the month of April. In May, the Mansion House was again made generally available. It was a month in which hostility to the Government and disillusionment with the Irish Party reached a new pitch. On 8 May the extent of the opposition to the partition of the country was emphasised by the joint declaration of protest by the Catholic bishops and three Church of Ireland prelates. Next day, in the South Longford by-election, the Sinn Féin candidate, Joseph P. McGuinness, a prisoner in England, defeated the favoured nationalist representative, Patrick McKenna, by 1,493 votes to 1,461. At the Dublin City Council, the news of the victory was greeted with jubilation by many members.

In the climate of disaffection, political meetings at the Mansion House could prove hazardous. This was borne in on Lord Mayor O'Neill during that month of May, when a public meeting was taking place with regard to the treatment of Irish prisoners in English prisons. He noticed on the way in a number of young men showing each other revolvers as they followed six "g men" in plain clothes (detectives of the Metropolitan Police) into the meeting. Subsequently, when in his study, he heard loud commotion in the distance. He rushed to the balcony, and saw revolvers pointed at the policemen. He shouted to attract attention, which succeeded, and the police were brought to a place of safety. Next day there were sensational headings in the press, 'Police shot at in the Mansion House', followed by letters in the papers claiming the Lord Mayor's interference was the cause of all the trouble.

Despite the criticism, O'Neill felt satisfied that his action 'prevented murder from being committed in the Mansion House that night'. He seriously considered closing the building against all meetings, but, on reflection, decided it was not right to punish the many for the faults of a few. He made representation to the Castle Authorities, however, that it was very injudicious to send police into public meetings in the Mansion House, a practice, which, to his relief, was discontinued.[29]

Introducing a national convention

On 16 May, Lloyd George interposed a politically persuasive distraction, announcing the immediate application of the Home Rule Act, with the exclusion for five years of six Ulster counties, unless an All-Ireland Convention produced an agreed self-government scheme. On 21 May he introduced his "Convention of Irishmen of all parties". It was a well-calculated move: causing disarray among those seeking self-government, disarming the Irish lobby in the United States of America, while privately the Northern Unionists were assured that the Convention would leave them undisturbed. Following the announcement, there was a disputatious gathering, which resulted in violent actions, at the Mansion House. On 22 May, a concerned Commissioner of the D.M.P. informed the Lord Mayor that 'in view of the disorder which took place at the close of the meeting in the Mansion House last night, it is apparent that a certain section of the Dublin public cannot be brought together with safety'. Meetings that were 'likely to cause any public excitement' were a danger at the present moment. Accordingly, the meeting that was advertised for that night (22 May) at the Mansion House 'should not, in the interests of the peace of the city, be permitted to take place'.[30]

Next day, Lord Mayor O'Neill received a very different kind of letter. William O'Brien, M.P., wrote from London urging him to take an active part in Lloyd George's convention. Its format was not yet decided: whether a small conference of 'a dozen non-party Irishmen' or a large miscellaneous convention, which, in O'Brien's view, was 'bound to end in fiasco'. 'In this most critical juncture', he assured O'Neill, 'your position as Lord Mayor of Dublin, uncommitted to any party or section, gives you an enormous influence' and he hoped O'Neill would not hesitate to use it in support of a small conference, such as proved successful in the Irish Land Conference (1902-3). He proposed some fifteen names from which twelve could be chosen. He singled out the prominent businessman and press magnate, William Martin Murphy, as a key figure. He and the Lord Mayor might decide how best to press their case, whether by letter to the *Independent* or *Times* or by an interview with the Press Association. 'Murphy's influence', he added, 'both with Mr Duke and Lord Northcliffe, is very great.' [31]

Negotiating the release of prisoners

In the succeeding weeks, increased attention was focussed on the release of the 120 prisoners in British custody. O'Neill negotiated patiently with the Chief Secretary on their behalf. His efforts were hindered on 10 June, when a police intervention, at a rally seeking the release of the prisoners, resulted in a police inspector, John Mills, being fatally injured. He left a widow and three children. There was much public sympathy. A fund was set up to assist the family. O'Neill, as Lord Mayor and Chief Magistrate, served on the organising committee that was largely composed of Unionists and members of the Irish Party.[32] On 16 June, however, he was relieved to receive a telegram from Mr Duke: 'Arrangements incidental to release are in the hands of the Commissioners at the Home Office. I am communicating with the Home Secretary. If you inform me, through Sir

Edward O'Farrell, of any views or proposals you would like to have considered I will submit them. Sir Edward will telegraph at once and I will take care to be at hand.[33] Two days later, the release of prisoners took place. On their arrival in Dublin, they were met by an enthusiastic crowd, and conveyed by wagonettes past the General Post Office to a luncheon in Gardiner Place, before being received by the Lord Mayor at the Mansion House.[34]

Reflecting on the released men, O'Neill observed that they came from every part of Ireland. Many of them were 'young fellows who had never travelled beyond the confines of their own parish or county', and, being interned, got a glimpse of the wider world and came under the discipline of leaders who had escaped the ultimate penalty of Easter Week. They learned the Irish language and received lectures on Irish history. Some joined the I.R.B. but all bound themselves to promote an Irish Republic. They arrived at the Mansion House as bearded men. 'From Dublin they scattered to their homes, and from then on could be seen on every dead wall throughout the country, "Up the Republic", and men marching in military formation to the strains of the newly adopted anthem, *The Soldiers' Song*.'

The Lord Mayor and the National Convention

On the 18 June, the very day of the celebration in Dublin, Prime Minister Lloyd George, announced the Government's intention "to summon immediately...a Convention of representative Irishmen in Ireland, to submit to the British Government a constitution for the future government of Ireland within the Empire". On 22 June, the Lord Mayor of Dublin was invited to be a member of the Convention. Invitations were extended to a wide range of public bodies and organizations, to representatives of the main churches, of the peers of Ireland, and of the main political parties, including Sinn Féin.

The leaders of Sinn Féin were suspicious of Lloyd George's intentions and declined to participate. On 1 July, the party rallied over 30,000 people to an "All Ireland" meeting in the Phoenix Park to protest against the partition of Ireland and against a nominated rather than a truly representative convention. Ten days later, support for the party was emphasised by countrywide celebration on the success of Eamon de Valera in the East Clare by-election. As if in response, Sir Edward Carson was appointed to the British Cabinet. Nevertheless, all during July the newspapers made frequent references to the Convention and its preparations. An air of excitement and expectation was generated. The Chief Secretary, H.E. Duke, informed the Lord Mayor, on 13 July, that he had agreed to act as chairman at the setting up of the Irish Convention, prior to the election of the chairman and other preliminary matters. [35] On 20 July, Lloyd George gave a reserved assurance to William O'Brien, M.P., 'that if there was good ground for believing that the Convention's proposals met with the support of the Irish people, His Majesty's government would do their best to give legislative sanction to the scheme'.[36]

On the same date, William Martin Murphy, writing to O'Brien, expressed the view of probably many nationalists participating in the Convention, namely, that Great Britain was never under such pressure as at present to placate Ireland, and that they could get many of the southern Unionists to support their view, not only about partition but for a full measure of self-government.[37] Laurence O'Neill later observed that he accepted the Prime Minister's invitation, after 'a great deal of hesitancy', because he believed the Convention was 'the last time constitutional methods would get a chance'. [38]

The Convention opened on Wednesday, 25 July, at Trinity College, Dublin. On his way into the college grounds, O'Neill 'was pounced upon by some of the northern delegates', who requested him to allow his name to go forward for the chairmanship of the Convention. After a few minutes conversation, it became clear to him that the request was not out of regard for himself but out of a desire, 'for some reason', to prevent Sir Horace Plunkett gaining the position. O'Neill declined the offer. The Chief Secretary, H.E. Duke, opened the proceedings, and Sir Horace Plunkett was elected chairman.[39] Before long, because of the unwieldy membership of over ninety participants, a working party of twenty, entitled the Grand Committee, was established. The Convention's deliberations lasted for nine months, and continued throughout to receive generous press coverage.

The two key persons singled out by William O'Brien as likely to have most influence in promoting the proposed convention, Lord Mayor O'Neill and William Martin Murphy, played a role outside the convention meetings in promoting good will and greater understanding, and in influencing major members of the government. Murphy, in fact, despite poor health, and personally involving himself in his newspapers' support of the Convention and trenchant opposition to partition, also held, at his residence, Dartry Hall, social gatherings of people likely to have political influence, including the Chief Secretary.[40] He, most likely, contributed to H. E. Duke's personal disapproval of partition and of conscription.[41] Lord Mayor O'Neill, for his part, availed of his office and personal reputation to invite a variety of people of different views to meet with members of the Convention for "conversations" at the Mansion House. The invitations met with a positive response from different sections of the public, and from different parts of the country. Among those invited was John Redmond, M.P. The very ill leader of the Irish Parliamentary Party replied on 5 August that, while he would like to have attended the "conversation" on Monday next, he found himself at present 'unable to attend any social gathering'. He was sure, however, that the Lord Mayor was 'doing a most valuable thing in giving this entertainment. The more men of different views meet socially the better'.[42] In fact a considerable body of people of different views came to the conversations in the Mansion House. They included: The lords mayors of Belfast and Cork, the mayors of Derry and Limerick, Lieut. Colonel Jackson Clark, Maghera, Mr Andrew Jameson, the Marquis of Londonderry, the Archbishop of Dublin, the Bishop of Down and Connor, the Moderator of the Presbyterian Church Belfast, the Lord Primate of Ireland, the Bishop of Raphoe, Sir George Clark, Belfast Shipyard, the Earl of Dunraven, the Duke of Abercorn, Joe Devlin, M.P., William Martin Murphy, and many others. [42]

O'Neill's participation in the Convention was spasmodic, because of the demands of his office. He retained in memory, however, a very successful visit of the Convention members to Belfast, and how for the first few weeks there was 'a spirit of forgive and forget'. Subsequently, he had felt obliged to publicly criticise Dublin Castle for patent hostility, under a Major Price, which was generating bitterness and anger, and undermining the Convention. The Irish National Volunteers' office was raided, rifles, deposited with the agreement of the authorities, were seized, hockey sticks were confiscated as offensive weapons, Sinn Féin meetings were proclaimed, arrests were made, and, the final provocation, Ulster troops were used for the seizures. The London *Daily Express* strongly criticised 'such ill-advised procedure', and the London *Nation* commented that Nationalist Ireland was amazed at this line of action so fatal to the Convention, where there was 'something of a break in the obduracy of Ulster, as well as a certain softening of the ruder side of Sinn Féin', and Mr Duke was 'a conciliator'. The only explanation was that the Castle wanted the Convention to fail.

Availing of the criticism expressed by the *Daily Express* and the London *Nation*, a Liberal and a Tory paper, Lord Mayor O'Neill addressed the Corporation in measured tones on 17 September 1917. A lengthy extract from his speech, was quoted, and commented on, in *The English Review*, a high quality literary magazine (founded 1908) which also covered politics. He kept a copy.

I fully realize the danger it is for any individual to find fault with the military authorities in this country at present, but when English newspapers point out that the action of the military authorities is nothing less than provocative, and will lead to rioting and an atmosphere of anger and recrimination, I think the time has come when public representatives should speak out their minds, as to what they think of the situation also. From my own knowledge of Irishmen and Irish affairs, I consider the action of the military authorities at present, instead of allowing a friendly feeling to exist, and the seeds of brotherhood between all parties in this country to be sown, will, in the first place endanger the success of the Convention, and, in the second place, will create an atmosphere of hatred throughout the country.... I do think that the present policy of the military authorities is one that is not for the best interests of the general peace of the country.

As no doubt he intended, his carefully chosen words evoked a sympathetic response from the English press. *The English Review* observed that it was important 'that we in England' should know what the Lord Mayor thinks about conditions in Ireland, 'because so little news percolates through to this country, and the situation there...is generally misunderstood'. The Lord Mayor was 'an eminently peaceful man, loyal, and held in high esteem', and if he felt himself constrained to utter such a note of warning, 'we may be sure that his reasons are valid, (and) that his motives are beyond cavil'. After further comment, the *Review* observed that the Convention was sitting for good or evil, and that it was contrary to common sense to 'allow Major Price to promote irritation by a police policy which is not consequent and equitably applied. Every arrest simply makes Sinn Féin stronger[44].

Growth of Sinn Féin and a unionist reaction

That final comment was an acknowledgement of the Irish reality, reflected in 'the old maxim' to which O'Neill had referred in his election speech – 'the lower the degradation by English methods, the higher the elevation in the esteem of the Irish people'. The Sinn Féin members incarcerated in Irish jails, now became the occasion of a new popular campaign for the release of 'political prisoners'.

The strength of Sinn Féin and its replacement of the Irish Party in public popularity was heralded by the extent of de Valera's victory in the East Clare by-election, by 5,010 votes to 2,035, and the extent and the intensity of the popular rejoicing that followed. A month later, 10 August 1917, Laurence O'Neill and many in the Corporation rejoiced at the election of William T. Cosgrave, in the Kilkenny City by-election. It was Sinn Féin's first urban seat.

Among those not rejoicing was Ald. David Quaid, a strong minded unionist. Early in the war he had been influential in removing from the roll of honour of Freeman of the City of Dublin, Professor Kuno Meyer, whom he described as a German spy, and in rescinding a resolution of the Paving Committee to have erected a stone commemorative of the Bachelor Walk fatalities, and he had also suggested that there was corruption amongst his colleagues. This roused the hostility of many in the Corporation, especially the influential P.T. Daly, who successfully moved that he 'not be heard' in the council on the grounds of comments he made at a previous meeting 'relative to members of this council'. The motion was carried overwhelmingly. One of those supporting it was the

Lord Mayor.[45] Quaid was almost unique in rousing O'Neill to angry comment. On 9 June Ald. Quaid threatened legal action if the resolution against him was not rescinded. At the council meeting of 13 August 1917, Quaid having withdrawn his accusation of corruption, it was proposed that the order of 7 May be withdrawn, 'the Council being of the opinion that Alderman Quaid has already been sufficiently punished for the offence he committed'. The motion was carried by 21 votes to 8, the Lord Mayor not voting. [46]

Personal political attachment

Although Lord Mayor O'Neill, as has been seen, made a particular effort to reach out to representatives of the government and of the unionist community generally, it was clear that his personal political attachment was to an independent Ireland. This was suggested by his motion in tribute to the late Thomas Edward O'Dwyer, Bishop of Limerick, who had publicly defied the commander–in–chief, General Maxwell, in 1916, and criticised him for the execution without trial of the leading insurgents. The Lord Mayor extolled the greatness, manliness, versatility and utter fearlessness of the dead prelate, whom Clr. William T. Cosgrave, seconding the motion, described pithily as 'as independent of party as he was of the terrorism of force'. [47] Again, there was the symbolism of O'Neill's chosen emblem of office, the Red Hand of the O'Neills of Ulster, but adapted to apply to the whole country: *Lamh Dearg na hEireann* – 'The Red Hand of Ireland'. Within the symbol there was implicit another attachment. The workers' badge in 1913 was of a red hand.

II

Responses to Political Prisoners
and to Municipal Problems.
August to December 1917

Political prisoners and hunger strikes

O'Neill's commitment to political independence, and his sharp, if brief, experience of incarceration, fostered his active sympathy for 'political prisoners'.

In September, he availed of his office as Lord Mayor and Chief Magistrate to gain access to such prisoners in Mountjoy jail in Dublin. The leading figure among them was Thomas Ashe, president of the Irish Republican Brotherhood (IRB), a striking personality, with an almost legendary standing as the only successful military commander in 1916. He had been arrested on 18 August, 1917, and sentenced to two years hard labour for seditious speeches. In prison he followed the practice of non-cooperation with the prison authorities, much as he had done in Lewes prison in England when he acted as de Valera's second- in- command.

On O'Neill's first visit to Mountjoy, he was informed by another prisoner, Austin Stack, that he feared that Joe McDonagh (brother of Thomas McDonagh, executed after Easter Week) was seriously ill, because he had been taken away from them. The Lord Mayor requested the Deputy Governor, Mr Boland, to take him to McDonagh. Boland consulted the Head Warder, who was nearby. O'Neill could see 'there was consternation between them'. They told him that McDonagh had been placed in an underground cell, owing to insubordination, and could not be seen. The Lord Mayor, sensing something was wrong, insisted on seeing him. Laurence O'Neill's papers relate what he found and his reaction:

'Found McDonagh downstairs, in a cell almost dark, although it was a bright morning. Called, no answer. Had to strike a match to see him. He was lying insensible, on, so far as I can remember, a stone floor, saturated with water; the water having been thrown over him, evidently with the object of reviving him, and left alone. A shocking sight. I at once took the law into my own hands, and gave orders for a doctor to be sent for at once, and helped to carry him over to the Prison Hospital. Only for Austin Stack's intimation to me, McDonagh would undoubtedly be added to the list of dead.' [48]

The Lord Mayor's next visit appears to have been in response to a report of hunger strike among prisoners. Their leader, Thomas Ashe, had refused to sew mailbags and insisted on talking to fellow prisoners in the exercise yard, in assertion of his right to be treated as a political prisoner and not as a common criminal. The prison authorities responded by removing his mattress from his cell and depriving him of reading matter. The other Sinn Féin prisoners joined in the protest. The authorities retaliated by raiding their cells, stripping them of bedding, boots, and personal belongings. On 20 September, the prisoners embarked on a hunger strike. The Prison Board made it clear that it would resort to forced feeding to break the strike. An attempt was made to suppress news of the strike, but Ashe managed to get word to the Lord Mayor.[49]

The latter got in touch with Sir John Irvine, chairman of the Visiting Justices, and together, in company with the Deputy Governor, Mr Boland, the head warder, and two other warders, they visited many of the prisoners on the morning of Saturday, 22 September. Among those visited, was Ashe. He was lying on bare boards in a corner of the cell. There was no bedding or furniture of any description, and his boots had been taken away. O'Neill, who had known Thomas Ashe previously, asked him if he had any complaints to make. He said that the only complaint he, and the other Sinn Féin prisoners, had was that they were being treated as common criminals. They had gone on strike on Thursday on this sole issue. After visiting Ashe and some other prisoners, the Lord Mayor informed Sir John Irvine and the Deputy Governor that he wished to meet with the Castle authorities. They met with the Chief Secretary, who sent for the Chairman of the Prison Board, Mr Max Green (a brother-in-law of John Redmond, M.P.). O'Neill told them what he had found in the prison, but without specifically mentioning Ashe. He did single out Joseph McDonagh and the circumstances in which he had found him. He emphasised that, from his conversations with the prisoners, it was clear that their one complaint was that they were being treated as criminals.

Mr Duke seemed very sympathetic and anxious to do something, but the Chairman of the Prison Board declared that these men were handed over to him as criminals, and that he had no alternative but to treat them as such. The Lord Mayor told them they were shouldering a dreadful responsibility and that if anything happened, the consequences would rest on their shoulders.

Thomas Ashe, his death and the public reaction

O'Neill did not see the prisoners on Sunday, 23 September, as he was attending a meeting of the National Convention being hosted by the Lord Mayor of Cork. He phoned the prison, however, and was informed by the Deputy Governor that the prisoners were very well. On Monday morning, he and Sir John Irwin visited the prison and, in company with the Deputy Governor and warders as before, saw many of the prisoners, including Ashe. When they entered Ashe's cell, he was standing erect. The Lord Mayor commented on his bed and bedding being restored. Ashe replied that they were restored on Saturday evening, following the visit of the Lord Mayor and Sir John Irwin. Ashe then explained that he had broken some panes of glass in the cell in order to get some air. The Lord Mayor asked him how he was, and he replied that he was well, but was being put through the revolting operation of forcible feeding. He also stated that an outside doctor had informed him that his throat was somewhat delicate, and he feared that if they persisted in feeding him as they had done that morning, the end would be fatal.

The Lord Mayor reasoned with him about endangering his health so much, now that he had made his protest, and that the authorities to a certain extent had given way, and would he not consider it best for his life to take his food. Ashe replied: 'No. They have branded me as a criminal. Even though I die, I die in a good cause'. There was 'loud applause' from other prisoners. Sadly, it was the last time Lord Mayor O'Neill saw Thomas Ashe.[50] He died the following day, Tuesday, 25 September, as a result of damage to his lungs while being forcibly fed.

News of his death gave vent to an outpouring of grief and anger. An application was made to the Estates Committee of Dublin Corporation by the Wolfe Tone Memorial Committee for the removal of Ashe's body to the City Hall where it would lie in state. The elegant Georgian building that was the City Hall, was under permanent military guard ever since its occupation by the insurgents in 1916. Meantime, on 26 September, the body was escorted in solemn procession from the Mater Hospital to the Pro-Cathedral, accompanied by a body of Volunteers, a large cortege of people, and about fifty Catholic clergy, some of whom had travelled long distances to be present.[51]

The following day, 27 September, a concerned Dublin Castle sent a pointed letter to the lord mayor. W.P. Byrne, the Under Secretary, writing from the Chief Secretary's Office, observed that rumours had reached him that an application was to be made to the Lord Mayor for the use of the City Hall, or the Mansion House, for the lying-in-state of the remains of Thomas Ashe, which, it was to be feared, would lead to the collection of great crowds, to much excitement amongst Ashe's sympathisers, and possibly to disorder in the street. It would be much safer if the watching of the remains took place in a church and had the character of a religious ceremony. He concluded with a sharp reminder: 'The Irish Government would hear with grave concern that any public demonstration of a non-religious character was contemplated; - and I venture to express the hope that you share this view and will, in the interests of the well-being of the city, discontinue any such proceeding'.[52]

The die, however, was already cast. The Estates Committee had granted the request of the Wolfe Tone Committee. It could scarcely have done otherwise. The tide of public opinion made any other decision unthinkable if peace were to be preserved. Thomas Ashe had already passed into the pantheon of dead martyrs. His words to the Lord Mayor were widely quoted – 'Even if I die, I die in a good cause', as were the words of the hymn/ballad he had composed, "Let me carry your cross for Ireland, Lord". The plan was to move the remains from the Pro-Cathedral to the City Hall for the lying-in-state, and thence back to the church for the funeral Mass. The problem was the presence of the armed guard at the City Hall. The Lord Mayor feared that their presence would provoke a serious breach of the peace among the highly-charged crowd.

He, and two conservative nationalist members of the Estates Committee, Patrick Corrigan and Sir Patrick Shortall, met Under Secretary Byrne and senior officials in Dublin Castle, shortly before the procession from the Pro-Cathedral to City Hall was ready to leave. O'Neill proposed to the administration that they avert a likely crisis by withdrawing the military guard temporarily from the City Hall. The Under Secretary was unyielding. He expressed surprise at people in authority expressing sympathy with 'criminals' and 'suicides', and he made it clear that a regiment of soldiers heavily armed was stationed in Castle yard. Fortunately, the commander-in-chief, Sir Bryan Mahon, entered the room and, having listened attentively to the deputation, at once gave the order to have the military sentries withdrawn from City Hall. 'Had it not been for Sir Bryan's foresight', the Lord Mayor observed, 'the streets of Dublin that day would have been turned into a shambles, and God alone knows what the consequences would be through the country.' [53]

As thousands passed by the bier in the City Hall, the prisoners continued their hunger strike and the authorities persisted with forced feeding. Very concerned for the men, the danger of another death and its effect nationally, O'Neill visited the men on Friday, 28 September, and on the Saturday. Austin Stack informed him that through one of the prisoners, J. J. Liddy, a list of their demands for presentation to the government had been drawn up. The demands dealt with matters of leisure, food, visitation, and communication; concerns which would differentiate them from the common criminals. A copy was given to the Lord Mayor, who, as intended, had it communicated to the Chief Secretary. About 8.0'clock on the Saturday evening, 29 September, Mr Duke phoned the Mansion House. He wished to see the Lord Mayor straightway. The latter said he would meet him about 9 o'clock, as he had an appointment in the meantime with the Archbishop of Dublin. When he informed Dr Walsh that he was meeting the Chief Secretary, he received the circumspect advice: 'Be careful, and any agreements come to, let them be on paper'.

It was a memorable night for O'Neill. 'As I drove up the avenue to the Chief Secretary's Lodge, a glorious night in September, everything looked so peaceful, but amidst the peaceful looking surroundings, bayonets glistened…' When he was ushered into the large room in which Mr Duke was sitting, the latter 'looked to be the picture of misery and loneliness, and when he came to greet me he seemed relieved, like a man who wanted to get a great weight from his mind'. They discussed Ashe's death, the hunger strike situation, and the prisoners' demands. Duke produced the Privy Council's order, made that day. They compared it carefully against the demands, and the Lord Mayor took a note. Duke arranged that at once the prisoners could have any class of food they wished supplied from outside. 'He looked and spoke like a man, who would, if he could, send them to the best hotel in the country to get rid of them'.

In retrospect, O'Neill reflected that the Chief Secretary was 'a fair minded man, placed in an almost impossible position, and the pity of it all was that he was not in a position to grant all these concessions when Irwin and I myself called and warned him of the consequences. No, order had to come from Downing Street, London. But it was ever thus in this country, some noble soul must perish before just demands are granted'.

The Lord Mayor left Mr Duke very late at night and made his way to Mountjoy prison. He informed Austin Stack that their demands had been granted, with slight alterations. Stack would not accept the Chief Secretary's word, but he took O'Neill's assurance, which left on the latter 'a responsibility and a duty' regarding the carrying out of the agreement. It was to cause him, he recalled, 'nights and days of ceaseless trouble'. Before he left the prison at 12.30 a.m., however, he 'had the satisfaction of seeing all the prisoners taking light refreshment'. He called on the archbishop on his way back to the Mansion House. At that very late hour, 1.0 a.m., Dr Walsh was waiting to meet him. 'He was relieved that the hunger strike was off, and that the men had come out of it with honour.'

Later that Sunday morning, O'Neill called at the National Aid Office with the news that the concessions had been granted, He described his welcome:

> A dark, strongly built young fellow, with a slight scowl on his
> face, came to meet me, and with a "well-what-do-you-want"
> tone of voice informed me 'I am in a hurry'. At this
> period neither of us was personally known to the other. It was
> the first time I met Michael Collins, who was to loom so much
> in the affairs of our country in such a short time, and one
> with whom after, in my position as Lord Mayor, I had
> many delicate negotiations.[54]

That Sunday, 30 September, the massive funeral took place without incident. Nine thousand Volunteers, from all over the country, along with the Irish Citizen Army, marched in the procession, and were joined by 18,000 trade unionists and representatives from various public bodies and from every Catholic fraternity and every trade and business association in Dublin. The *Irish Independent* commented next day on 'the real significance of yesterday's unprecedented demonstration', namely, that 'the people from the archbishop down to the humblest citizen, while paying tribute to the memory of the dead also desired to register a protest against a regime and practice which they regarded as needlessly vindictive and harsh'.[55]

At the graveside, after three volleys had been fired and a bugler had sounded the last post, Michael Collins stepped forward and gave the briefest of orations over an Irish patriot's grave. He delivered a few words in Irish, which were not recorded, and then declared in English: 'Nothing additional remains to be said. That volley which we have just heard is the only speech which it is proper to make above the grave of a dead Fenian'.[56] That ended the official ceremony; but the example of Thomas Ashe was to stay with thousands of young men and women and, in a special way, with subsequent prisoners.

Prisoners and concessions

The prisoners' issues were to hold attention for the remainder of the year. On 29 September, the General Prisons' Board, with the approval of the Privy Council in Ireland, exempted prisoners under the Defence of the Realm Act from most of the rules applying to other classes of prisoners. They were to be treated, henceforth, as political prisoners. Lord Mayor O'Neill, given his sense of responsibility for the implementation of the concessions, continued to visit Mountjoy on a regular basis. Reflecting on that time, his memory was of prisoners reaping the benefit of the concessions. 'They had a special enclosure allotted to them, where they could play games for the length of the day. They had the full run of the prison wing, their cell doors were left open until late at night, they had absolute freedom within the prison walls. What a change from a few days before. They were now the warders masters.' Asking one man how he was getting on, he received the answer that he was 'as happy as a lamb with two mothers'. Enquiring generally if they had any complaints, 'one complained about the flavour of one of his eggs; another that he had a lump of fat in his soup'. Subsequently, enquiring from Austin Stack, in the presence of J.J. Walsh and Finian Lynch, what was the cause of the prisoners raising such petty complaints about eggs, soup and so on, he received the blunt response, which later he had cause to remember: 'Our great object is to break down the prison system'.

The prisoners, however, expressed their gratitude to Lord Mayor O'Neill by presenting him with an inscribed scroll, signed by all who took part in the hunger strike from 20-30 September 1917, in which they conveyed:

> Our sincere thanks for your efforts on behalf of our gallant
> comrade, Thomas Ashe, … and on our own behalf during
> that trying period and subsequently when you spared no
> efforts to have the concessions which we won – to be treated
> as political prisoners – carried out.[57]

The prisoners' distrust of the authorities ran deep. Within a few days, on 3 October, they threatened to resume their hunger strike because the implementation of certain of their privileges had not taken place – permission to smoke, write letters, receive newspapers and books. The Lord Mayor made his way across the city to the prison, met the prisoners, and then consulted Mr Duke. Next day, 4 October, O'Neill announced that the outstanding concessions would be granted at once.[58] He brought the draft of the rules to Austin Stack on the morning of 6 October. That evening, Austin Stack sent a message that he had not had sufficient time to study the document fully. He now wished to inquire whether, in addition to such items as smoking, visits, and diet, the prison board's concessions included – ' cells not to be locked' till 9.45 p.m.. Lights in cells 'till 9.45 p.m.' 'It is most important', Stack declared, 'that we should see and approve of the whole of the regulations and scale of diet before the same are finally issued. I hope to receive the copy, which you are to have made for me by Monday.' Then, acknowledging that he and the prisoners' demands had been burdensome, he concluded: 'The whole matter has been a source of much trouble to you and I must apologise for continuing to bother you about it'.[59] These requirements resulted in further concessions before the political prisoners were moved to Dundalk on 12 November.

O'Neill felt very strongly not only about Under Secretary Byrne's remarks on the occasion of the deputation seeking the withdrawal of the military from the City Hall, but about his denial that he made them, thereby casting doubt on the truth of O'Neill's account. Hence, when on 1 November he received a letter from the Under Secretary, offering an indirect olive branch in the form of congratulations on his recent public offer to act as mediator in the city's industrial disputes, and assuring him of such government assistance as might be required,[60] Lord Mayor O'Neill's instinctive response was short and sharp. In the draft of a letter he sent or intended to send, he stated bluntly: 'Until you publicly withdraw, and apologise for the insult you recently offered to a vast percentage of my fellow country men and women, living and dead, by the words "criminals" and "suicides", I wish to have nothing to do with you; and I should be … to steer the affairs of this city to the best of my ability without your help'.[61]

O'Neill also decided that it was important to place before the Corporation his account of what had taken place. On 5 November he explained that he wished to give his account because the matter had developed into a very grave question of principle affecting 'not alone the high dignity of his office but as well the credit of the citizens and the peace of the country'.[62] Following his account, Ald. Thomas Kelly moved, and Clr. John T. O'Kelly seconded the motion: 'That we express our sincere appreciation of the action of the Lord Mayor during the tragic circumstances of the forcible feeding of the Irish political prisoners in Mountjoy Jail, followed by the lamented death of Thomas

Ashe'. The motion was passed, and then, Clr. Wm. Cosgrave perceptively proposed an *addendum*, which was accepted, 'That this council accepts unreservedly the statement now submitted by the Lord Mayor in connection with the interview with the British Under Secretary'. The motion with the *addendum* was then put and was carried unanimously.[63]

At the same meeting, the growing mood of independent Irishness was reflected in two letters seeking approval. One was from the Gaelic League, which sought the support of county councils and public bodies to ensure that any company wishing to erect signposts should recognise the Irish language by being, at least, bilingual. A motion to that effect was moved and carried.[64] The second letter was from Thomas Kent, Hon. Secretary of a Sinn Féin club, which requested that the Corporation stipulate 'that Irish stone only will be used in the work of re-construction of the destroyed areas'. This, too, received approval. Sinn Féin's public standing had been emphasised at the Mansion House less than a fortnight previously.

On 25 October, the Lord Mayor hosted what came to be a historic Sinn Féin convention. Some 1,000 Sinn Féin clubs, and 1,700 delegates, attended from all over the country. O'Neill noticed much disparity between the clubs, but that there were two general groupings: those looking to Arthur Griffith and John McNeill, and those drawn to Cathal Brugha and Count Plunkett. It was apparent to him that even before the meeting commenced, 'cliques and jealousies were maturing, as it was common property that Arthur Griffith was going to be superseded as president of Sinn Féin, and canvassing for seats (on the executive) was going on'.[65]

The meeting opened with Arthur Griffith taking the chair. But he immediately announced he was withdrawing from the presidency in favour of Mr Eamon de Valera. Count Plunkett, who had also been nominated for president, did likewise. All sides found a form of unity behind the romantic figure of de Valera, who, by association with 1916 and his leadership during internment in Britain, had caught the public imagination. In the other administrative elections: Griffith and Fr Michael O' Flanagan were elected vice-presidents; W.T. Cosgrave and Laurence Ginnell, honorary treasurers; and Austin Stack and Darrell Figgis, honorary secretaries. In the election for the twenty-four members of the executive, the counting of the votes went into the early hours of the morning. Clr William Cosgrave, M.P., kept O'Neill informed on the progress of the count as old stalwarts like Ald. Tom Kelly were cast aside and young men and new policy made a bid for supremacy. In the final count, Eoin McNeill easily topped the poll, Cathal Brugha came second, and the last elected, with the lowest vote of the twenty-four, was Michael Collins. As the figures were announced, each name received its share of cheering, but the cheering for McNeill was more prolonged, reflecting victory over the almost hysterical opposition to him conducted by Countess Markievicz and most of the women. Griffith had defended McNeill as having done the best for Ireland as he saw it, and he asserted that he would stand or fall with John McNeill. As Lord Mayor O'Neill heard the result of the election, he thought – 'A victory for Arthur Griffith, but for how long?'[66]

Prisoners again

The Corporation's support for the Lord Mayor on the issue of Thomas Ashe and the hunger strikers, at their meeting on 5 November, was far from signalling the close of prisoner problems. On 13 November, the day after their removal to Dundalk prison, Austin Stack wrote to the governor of the prison announcing a hunger strike. His letter angered Lord Mayor O'Neill because it appeared to rank him as working for the British government, an association that would undermine his standing and credibility with many citizens. Stack had written: 'Owing to the repeated attempts on the part of the prison authorities to break through the agreement made by the Lord Mayor of Dublin on behalf of the British government with ourselves, which culminated today when we were offered breakfast according to class "D" on dietary scale for ordinary prisoners, we have decided to hunger strike until the British government have fulfilled the following conditions.' The conditions required the drafting of new rules embodying all the terms of the previous agreement, to be printed and published within seven days; these included the restoration of a dietary scale, such as existed in Mountjoy from 3 September, – and he named, in detail, the food to be provided at breakfast, dinner, and tea; and a clause was to be added 'to the effect that the prisoners shall not be sent out of Ireland pursuant to the undertaking given by the Lord Mayor of Dublin on behalf of the Chief Secretary', and that 'visits be allowed each day including Sundays'.[67]

That same day, 13 November, the Lord Mayor, as the party trusted by both sides, received permission from the chairman of the General Prison Board to see the prisoners at Dundalk prison. During his visit he made it clear to Austin Stack his concern at the wording of the latter's letter to the governor, and he required a letter from Stack exonerating him from any suggestion of collusion with the government. The following day, Stack sent his letter of apology. With reference to the letter he addressed to the governor of the prison the previous day, he wished to assure the Lord Mayor at once that nothing was further from his intention than to suggest that he (the Lord Mayor) was 'acting on behalf of the British government or for the English Chief Secretary'. 'What I meant,' Stack continued, 'was that the agreement between the British government and ourselves was arrived at through you… From beginning to end I could see that you acted entirely in our interest.' O'Neill was at liberty to make any use of the letter that he thought fit.[68]

Later, Lord Mayor O'Neill jotted down some impressions of Austin Stack: 'I look upon Austin Stack as one of the most determined and indurable (sic) men I have met or had dealings with. Yes, Austin Stack was a superior type of man'. He had a strong will-power, and though outwardly distant he had underneath a warm personality and was 'all good nature to those who led or helped towards the independence of his country'.[69]

On his visit to Dundalk on 13 November, O'Neill found the prisoners on hunger strike. Having satisfied himself that they had right on their side, he returned to Dublin and phoned the Chief Secretary. He 'taxed him with the Ashe agreement having been broken'. Mr Duke 'plaintively wailed' "What can be done?" O'Neill suggested that the easiest way out of the difficulty was to release the men. Whether or not there was any connection, eight men were discharged from Dundalk a few days afterwards.[70]

Municipal Problems

Prior to, and during these demanding situations, Lord Mayor O'Neill was faced with a variety of issues of major importance to the ordinary citizens of Dublin. Quite early in the year, the urgency of the housing question was underlined by a representative committee, chaired by Dr Walsh, Archbishop of Dublin, and including six members of parliament, among them Edward Carson, and representatives of the Chamber of Commerce and the Dublin Trades Council. It requested the Lord Mayor 'to convene a representative conference to consider the question of Dublin housing with a view to preparing a plan for its settlement to be put into operation when the war is over'. The committee was careful to emphasise that it did not wish that any approved plan of the Corporation be abandoned or suspended. On 3 March, 1917, the Lord Mayor responded positively to the request. He invited Dublin Corporation to nominate twelve delegates to the representative conference.[71] As with all attempts to solve the housing problem, it was clear that the cost and work involved would require considerable government funding. Circumstances were to dictate that the hoped for government assistance would not be forthcoming.

More immediately pressing as the weeks went by was the high cost of living, shortage of food and fuel, unemployment and industrial unrest. On 4 June 1917, the city council expressed concern at the privation and suffering being experienced by many of the poorer citizens, and intense alarm at 'the recently imposed restrictions on the manufacturing and output of brewing and distilling', which 'were certain to bring about untold unemployment and poverty and throwing thousands of workers on the rates'. The council formally protested against the threat of state control to the breweries. [72]

By the 1 November, Lord Mayor O'Neill felt it necessary to write to the *Freeman's Journal* expressing disquiet at the serious disputes between employers and employees in the trade of the city. He asked all to stay their hands, and offered to arbitrate 'as far as might be desired'. 'We are passing through times of great stress', he concluded, 'and I sincerely hope that wise counsels will prevail'. Two days later the *Dublin Saturday Post* underlined the gravity of the situation in its editorial. 'There seemed to be no solution to the notices of strike from thousands of workers due to end this weekend.' It endorsed his Lordship's appeal and hoped 'that some definite steps would be taken at the eleventh hour'. 'The workers', the editor added, 'find themselves unable to pay the exorbitant prices demanded from them for the bare necessaries of life. Their protests to the government have been unavailing.' They felt that only by strong action could they hope to get an increase in wages 'to meet the present cost of living, which, according to the latest Board of Trade returns, is now 97 percent higher than the pre-war cost'.

On 17 November, the *Freeman* noted that the Lord Mayor had presided in the Mansion House between representatives of the Dublin Coal Merchants' Association and the Transport Workers' Union. By 21 November the paper was able to announce some improvement in the labour situation. 'This happy result is in measure due to the reasonable attitude adopted by both masters and men, and particularly to the good offices of the Lord Mayor, but for whose praiseworthy, indefatigable, and invariably successful exertions a crisis would have been precipitated at the most inopportune time of the year.' On 23 November, the paper reported a settlement in the Dublin printing trade in which the Lord Mayor played a central role. The *Dublin Saturday Post* of 1 December, under the heading "Labour Troubles Settled", explained that, after weeks in dispute, both parties in the printing trade agreed to recommend the Lord Mayor's award to their respective associations. The men had asked for an increase of ten shillings a week and a shorter week of 3 hours in some cases and 5 hours in others. The Lord Mayor awarded the men 5 shillings a week and a reduction of one hour. He had also, the paper explained, actively interested himself in other local labour troubles and, in addition, was doing his utmost to establish a wages and conciliation board for the city. His proposal had received warm support in many quarters. The idea of a permanent conciliation board had long been championed by Archbishop Walsh.[73]

Towards the end of November, Lord Mayor O'Neill delivered a severe indictment on an issue close to his own business interests. There was a 'hay famine'. The government, for war purposes, had commandeered or purchased large quantities of hay, and a number of farmers, besides, were holding on to their crop instead of bringing it to market. Hay and straw became scare in the city and their price rose. A public meeting was held at the Mansion House on 26 November for the purpose of 'requesting the War Office to remove all restrictions on the movement of hay and straw in the county of Dublin, and to release all commandeered or purchased ricks of hay'. By 15 December, the Lord Mayor was able to report that with the help of his esteemed colleague, Alderman Byrne, the hay question was improved from the previous week.[74]

The food shortage in the city became so acute at the start of December that the Lord Mayor requested the City Council on 3 December to consider what was best to be done to prevent a shortage of food supplies before it was too late. 'In his opinion there was plenty of food in the country at present if it were properly guarded and distributed.' It seemed to him that in every step the authorities had taken their object 'seemed to be to help the rich and the profiteers to the detriment of the middle classes and the poor of the city'.[75] A typical example was with the potato crop. 'There was a system of thimble-rigging between the Government and the growers. As a consequence, the city was left without potatoes, and he feared the same would happen as last year – the potatoes would be allowed to rot while the poor were starving.' He appealed to the public representatives to keep their eyes on the growers and to prevent potatoes from leaving the country till the needs of the people were satisfied. Turning to the price of oats, 'he found that buyers from England had gone beyond the controller's price, and that thousands of tons of oats were leaving the Irish ports'. After discussion, the Lord Mayor moved, and Ald. Byrne seconded, 'That a committee consisting of six members (named) of this Council, together with the Lord Mayor, … be appointed to consider food supply for the city'. An *addendum* was put forward by Clr. Patrick T. Daly – 'And that the committee be empowered to convene an all-Ireland conference to consider the whole question of Irish food supplies'. The motion, with the *addendum*, was put and carried.[76]

One of the most critical matters was the availability of milk, especially for the children of the poor. Already, at a council meeting on 3 September, Clr. Briscoe had protested at the price of milk being raised to 6 pence per quart. This raise, he stated, vitally affected the interests and health of the general body of citizens and meant that the children of the poor would suffer much hardship. He moved that 'we direct and empower the public health committee to take all steps necessary to enable the supply of milk to be continued to the citizens at a reasonable price'. Little seems to have been effected, for on 10 December the *Freeman's Journal* carried a letter from the Lord Mayor under the banner headline: "The Threatened Milk Famine. The Government's Duty to Secure City's Supply." In his letter, the Lord Mayor uttered a warning of the grave consequences 'for the poor and for the infant poor in particular' if an impasse were allowed to occur. It was the duty of the Government to see to an adequate supply, and he hoped that, even at this last moment, it would exercise its powers discretely to that end.' The government order fixing the price of milk was due to come into force on the forthcoming Monday. 'Drastic penalties' were 'threatened for infringement'.

In the week prior to the operation of the government order, 'members of the Dublin Dairymen's and Cowkeepers' Association declared they would continue to sell at 8 pence a quart.' There was also a tendency among them to reduce their herds, and 1,000 milch cows were due to be auctioned on the coming Thursday.[77] On Wednesday the shortage of milk supply was such that hundreds of families in the poorer districts were unable to buy the small quantity needed by them. On the Sunday, just before the government order came into effect, the Dairymen, under protest, decided to abide by the regulated selling price over the counter of 5 pence per quart and, if delivered to the house, 6 pence. 'This decision', in the view of the author of "The Citizen's Diary" in the *Dublin Saturday Post* of 15 December, 'was the result of the Lord Mayor's intervention in the interests of the citizens generally, and of the poor in particular (especially expectant mothers and children)'. 'In the meantime, the books of the selected milk vendors' were 'being examined for the purpose of ascertaining whether or not milk could be supplied at the government price.' The Council's Commmittee on Food had met with milk vendors from Louth, Meath, Cork and Tipperary, all of whom claimed they could not survive if they kept to the regulation prices. Finally, with regard to another essential item, the "Citizen's Diary" relayed the good news that, thanks to the strong action of the council's special committee, a better supply of potatoes was coming to the markets.

In an era without a state- welfare system, voluntary organisations and generous individuals played an important role in alleviating poverty and sickness. Lord Mayor O'Neill acknowledged this on 5 December with respect to the Dublin branches of the Women's National Health Association of Ireland. At the annual meeting of the executive of the city and county, held in the Mansion House, he paid tribute to their efforts 'to relieve the suffering of the poor, to bring happiness into their homes, and to grapple with the deadly disease of tuberculosis'.[78] Among the individuals who involved themselves generously in assisting the less well-off was the Lady Mayoress. She was patron of Sunshine House, which catered for boys from deprived families, some of whom sold newspapers on the streets, and arranged for a sea-side holiday for them each year. Dublin press photographers showed her crowning the children's May Queen at the civic playground, Constitution Hill, and visiting and inspecting one of the city's cooked food depots, at Belvedere Court, Upper Gardiner Street, which supplied cooked food at cost price to working class people. She played a key role as companion and friend to Laurence O'Neill, as well as accompanying him to certain functions, and with their two daughters making the Lord Mayor's guests welcome at the Mansion House.

Intense political feeling

In the final months of the year the socio-political scene continued to undergo significant change. Less than four weeks after his election as president of Sinn Féin, de Valera was elected president of the Volunteers. Significantly for the future, he now led both the political and para-military wings of the movement. A section of the latter wing had little patience with politics or contrary authority figures such as Cardinal Logue, who, in a pastoral letter had criticised republicanism as utopian and dangerous. As a result, de Valera appears to have had difficulty in restraining the impatient militancy and critical tendencies of a number of his men. Writing to a trusted supporter, Bishop Michael Fogarty of Killaloe, on 28 November, he bemoaned criticism by the bishops as encouraging hostility to the Church among members of the movement 'who love their country passionately, and who cannot understand why what is a virtue in Belgium, France, Poland, England and Germany should be a crime in Ireland'.[79]

A colleague of Laurence O'Neill, who also loved his country passionately, was a committed socialist and Christian, and was jailed for his participation in the 1916 rising, Clr. William Partridge, wrote from prison in England to the members of Dublin City Council. His letter was read at the council meeting of 30 April, 1917. He expressed the hope that political prisoners would not accept a compromise in order to gain release. 'For myself', he asserted, 'I would certainly prefer to finish my full sentence – or indeed I would rather die a convict and be buried inside prison walls – than consent to have my freedom purchased by the smallest portion of such a price.' To Alderman Laurence O'Neill he sent his heartiest congratulations upon his well-merited election to the mayoral chair. With all good wishes for a successful term of office, he prayed his mayoralty 'may witness the termination of this terrible war, and the restoration of peace and prosperity to brave old Dublin and that dear old land of which Dublin is the capital'.[80]

He did not survive the year; [81]no more than O'Neill's mayoralty witnessed "the termination of the terrible war and the restoration of peace and prosperity" to Dublin and the country. Nevertheless, it was almost universally agreed that Alderman O'Neill had a very successful first term of office in trying times. Despite shortness of stature and a less than imposing appearance, his assured ease of manner and his interest in people and his commitment to his office seldom failed to impress. He assumed good in others and that he could get along with them, irrespective of their reputation or background, and that they would like him. And this somehow seemed to elicit a positive response from them. Laurence O'Neill, therefore, at the close of his first year in office was acceptable to virtually all sectors of society, and was popular with press, people, and the vast majority of his colleagues.

He and the Lady Mayoress made the Mansion House a welcoming focal point in the city. It was open to all kinds of people and organisations, and was a place which drew visitors from many parts of Ireland and overseas. The range of people calling to the Mansion House during Laurence O'Neill's term of office is suggested by the names in the visitors' book for 1917-1918. Irish citizens, lay and clergy, male and female, irrespective of religion or political allegiance, were made welcome as much as dignitaries such as Major General Fry, the Royal Hospital Kilmainham, the Countess of Fingal, or the Royal Italian Consul. The plurality of visitors is best indicated by listing the names of a great many of them largely as they occur: Dr Denis Coffey, president University College Dublin, and Mrs Coffey, the Bishop of Clonfert, Dr Thomas P. Gilmartin, Major Dease, Thomas Bodkin, the Earl of Granard, Horace Plunkett, Erskine Childers (with an address in Chelsea), Lord Middleton (twice), R.V. Vernon (the Under Secretary's Lodge), Lieut. Col. J.J. Clarke, the Earl of Desart, Lord Aranmore and Browne, Sir William Goulding, S.B. Quin, Mayor of Limerick, Lord Smithborough, Bishop Patrick Finegan, Kilmore; and there was a stream of overseas visitors from Australia, the United States of America, Rhodesia, South Africa, New Zealand, and from Rome a number of Irish clergy. In 1918 the nation-wide anti-conscription movement was to result in a more concentrated range of visitors – politicians, clergy, trades unionists from different parts of the country and different traditions.[82] In that year, Laurence O'Neill became a national figure.

Notes

1   *Dublin Saturday Post,* 27 Jan. 1917

2   *Evening Herald,* Tues. 23 Jan. 1917

3   Idem

4   *Dublin Sat. Post,* 27 Jan.1917

5   The Irish Times of 6 March would report that the Corporation had received 1,200 applications for 269 plots.

6   Before the end of the year, the desired Local Government (Allotments and Land Cultivation) Act was introduced. See P. Yeates. *A City in Wartime,* pp. 182-3.

7   *Dublin Sat. Post,* 24 Feb. 1917

8   O'Neill Family Papers (ONFP). Among reminiscences of his years as lord mayor.

9   Family memory

10 Information from family members. There is some confusion about this, as will appear later. He appears to have received some funding from the Corporation as lord mayor.

11 Mins. of Dublin City Council, 1917, no. 268, p. 164

12 Idem. P.165

13 O'Neill Family Papers (ONFP). Notes on Mr H.E. Duke. Also NLI. O'Neill papers, Duke- Lord Mayor, 19 April 1917, Ms. 35,294/1.

14 *Evening Telegraph,* 11 June 1917

15 ONFP. "Attempts to bring the Mansion House and the Viceregal Lodge into social intercourse".

16 Yeates. *A City in Wartime,* p. 179

17 Yeates. op.cit., pp. 180, 188

18 Cornelius F Smyth. *The History of the Royal Automobile Club 1901-1991*, p. 61

19 Idem, p. 87

20 P. Yeates. op. cit., pp. 11ff.

21 *Evening Telegraph,* 13 April.

22 ONFP. *"Stoppage of Horse Racing".*

23 ONFP. "Unemployment"; and NLI O'Neill papers. Ms. 35,294/1: W.P. Byrne- Lord Mayor, 26 June 1917.

24 ONFP. "Irish Cyclists 'Old Timers'." June 1917

25 ONFP. Idem.

26 DCC. Municipal Council Minutes. Special Meeting, no. 280, pp. 172-3

27 ONFP. "Proclamation by the Military. Ban on all public meetings"; and see Yeates, op. cit. p. 191

28 NLI. O'Neill papers, Ms. 35,294/1, 22 April, 1917.

29 ONFP. "Revolvers in the Mansion House", May 1917

30 NLI. O'Neill papers, Ms. 35,294/1. 22 May.

31 Idem. W.O'Brien-Lord Mayor, L. O'Neill, 23 May 1917.

32 *Irish Times*, 11,13 June 1917

33 NLI. O'Neill papers. Telegram 16 June, from Chief Sec. Duke. Ms. 35, 294/1

34 Yeates. op.cit., p. 196

35 NLI. O'Neill papers. Ms. 35,294/1.

36 *Freeman's Journal,* 24 July 1917

37 Wm. O'Brien papers, Ms 8557/9. Pos. 8425. W.M. Murphy- Wm O'Brien, 20 June 1917.

38 ONFP. Typed notes on "The Convention"

39 Idem

40 T.J. Morrissey. *William Martin Murphy,* pp.86-7

41 Idem. *Thomas Finlay,* S.J., 1848-1940, p. 115; and T.M.Healy. *Letters and Leaders of My Day,* vol.2, T.M. to Maurice Healy, 2 June 1917, pp.582,599

42 NLI. O'Neill papers. Ms. 35,294/1, Redmond to Lord Mayor, 5 Aug. 1971

43 ONFP. "Conversazione at Mansion House", Aug. 1917

44 ONFP. Typed notes on "The Convention".

45 Mins. Dublin City Council (DCC), 7 May, no.333, p. 218

46 Mins.DCC. 13 Aug. 1917, pp. 333-335

47 *Freeman's Journal,* 30 Aug. 1917; DCC. No, 505, p. 346

48 ONFP. Typed document – "Case of Joseph McDonagh"

49 Yeates. op. cit., p. 203

50 ONFP. Under heading "Sean McDonagh". Much of the material is as given in O'Neill's witness at the Thomas Ashe Inquest.

51 *Irish Catholic Directory,* 1918, with reports on 1917, 26 Sept.

52 NLI. O'Neill papers. Ms. 35294. Wm. Patrick Byrne-Lord Mayor, 27 Sept. 1917

53 *Dublin Saturday Post,* 10 Nov. 1917 reporting in "A Citizen's Diary" on the City Council meeting 'at which the Lord Mayor placed before his colleagues the full facts of his interview with the Under-Secretary, Sir William P. Byrne, on the occasion of the lying-in-state of Thomas Ashe'.

54 ONFP. Typed notes on "Hunger Strike"

55   Cit. Yeates, op. cit., p. 208

56   *Irish Independent,* 1, 4, Oct. 1917

57   The scroll is displayed in Kilmainham Jail museum.

58   *Evening Herald,* 4 Oct. 1917

59   NLI. O'Neill papers. Ms. 35,294/1. A. Stack-Lord Mayor, 6 Oct. 1917

60   NLI. O'Neill papers. Ms. 35,294/1. W.P. Byrne- Lord Mayor, 1 Nov. 1917.

61   ONFP. No date on the document. That he may not have sent the letter is perhaps suggested by a scribbled note attached to the letter – 'Remorse'. Mr Byrne 'in a new role'. The word after 'I should be' is illegible.

62   *Dublin Sat. Post.* "A Citizen's Diary". 10 Nov. 1917,

63   Mins. DCC. 5 Nov. 1917, no. 684, p. 464

64   Idem, no. 717, p.475

65   ONFP. Typed notes: "Sinn Féin Convention, Mansion House, 25 Oct. 1917"

66   Idem.

67   NLI. O'Neill papers. Ms. 35,294/1. A. Stack-Governor of Dundalk Prison, 13 Nov. 1917

68   Idem, A. Stack- Lord Mayor, 14 Nov. 1917

69   ONFP. "Austin Stack".

70   *Freeman's Journal,* 20 Nov. 1917

71   Mins. DCC 1917, no.178, pp. 108-9

72   Mins. DCC. 4 June 1917, no. 381, p. 250

73   T.J. Morrissey. *William J. Walsh, Archbishop of Dublin,* 1841-1921, pp. 188-191

74   *Dublin Sat. Post,* "A Citizen's Diary", 15 Dec. 1917

75   *Evening Telegraph,* 3 Dec. 1917

76   Mins. DCC. 3 Dec. 1917, no, 731, p. 484; and *Dublin Sat. Post,* 8 Dec. 1917

77   *Freeman's Journal,* 10 Dec. 1917

78   *Freeman's Journal,* 6 Dec. 1917

79   Killaloe Diocesan Archives. F.4, F.10, De Valera- Bp. Fogarty, 28 Nov. 1917.

80   Mins. DCC., Dec. 1917, p. 324

81   He died on 26 July 1917. The Lord Mayor moved the motion of deep regret at the council meeting on 13 Aug.1917, no. 481, p. 324.

82   On 18 April 1918, the anti-conscription convention at the Mansion House brought together Joseph Devlin, M.P., William O'Brien, M.P., John Dillon, M.P., T.M. Healy, M.P., Eamon de Valera, M.P., Thomas Johnson and Michael Egan representing the Irish Congress of Trade Unions, and Clr. William O'Brien, socialist and trade unionist. During 1918, the entries include many prominent republicans as well as de Valera (a regular visitor), Cathal Brugha, Terence MacSwiney, many clergy including Dr Walsh, Archbishop of Dublin, Dr MacRory, Bishop of Down and Connor, Dr Thomas Gilmartin, by then Archbishop of Tuam, Sir Charles Barrington, Bart., Glenstal, Dr Kathleen Lynn, four members of the Malon family, Keady, Co. Armagh, and an interesting contrast – four men from the auxiliary division of the Royal Ulster Constabulary and Michael Collins. A fairly frequent visitor was Rev. Michael C. Curran, secretary to Archbishop Walsh and subsequently assistant-president at the Irish College Rome. [NLI. Ms. "Visitors to the Lord Mayor and Lady Mayoress, the Right Honbl. Laurence O'Neill 1917-1918"]

8.
1918:
Defying Conscription.
Negotiating for Prisoners, Industrial Peace, and the invitation to the American President.

On 23 January 1918, Alderman Laurence O'Neill was re-elected Lord Mayor of Dublin with but one critical voice, that of the dedicated unionist, Ald. Quaid. In moving the re-election, Ald. Corrigan spoke of the dignity with which O'Neill conducted the business of the council, his settling of many business disputes in a manner which left no bitterness on either side, and his efforts to provide food for the people at a reasonable rate. 'He had succeeded in being a Lord Mayor for all the citizens of Dublin and not a section.' Clrs. MacAvin and Sean T. O'Kelly spoke in a similar vein, referring to him as a 'friend of the poor' and to his humanity in dealing with the hunger strikers.

Ald. David Quaid, however, disagreed that O'Neill represented the entire body of the citizens. Moreover, he did not approve of a second year in office, he objected to a testimonial (including a material gift) being presented by labour employees in the Mansion House to Clr. P.T. Daly, and he considered that the Lord Mayor had interfered with the independence of the council by appointing one of its members as his secretary. He was not, he insisted, speaking disparagingly of the Lord Mayor's secretary, nor denying the personal qualities of the Lord Mayor.

Ald. O'Neill, in an undistinguished speech, feared that the acute food problem would get worse in the next twelve months, but he was more optimistic about the world of labour, where he found a better spirit emerging. As to Ald. Quaid's comments, particularly his justifiable criticism of P.T.Daly, O'Neill treated them as a 'groundless assertion' and remarked disparagingly that 'they could treat with contempt the foul things which came from Ald. Quaid'.[1] Not for the first, or the last time, O'Neill shed urbanity and detached judgement when it came to Quaid.

The Lord Mayor received many congratulations on his re-election. He preserved two of them: one from Dr Walsh, the Archbishop, expressing his delight that the Municipal Council had not only 'done the right thing, but done it so well';[2] the other, on 25 January, from the Commander-in-Chief, who signed himself simply as Bryan Mahon, invited O'Neill to dine with him at the Royal Hospital Kilmainham, and congratulated him on his re-election, adding – 'I should rather say that I congratulate Dublin, as I do not suppose your position is an easy or envious one'.[3]

The New Year had opened with the welcome news that the export of butter from Ireland was to be prohibited;[4] and, at a council meeting on 7 January, O'Neill had assured a deputation led by William O'Brien, on behalf of the Dublin United Trades Council and Labour League, that measures were in contemplation to convene an All-Ireland Conference on the conservation of food supplies in the country.[5]

On 28 January, O'Neill presided over a large representative gathering from all over Ireland. Food was scarce, he warned, despite a good harvest and increased tillage. 'In most cities and towns they were coming nearer to a dreaded famine' due to the mismanagement of the government 'who rule our destinies in London'. The aim of the meeting was to set up some sort of machinery so that food supplies might be properly and evenly adjusted. Representatives from various parts of Ireland made reports and offered suggestions. The reports from Kilkenny and Limerick,[6] in particular, indicated much progress in meeting local needs. Seamus Hughes was the representative speaker for a combined group of Sinn Féin, Labour, and cooperative organisations and traders in Dublin city. He outlined an overall scheme which won approval. He suggested the appointment of town and county committees. The particulars about the surplus of food were to be sent to a county committee which would forward the returns to an All-Ireland committee to be tabulated and entered for the information of other localities. The conference which he represented, he explained, had come to the conclusion that the stopping of exports by violence was not an effective solution to the problem. Mr W.T. Cosgrave, M.P., stated that if the scheme were elaborated 'the Sinn Féin executive would put down £1,000 in order to carry it into effect'.[7] In the subsequent months the scheme was actively promoted.

Regarding the fuel problem, the Lord Mayor informed the conference that he had visited the Coal Controller the previous Saturday, and that that gentleman, who had executive power, was able to inform him that after the first of February he would be able to have their coal delivered at 10 shillings a ton less than they were currently paying for it. O'Neill suggested that similar executive powers be given to the Food Central Committee.[8]

To London with Convention

Meantime, the meetings of the National Convention were proceeding with mixed enthusiasm. Hopes for a worth-while settlement were fading, but the chairman, Sir Horace Plunkett, kept struggling on. O'Neill lost patience with the chairman reporting that 'he had letters from the Prime Minster, he had conversations with the Prime Minister, and the Prime Minister had written to him stating "that before decision was come to by the Convention on certain issues, he and his cabinet would be happy to confer with leading members, representing different sections".' O'Neill interjected rather abruptly, 'for goodness sake go over and see him'. A deputation was appointed from different sections to visit Lloyd George. To his surprise, O'Neill was selected, even though he was not a representative of any section. The deputation was composed of Dr. O'Donnell, Bishop of Raphoe, and Messrs. J. Devlin, M.P., William Martin Murphy, J. Gubbins, chairman of Limerick County Council, and the Lord Mayor of Dublin.[9]

On 29 January Horace Plunkett informed the Lord Mayor that the 6 February would be a provisional date 'for the opening of discussions with the war-cabinet in London', and that the Lord Mayor should be in London before that date[10]. On 2 February he expressed the hope that the Lord Mayor would accept the invitation from Sir Charles Russell and some representative Irishmen to dine with them in London on Wednesday, 6 February, to meet Lord Morley and General Smuts. In the same letter he confirmed that the meeting with his Majesty's Government had definitely been arranged for 6 February.[11] The meeting, however, was postponed. On 13 February, O'Neill, staying at the Savoy Hotel, received a telegram from Plunkett – 'Please come to Prime Minister's, 10 Downing Street, at eleven o'clock'.[12]

O'Neill's later memory of what took place was possibly coloured by subsequent events. 'We were ushered into the Prime Minister's room, where so many acts of fame and infamy were enacted in the building up of the British Empire. Lloyd George bounded into the room, meekly followed by Bonar Law, two men, whom you could see at a glance were of very different calibre: Lloyd George , with a clap on the back, how the devil are you, old man, salute; Bonar Law reserved and very cool.

The talking then commenced, George attempting to throw dust in our eyes all the time.' Lloyd George spoke of 'the glorious opportunity given the Convention to heal all differences between England and Ireland; how pleased the King, Parliament, and all the commoners in England would feel if an agreement were reached after seven hundred years of strife', and 'a lot of twaddle of this sort'. After an hour of talking, O'Neill put a question to the Prime Minister concerning (the control of) customs. He answered: 'Oh yes, Lord Mayor, that can be easily done', but at that Bonar Law intervened, addressing him: 'I fear, Prime Minister, you have made a mistake, that cannot be done'. The gentle rebuke, in O'Neill's eyes, had a world of meaning. 'I don't know what my colleagues' feelings were, but after our interview I felt the Convention must soon end, and that Lloyd George was not honest about Ireland.'[13] His colleagues returned home with different versions as to what the Prime Minister said.[14]

Laurence O'Neill recalled that 'with the reports of the interview with the Prime Minister the Convention ended, after sitting fifty one days, with innumerable committee meetings, from 2 July 1917 to 5 April 1918'. He defended its members against the critics of the Convention:

> Let no one say a hard word of the members of the Convention.
> With few exceptions, everyman who entered it believed he was doing his
> best for his country. For months they left their homes, coming long
> distances, neglecting their business or their professions.
> But from the first the dice was loaded against its success, and with it there
> perished the last attempt to gain a measure of freedom
> for our country by constitutional methods.[15]

O'Neill's final words about the convention were in relation to the person who impressed him most among the members. Responding to a question in this regard from 'a highly placed churchman', he observed that it was difficult to express an opinion about a body with so many great personalities, but the man who impressed him most, even though he seldom spoke, was:

> A man of quiet demeanour, enthusiastic without showing
> it, a hard business man as he had need to be, his arguments
> (were) sound, logical, and full of common sense, a good
> fighter, as he had proven, he held aloof from the many little
> intrigues, as far as I could see. One could plainly see his
> whole desire was a settlement, as he was in a position to
> gauge and realise what would happen if the Convention
> failed. A handsome, well-groomed old gentleman, Mr
> William Martin Murphy.[16]

O'Neill's testimony was all the more striking in that he was known as being favourable to Labour and he had been a firm supporter of James Larkin in 1913.

Political prisoners again

In the month prior to the end of the National Convention, the Lord Mayor was immersed in many matters. The treatment of political prisoners became an issue once more. In a familiar pattern, they resorted to hunger strike. O'Neill wrote to the newspapers declaring that the treatment of prisoners had become a serious problem. On 5 March he received a stark letter from former prisoner, Joseph Mac Donagh, charging him with not openly stating that Mr Duke had broken his word, and declaring that if anyone died in the current hunger strike he, the Lord Mayor, would be regarded as a man 'who was afraid to declare the truth' and a great deal of responsibility would lie at his door.[17] A large public meeting was held in College Green to protest at the treatment of the prisoners, and afterwards a deputation, consisting of de Valera, Griffith, Stack, Count Plunkett, and Countess Markievicz, called on the Lord Mayor.[18]

Later on that day, 5 March, O'Neill wrote to Mr Duke reminding him of the concessions granted to prisoners which, he had now learned from friends, were not being implemented. There must be some blunder because he could not believe that Mr Duke would be a party to breaking the agreement.[19] Duke replied the next day that the prisoners in question went on hunger strike not because 'of a failure to apply to them any special treatment but for the purpose of compelling their release, and for no other reason or purpose'. They could not be released. He pointed out, moreover, that the weapon of hunger strike was being widely abused. He instanced eight criminals who were protesting against their arrest by using hunger strike.[20] That night, James O'Connor, the Attorney General, an old friend of O'Neill from the cycling days, called to the Mansion House, declaredly on his own responsibility, 'to see what could be done about settling the … hunger strike'. By a coincidence Austin Stack was in the house at the time. This eased the problem for the Lord Mayor. Stack and O'Connor settled the matter to Stack's satisfaction. The Lord Mayor sent a letter to the Governor of Dundalk Prison conveying the agreement. The Governor, in acknowledgement, stated that the contents of the message were relayed to the prisoners and Mr Stack's orders to them.[21]

On 12 March, however, Dublin Castle issued an official statement 'that there was no truth in the statement that anybody representing the Government carried on negotiations with the Lord Mayor... in regard to the treatment of the prisoners on hunger strike in Dundalk or elsewhere'. When questioned by O'Neill about his being over-thrown by the authorities, O'Connor stated that he had not been acting officially for the Government when negotiating with Austin Stack. Subsequently, O'Connor was transferred to another position; and it turned out that different departments in the Castle, which were dealing with the question of the prisoners, were not communicating with each other regarding the Ashe agreement. [22]

On 20 March, Stack sent a letter to O'Neill which he had received from Terence MacSwiney in Dundalk Prison, and which stated that 'all the men had agreed to abide by Stack's letter, namely, to protest but not to take any further action' pending his negotiation in Dublin. The nine men accused of criminal activity were supported because their actions were seen as 'political'. The governor expected their case to be settled in a few days.[23]

Death of John Redmond

While O'Neill was negotiating with Mr Duke, John Redmond, in the aftermath of a successful major operation, died unexpectedly. The press gave much space to his death and career. The Dublin City Council, on 11 March, expressed its deep sense of the great loss which Ireland has suffered through his demise, and adjourned its meeting until 25 March as a mark of respect to his memory.[24] O'Neill, in his reflections on Redmond, recalled being on a visit to Belfast with him and Joe Devlin as members of the Convention. The three of them had a few drives together, during which Redmond was very quiet and obviously ill. His death moved O'Neill to muse on tragedy in Redmond's career – 'a honest man deceived, too trustful of the word, schemes or promises of English rulers of this country'. What tragedies were associated with the deaths of most Irish political leaders during the past 120 years! Popularity was so fickle. He had often thought there was 'too much of the personal in the political life of this country, too much attachment to personalities, very often to the detriment of great principles'. 'Whatever about Redmond's actions, sometimes mistaken, not even his most bitter enemy could question his motives.'[25]

Corporation business

The work of the Corporation continued from day to day. Meetings were taken up with reports from various committees and deputations on issues such as wages, housing, food shortage, and the annual problems of budgets and rates. The most prominent councillor in many ways was P. T. Daly, supporter of Labour and Sinn Féin, who proposed or seconded motion after motion, amendment after amendment. The city's estimates and rates were given a stormy reception on 25 March. The *Freeman's Journal*, the following day, carried the large heading: "City's Burden of Rates. Citizens' Deputation Indicts the Corporation". The Council had received a deputation from the Dublin Citizens' Association, a number of whom resided in the independent suburbs of Rathmines and Pembroke but had business premises in the city. The chairman of the Association pointed out that expenditure exceeded the estimates, and that the resulting rates were the highest rates in the history of the Council. The various Corporation departments were not being kept within their estimates. Mr W.J. Shields of the Association claimed that the Corporation was not doing its business in a proper fashion and had too many officials.

The Lord Mayor intervened at this point: 'Now we are getting down to business. Will you give us the names of these officials?' Mr Shields said he was not in a position to do so. Mr Howard Hely stated that 'speaking inferentially, Rathmines and Pembroke would not come into the city because they were satisfied things were not conducted as they might'. The Lord Mayor responded that men living in those areas made use of the city. They used 'an office for which they paid three shillings and sixpence a week, and earn thousands of pounds'. Mr P.T. Daly interjected – 'including some of the deputation'. The Lord Mayor continued: 'And they live in Rathmines and Pembroke, I am speaking inferentially also' (laughter).

The Lord Mayor then declared that 'the views of the Deputation would be taken cognisance of, and the estimates would be cut down to the lowest possible point. The Deputation, however, should remember that the members of the Council were ratepayers also. If the rate was high, they suffered as others did, and it was to their interest to see that the rates were cut down to the lowest possible figure'. To add to the difficulty of pleasing all the citizens, a further deputation, this time from the Dublin Trades Council, made it clear that they opposed any reduction of the rates.[26]

Whatever the drama and pressure on the Lord Mayor during March, he was to face far more in the next month. April was to prove one of the most challenging and exciting months of his life.

The Challenge of Conscription

The other populations of the United Kingdom had experienced compulsory conscription since 1916. The Easter Rising had deferred decision regarding Ireland. The need to impose it in Ireland seemed imperative to the British Cabinet following the breaking of the military deadlock in March 1918, when German troops crashed through the Allied lines. Word of the Government's intentions circulated widely in Ireland. There was concern and panic at the prospect of conscription being enforced, but uncertainty as to what to do.

Dublin Corporation stepped into the breach on 8 April.[27] Ald. Alfred Byrne proposed the following motion, to which Ald. Sherlock moved an *addendum*.

> That this Council, representing all sections of the City of
> Dublin, hereby warns the Government against the disastrous
> results of any attempt to enforce conscription in Ireland, and
> we earnestly request them not to be driven by a hostile
> Anti-Irish press campaign against considering any such insane
> proposal, which, if put into operation, would be resisted
> violently in every town and village in the country, ending in a
> a great loss of life and the establishing of a battle front in
> Ireland that would not be any advantage to the Allies or the
> cause which they are fighting for.

The *addendum* requested the Lord Mayor 'to invite Mr John Dillon, M.P., Mr de Valera, M.P., Mr Joseph Devlin, M.P., Mr Arthur Griffith, and representatives of the Irish Trades Union Congress, to meet him in conference to arrange for a united-Ireland opposition to conscription, and to consider the advisability of establishing an All-Ireland Covenant against it'. The motion and *addendum* were passed by 40 votes to 3. Those opposing were Aldermen Quaid and Dinnage, and Clr. Caultier.[28]

Two days later, 10 April, Horace Plunkett handed in his reports on the Convention, and, that afternoon, was sitting in the House of Commons when, to his dismay, he heard Lloyd George introduce a Military Service Bill which gave the Government power to raise the military age in Britain to fifty-one years, and to extend the principle of conscription to Ireland. The Prime Minister coupled it with a pledge to introduce a Home Rule measure before the conscription provision came into effect.[29] As few at this stage trusted British promises, the attention of all in Ireland, apart from unionists in the north-east, was focussed on conscription.

That same day, Laurence O'Neill sent out invitations to an anti-conscription conference. In addition to the names proposed by the Council, he invited Mr T.M. Healy, M.P., and Mr William O'Brien, M.P., as he considered that a conference without them would be incomplete. He also suggested that Labour be represented by members from the three main cities- Dublin, Belfast, and Cork. Interchanging letters and telegrams with members of different political parties, and then finding an agreed date for the conference, proved a delicate and tedious exercise.

On 12 April the impetus towards unity received a boost by a declaration from the Catholic hierarchy, which referred to rumours about conscription 'as yet unconfirmed', but which, given the War Office's lack of real touch with Irish conditions, might now be proposed. 'To enforce conscription here without the consent of the people', the bishops warned, 'would be perfectly unwarrantable, and would soon and inevitably end in defeating its own purpose …'

As days passed, the country became impatient with the delay in providing a common front. It was particularly difficult to get John Dillon to agree to a date. He claimed that conscription would be best fought in the House of Commons. Griffith and de Valera suggested that the conference go ahead without Dillon. 'By a little tact and patience', as O'Neill put it, 'the first meeting of the conference was eventually held in the Mansion House on 18 April, all attending'. 'As I had summoned the conference', he continued, 'I was in the chair, and it took all the ingenuity I possessed to make a favourable start.' He recorded his memory of the participants. John Dillon was 'solemn, and no doubt realised that the power of his party was diminishing and that by attending the conference he was playing into the hands of Sinn Féin'. Healy, 'right way was insuppressable'. De Valera – 'loveable but voluble, at once pleading his inexperience'. Griffith – 'silent, but very little escaped him'. Devlin – 'carefully guarding Dillon from Healy's thrusts'. O'Brien (Mallow) –' with a look of paternal affection towards his comrade, Tim'. Labour – 'calmly surveying: Johnson (as secretary) taking notes; William O'Brien- pulling his well-trimmed beard and looking very dogged. A man with a dark exterior, and one who would go a long way to get his own back; but in my dealings with him during labour troubles, and as a member of Dublin Corporation, I always found him as straight as the barrel of a gun. Egan, T.C. (Cork) – a Justice of the Peace, a man of quiet and unassuming disposition. His great anxiety was how conscription affected Cork.'[30]

Despite their motley character, the members were borne up by the expectation of the great mass of the population. Initially, O'Neill had envisioned a conference representative of nationalist and unionist opinion, but, as he informed William O'Brien, M.P., he had had difficulty coming up with suitable unionist names.[31] The *Evening Herald* for that day, 18 April, carried the headline: "A Fateful Day. Momentous Meeting of the Irish… Leaders. A United Ireland." The text commented that the eyes of every Irishman and woman were turned to Dublin awaiting with feverish anxiety the decision of the conference, and there could be no doubt that the people of the country would stand by the decision … The Irish Hierarchy were meeting at Maynooth to discuss the situation. The people were advised to remain calm and continue to be united…'

O'Neill, prompted by Archbishop Walsh, arranged the conference to coincide with the meeting of the Hierarchy in Maynooth. A number of the representatives were concerned to have the bishops supportive of their decisions.[32] There were in fact a number of private meetings prior to the conference largely engineered by Dr Walsh. His secretary, Fr Michael Curran, informed de Valera and O'Neill that the bishops were meeting on 18 April. The *Daily Express* observed on 17 April that de Valera had a lengthy interview with the archbishop in recent times. On the evening of the 17 April,

Dr Walsh called to the Mansion House and arranged with the Lord Mayor that he, the Lord Mayor, would telephone towards lunch time the following day to arrange for the reception of the conference delegates by the bishops at Maynooth. In order to conceal this pre-arrangement the archbishop's name was to be kept secret.[33] On the morning of 18 April, de Valera brought to Archbishop's House a copy of the resolution he intended to have passed by the conference. Dr Walsh considered it safer not to see him. Curran met de Valera and heard his request that the bishops would say nothing which would hinder those who were prepared to defend themselves with arms to the last. Curran conveyed to the archbishop the tenor of de Valera's message.[34]

The Mansion House Conference approved a defiant declaration on the lines proposed by de Valera, asserting Ireland's separate and distinct nationhood and the principle that the government of nations derived their just powers from the consent of the governed, and hence the absence of authority on the part of the British Government to impose compulsory service in Ireland against the expressed will of the Irish people. 'The passing of the Conscription Bill by the British House of Commons must', therefore, 'be regarded as a declaration of war on the Irish nation.'[35] De Valera then mentioned the desirability of meeting with the Catholic Hierarchy, and William O'Brien, the trade unionist and socialist, proposed that a deputation be appointed to go to Maynooth. Arthur Griffith seconded the proposal. The appointed deputation consisted of de Valera, John Dillon, Tim Healy, William O'Brien (Labour), and the Lord Mayor. O'Neill, meanwhile, had hired two cars to bring the deputation to Maynooth. Who was to travel with whom became a problem. The Lord Mayor, presumably tongue-in-cheek, remarked to T.M. Healy: 'Mr Healy, I don't suppose you'd like to travel with Mr Dillon?' 'Well', Healy replied, 'as the American colonel said, I can eat crow but I don't like it.' Dillon, the Lord Mayor, and O'Brien went in one car, and de Valera and Healy in the other. Healy's car had a puncture on the way to Maynooth, and Dillon's on the way back, which O'Neill thought was 'a fair distribution of the favours of Providence'.

On their arrival, they were warmly received by the bishops and invited to lunch. As O'Neill remembered the occasion, the conversation was somewhat restrained because Mr Dillon was present and Archbishop Walsh sometime previously, in connection with the Longford by-election, had publicly stated that the country had been sold.[36] William O'Brien remembered a discussion on two topics, whiskey and petrol.[37] After lunch the official meeting took place. In O'Neill's recollection of the event, he as chairman was placed on the cardinal's right, with Dr Walsh on his left. 'In that simple and unassuming manner most of us knew so well, the Cardinal (Logue) said, "Well, Lord Mayor, what can I do for you?" I made answer: "Your Eminence, we have a little pledge we wish you to take", which I handed to him.

As well as their agreed declaration, the deputation had designed a pledge which they wished the public to take, preferably outside their churches. They viewed it as 'A National Pledge. Ireland's Solemn League and Covenant', to which people would sign their name and address. It stated:

Denying the right of the British Government to enforce compulsory service in this country, we pledge ourselves solemnly to one another to resist conscription by the most effective means at our disposal.

Having received the pledge, the Cardinal then asked: 'Do any of the Gentlemen wish to speak?' 'A little shuffling took place as to who would speak first. I called on Dillon, Healy, and de Valera in rotation. Healy's speech in my estimation made the greatest impression.'[38]

O'Brien recalled 'de Valera was very strong' that the bishops should not 'say anything that could be taken as condemnatory of the Volunteer movement, because he said no matter who decided anything the Volunteers would fight if conscription was enforced', and he added, pointedly, they had no use for passive resistance. Cardinal Logue, taking the point, responded: 'Well, now, Mr de Valera, when I talk about passive resistance, I don't mean that we are to lie down and let people walk over us'.[39]

After the presentations, the Cardinal requested them to withdraw while he consulted his colleagues. When they withdrew into the grounds, the seminarians and younger priests flocked around de Valera, the professors and older clergy around Dillon, and Healy had the president and vice-president by his side. O'Brien and O'Neill looked on 'at the different strata of greatness'.[40] The Cardinal, meanwhile, had been taken aback by the bellicose mood of some of the bishops. They agreed on the following statement:

An attempt is being made to enforce conscription upon Ireland
against the will of the Irish nation and in defiance of the protests
of its leaders… We consider that conscription forced in this way upon
Ireland is an oppressive and inhuman law, which the Irish
people have a right to resist with all means consonant with the
law of God.

Following this strong statement, they called for strict adherence to the Divine law and urged fervent and persevering prayer, a national novena in honour of Our Lady of Lourdes, and the recitation of the rosary in families every evening with the intention of 'bringing us safe through this crisis of unparalleled gravity'. [41]

After a relatively short time, the Cardinal sent for the deputation. He announced: 'Lord Mayor we have decided to take your pledge'. After some discussion, the deputation thanked the Cardinal and his colleagues and departed for Dublin. Lord Mayor O'Neill was elated. With the hierarchy's support, he felt that conscription was killed. He later wrote that he had not been surprised by the quick response of the bishops: 'With my many conversations with the Archbishop of Dublin, and twice with the Cardinal, I had a very fair indication as to the action the bishops would take.'[42]

The conference re-assembled at the Mansion House between seven and eight o'clock. By then, the crowd outside the building had reached 'enormous proportions'. The conference drew up a manifesto, which appeared side by side with the statement of the bishops in the press next morning. At ten o'clock the conference adjourned until 11.30 a.m the following day. On their emergence, the delegates received an enthusiastic reception from some ten thousand people in Dawson Street. There were warm cheers for all. De Valera was lifted on the shoulders of his supporters. Crowds followed Mr Dillon to his residence in North Great George Street. As he entered the house, Dillon gave a fitting valediction to the day: 'I only desire to say good-night, and if the Nationalists of Ireland hold together no power on earth will conscript them out of Ireland'.[43] There was, as the *Freeman's Journal* observed, a new and united spirit in Dublin.[44]

On the evening of Friday, 19 April, de Valera and T.M. Healy called on Archbishop Walsh to discuss what was being termed the National Defence Fund, the legal aspects involved, and to make arrangements by which the Archbishop and the Lord Mayor would act as trustees with a third person to be named by the Mansion House Conference.[45] On the Sunday, at every Catholic Church, the pledge was recommended and a forthcoming collection to help resistance to conscription was announced. A million people signed the pledge. There was no flag waving, no rhetoric or mob hysteria, just an unmistakable, deep, tense determination to fight conscription.[46]

At the meeting of the conference on its second day, 19 April, there was some disagreement among the delegates,[47] but key decisions were made. Representative local committees of defence, selected from those who signed the pledge, were to be set up immediately in each parish; the question of local conservation of food supplies was considered with a view to possible developments; it was decided that a detailed statement of Ireland's case would be presented to the world, and the Lord Mayor was requested to arrange to proceed to Washington and to present in person the statement to the United States of America.[48] O'Neill, at this stage, had become a national figure – the convener and chairman of what was being termed the 'National Cabinet'.

At the meeting with the bishops on 18 April, William O'Brien announced that there would be a day off for workers in the coming week to enable them to take the pledge.

What that meant was vividly illustrated on Tuesday 23 April when, all over Ireland, except Ulster, there was a general cessation of work. 'There were no trains, trams, cars, or papers. All shops without exception were closed. There were no trains to Punchestown races and jarveys refused all bribes to carry passengers. In the hotels the guests had to cook and serve their own meals. It was a very effective and powerful warning of the resistance that could be offered on a large scale if necessary.'[49]

The strength of opposition to conscription gave rise to a concerted attack in the British press on nationalists and against the Irish clergy, the bishops, and the Vatican. The rabid Anti-Catholic (no popery) campaign continued in fury for a fortnight and was assisted by patriotic Roman Catholic Englishmen such as Lord Edmund Talbot, Lord Denbeigh, James Hope, and the Catholic Union of Great Britain.[50] Such criticism only stiffened resistance in Ireland. O'Neill, however, availed of the opportunity to bring some urbanity to the situation when he was approached by the *London Daily Express* for an interview. His was a disarming propagandist performance.

The special correspondent of the *Daily Express* reported in the Saturday issue, 4 May 1918, on his interview with 'one of the men of the moment in Ireland, Alderman Lawrence O'Neill, Lord Mayor of Dublin'.

> 'Here am I', he said, 'at the age of forty-seven, a plain man who never appeared on any political platform, unskilled in the arts of diplomacy, and not concerned to learn them, suddenly saddled with great responsibility for my country's sake. I am expecting my passports any day for my trip to Washington as the special representative of Ireland. My task is the simple one of stating Ireland's reasons for resisting conscription. President Wilson, I feel sure, will listen to me, as Mr Lloyd George and Mr Bonar Law did in London recently.'

'Leaving the room for a moment, Mr O'Neill returned with a photograph of his son in the uniform of an R.A.M.C officer'. He continued: 'Consider the paradox; I am serving my second year as Lord Mayor of Dublin by the unanimous selection of the Council. I am chairman of the Mansion House Conference opposed to conscription. During the Easter rebellion of two years ago I was imprisoned for ten days. Now I expect to go to America on what some would describe as an errand of disloyalty, and yet' – pointing proudly to the photograph – 'as you see, I have a son in the British army.'

> Mine is a typical case. Ireland's present hostile attitude to conscription is, no doubt, largely due to the blundering methods of the Intelligence Department in England…

Concluding the interview, Mr O'Neill remarked; 'The present is the most serious and yet the most hopeful crisis in the chequered relations of the two countries. Sane measures will be strongest. Force would be fatal.'

On the same date, 4 May, the *Daily Express* announced a radical change of government in Ireland: Field-Marshal Viscount French replaced Lord Wimborne as Lord Lieutenant, and Mr Edward Shortt, K.C. M.P. replaced Mr H. E. Duke as Chief Secretary. There had been divisions within Dublin Castle on the issue of partition and conscription,[51] and in the ranks of the police.[52]

The change in Government presented initial problems for the Lord Mayor. He had come to view Mr Duke and especially Sir Bryan Mahon as friends. The latter wrote to him on 13 May to wish him 'good-bye and good luck'. He was sorry to leave Ireland. 'You and I have seen one or two troublesome affairs through, and I will always be grateful to you for your support which you always gave me. *Au Revoir.*'[53] Mahon had been dismissed, in T.M. Healy's words, 'without the formality of as much notice as would be given a butler'.[54] O'Neill replied to his letter the following day, thanking Mahon for his foresight, energy, and courtliness, which enabled the 'troublesome affairs' to pass over without any ill effects. He regretted his leaving Ireland. But it was ever thus. When a man in a high position in Ireland endeavoured to do his duty in a fair and conscientious manner... dark happenings ...behind his back made it impossible for him to remain in his position. O'Neill concluded:

> You, Sir, and I may never meet again, and in the future
> a great gulf will naturally exist between us, but I shall
> always to the end of my days look back with grateful
> remembrance to your many kind acts – not alone to my
> country, but to me personally.[55]

The Mansion House Conference, in the meantime, continued its work of unifying and galvanising the opposition to conscription. On 5 May, de Valera and John Dillon shared the same platform in Dillon country, Ballahadereen, Co. Mayo. At the same time the seeds of division had been sown in the conference because of a parliamentary vacancy in Co. Cavan. Sinn Féin and Nationalist supporters were anxious to test their respective strengths in view of the general election due at the end of the year. The seat had been held by the Nationalists, Mr Dillon's party. He delayed in moving the writ for the by-election in order, as he said, to preserve unity in the conference. This angered Sinn Féin and also, for some reason, William O'Brien, and T.M. Healy. O'Brien raised the matter before the conference. Dillon refused to discuss it, saying that he had accepted the Lord Mayor's invitation on the understanding that the conference would deal with conscription only. The Lord Mayor then pointed out that the Cavan election was a question affecting conscription, and if there were any disagreement the morale of the people would be shaken. Dillon remained adamant.[56]

Concern about division was widely felt. Archbishop Walsh expressed to O'Neill the importance of having an agreed candidate[57]. O'Neill was widely pressed by people outside the conference to allow his own name to go forward. The Nationalist candidate, John F. O'Hanlon, apparently expressed willingness to withdraw in his favour. As Sinn Féin, however, was being very militant and the conference was blocked from dealing with the election, O'Neill felt that his stepping into the arena would do more harm than good, as it would lead to complications with Sinn Féin and weaken his position as chairman of the conference.[58] Arthur Griffith was nominated by Sinn Féin; John O'Hanlon by the Nationalists; and a vigorous campaign began.

Reports from within Dublin Castle reached the Mansion House that the Government planned to avail of the signs of division among the people, and that members of the conference were to be arrested and its funds seized. At the conference there were divided opinions about the reliability of the reports. Their trustworthiness was demonstrated on 17-18 May, when Sinn Féin leaders, including de Valera, Griffith, Darrell Figgis, W.T. Cosgrave, and Countess Markievicz were arrested, and, simultaneously, there was a vice-regal proclamation alleging Irish collaboration with Germany – the alleged "German Plot". Also detained were senior officers of the Irish Volunteers. Seventy-three persons in all were deported to England. With the leaders of anti-conscription removed, the collapse of opposition was expected. But substitutes for de Valera and Griffith had been nominated for the conference, namely, Professor Eoin McNeill, and Ald. Tom Kelly; and, one key figure had escaped arrest, Michael Collins. The new situation gave him a free hand to exercise his extraordinary gifts for organisation and motivation, and his capacity for ruthless action.

The work of the conference at this point was carried on by a standing committee, under O'Neill, of Dillon, Tom Kelly, O'Brien (Labour), Johnson, with Healy involved from time to time. Despite their difference in temperament and background, they worked well together. When Healy was absent, Dillon appeared far less aloof and took a 'kindly interest' in all the others.[59] The Lord Mayor summoned a special meeting of the conference for 23 May to protest at the arrest of so many fellow countrymen and women without trial and without charge. The conference denounced the arrests and deportation, and deplored the attempt, in the proclamation of Field Marshal French, to poison the English mind against the Irish prisoners by the sensational allegations of "a conspiracy in Ireland to enter into treasonable communication with the German enemy".' The conference appealed to their fellow countrymen and women to preserve their imperturbable calmness and their unshakeable determination to be faithful to their pledge in the face of all hazards; and it drew the attention of all friends of human freedom in the civilized world to the present British attempt to force a civil war upon the Irish people on the false pretext of military expediency.[60]

The conference also dealt with other matters. It described the exclusion of women from local committees as highly undesirable,[61] and decided to make public the Lord Mayor's correspondence with Mr A. J. Balfour, Secretary of State for Foreign Affairs, regarding his travel to Washington.

On 23 April, O'Neill wrote for a passport. His request caused some disquiet in Washington as well as in London. The State Department of the United States, unwilling to embarrass Britain, opposed and delayed the granting of a visa. In the face of the strong Irish lobby in America, however, President Wilson, on 4 May, commented to William Phillips, a diplomat in the States Department: 'It is plain to me that there is no way in which we can head off the Lord Mayor of Dublin though I think his visit is most unwise from every point of view. We can only follow the best course we can devise amongst us when he gets here. If he knew how little he was going to get out of the trip he would stay at home!' Two days later, Robert Lansing, the U. S. Secretary of State, cabled Ambassador Page (in London), 'You may visa passport for Lord Mayor of Dublin'. Mr Balfour also granted a passport, but with the proviso that the documents O'Neill carried must first be approved by the Lord Lieutenant. The condition had the desired effect intended by Balfour.

O'Neill replied to him on 15 May, thanking him for the passport and requesting that he relax the regulation preventing people bringing documents to the United States. On Balfour refusing to do so, O'Neill responded on 22 May: 'My Conference have decided that as "the document" is a direct communication between the Conference and the President of the United States, they decline to have it submitted to the Lord Lieutenant.'[62] This marked the end of the Lord Mayor's chances of meeting the President as envoy of the Conference.

Challenging Mr Healy

Also during May 1918, O'Neill's position as chairman, and the very cohesion of the conference, was threatened from within. T.M. Healy, when present, was difficult to control. He seemed driven by the desire to pay off old grudges against Dillon. He wrote to his brother on 21 May: 'Snigs at Dillon and Devlin at the Mansion House Conference have made them squeal… meanwhile, I enjoy myself'.[63] The point was reached of both

Dillon and Devlin threatening to withdraw from the conference. O'Neill had the feeling that that was what Healy had in mind. To face down a person of Healy's political experience and cutting wit was a daunting task. O'Neill nerved himself to do so. After one such unpleasant meeting, as he explained: 'I had the temerity to speak to Healy as to the dangerous game he was playing, and pointing out to him what a reflection it would be on the members of the conference if it were broken up owing to personal spite and bitterness of the past, and that Irishmen and women would forever execrate our names; and, moreover, I said to him that I considered that his heart was not as bitter as his tongue.'

'My little intervention,' O'Neill continued, 'seemed to have the desired effect. By degrees all the animosities and hatreds of over twenty-five years seemed to be fading away, and in a short time every member of the conference was greeting each other in a friendly spirit. Healy and Dillon paid each other compliments and letters passed between them.' Dillon stated at the conference 'that I was the only man in Ireland that could have succeeded in bringing them together; a rather unique compliment, if deserved.'[64]

Government pressure. Seeking American support

During June governmental pressure became more pervasive. Those in detention in England were not permitted to communicate with their families, who were still in ignorance of their whereabouts. The Municipal Council protested against this on 3 June.[65] A week later, the Council expressed disapproval at the Lord Lieutenant's refusal to sanction a pension granted by the Corporation to a man retired with an incurable disease after twenty-five years service. The Lord Mayor requested the Lord Lieutenant to receive a deputation on the matter.[66] Later in the month, Lord Lieutenant French added to the public tension with the bald assertion: 'Conscription is not dead. The Government will do its duty.'[67]

The Mansion House Conference, meanwhile, opted to persist in its efforts to send its manifesto statement to the American President. Lord Mayor O'Neill was sent to the American Embassy in London to request that the document be conveyed to the President through embassy channels. O'Neill took the mail boat to England on the night of 18 June, accompanied by his daughter and his secretary Clr. Foley. On arrival, Foley arranged an appointment at the embassy for the Lord Mayor. On Thursday, 20 June, Lord Mayor O'Neill was met by Mr Irwin Laughlin, acting as *chargé d'affaires*, in the absence of the ambassador. O'Neill explained his role and purpose. Laughlin asked a number of questions, which O'Neill readily answered. The ambassador's representative then said he would cable the contents of the letter and its circumstance to the President and would request his instructions about despatching the document. He hoped to have an answer within a day or so and would contact the Lord Mayor at his accommodation, Charing Cross Hotel. On Saturday, Laughlin reported that President Wilson was quite willing that the address should be sent on to him. [68]

The address consisted of six printed pages. A covering letter from the Lord Mayor to the ambassador announced that it was not proposed to make any publication of the address in Britain or Ireland before the 4th of July, by which date it was hoped it would have reached Washington. The document, with its ten signatories, recalled that during the American Revolution, those seeking liberty appealed to the Irish parliament against British aggression, now it was Ireland's turn to appeal to the people of America. After this opening, there followed a summary of Irish history leading to its present demand for freedom. The address concluded with an expression of assurance that the President, whose assurances had inspired the small nations of the world to defend their liberties against oppressors, would not be among those condemning Ireland for its determination to achieve freedom.[69]

The address was carried in London's morning papers a week before it appeared in the *Weekly Freeman's Journal*, on Saturday 13 July. It evoked little comment. O'Neill, who had sent news of the conference to de Valera from time to time,[70] sent him and Arthur Griffith copies of the address on 3 August.[71] De Valera's acknowledgement on 19 August commented: 'It would be idle to add to the compliment paid to the address by the English newspapers …the significant tribute of their silence.'[72]

A further development of a more personalised nature was reported in the *Dublin Saturday Post* of 3 August. It noted that the Lord Mayor of Dublin had 'issued a writ for libel, claiming £5,000 damages against the *Irish Times* for its comments, on 26 June, regarding his conduct of the Mansion House Conference in relation to the petition to President Wilson'. He won the case, but was given minimal damages.

Influenza. Cosgrave and confronting Lord French

During July, influenza hit the Mansion House. On 19 July, W.T. Cosgrave, in the course of a letter from Reading Prison, expressed the hope that the Lord Mayor had quite recovered again and that the Lady Mayoress and all members of the family were quite well.[73] Soon afterwards, word came to O'Neill that Cosgrave was ill. Mrs Cosgrave at the same time was very unwell. She appealed to the Lord Mayor to get her husband home. He wrote to the Lord Lieutenant but got no reply. After a few days he wrote again, but got no response. He went to the Vice-Regal Lodge and taxed Lord French with his lack of courtesy. The latter assured him that he had not received the letters. He touched a button. A tall, sallow man appeared. 'Sanderson, did you receive any letters from the Lord Mayor?' Sanderson replied: 'Yes, Your Excellency, but you were too busy to attend to them'. This moved O'Neill to wonder how often the Lord Lieutenant was fooled by his subordinates. Sanderson was strongly rebuked in his hearing for daring to keep back the letters. Lord French touched another button, 'and speaking to the Irish Office London instructed that William Cosgrave be left out on parole at once'.

Cosgrave was returned home, but most of a month was spent in Jervis Street Nursing Home. He received an extension of a further month. O'Neill suggested to him that he would seek his discharge from prison. He had been speaking to James McMahon, the Under Secretary, who agreed to the idea. Cosgrave, however, 'thinking his comrades would think badly of him, preferred to return to jail'; but he was discharged in a few days.[74]

The reference to James McMahon is a reminder of the important role he played. He was greatly valued by Lord Mayor O'Neill. 'There were few men in Ireland who had a more complex and difficult position than James McMahon. Most of those he was associated with in the Castle were different in religion, and had a very different outlook on Irish life and Irish affairs.' Without being 'vainglorious', O'Neill continued, 'I accomplished a great deal in ameliorating suffering and agony of mind, many a mother, father, sister and sweetheart gained consoling news through the Mansion House about those taken from them, and many prisoners in English and Irish jails got parole and release. But I would have been as chaff before the wind only I had James McMahon and his most obliging secretary, Walter Doolin, behind me; and often if Mr McMahon could not grant a request himself, he was the silent factor that influenced the Lord Lieutenant, the Commander-in-Chief, and different Chief Secretaries.'[75]

The Lord Mayor, Lord French and Mrs Sheehy Skeffington

During August, the Lord Mayor had further occasion to call on Lord French. Mrs Hanna Sheehy Skeffington, whose husband, a pacifist, had been murdered by a British officer in 1916, was arrested on her return from America on the pretext that she had contravened some "passport rules". A formidable supporter and spokesperson on social justice issues and women's rights, she went on hunger strike when she was jailed in the Dublin Police Bridewell. The Lord Mayor, who admired her, called to see her and found her in the company of her sister, the widow of T.M. Kettle. Afterwards, he went to the Vice-Regal Lodge to meet Lord French. He told him of the 'absolute disgrace' of

Mrs Skeffington's arrest. French, 'in real soldiery fashion', asked him 'to take the damn woman off his hands and keep her quiet'. Knowing how strong-minded Mrs Skeffington was, O'Neill responded that he could not take her off his hands unless she were released unconditionally. He left with the tacit understanding that she would be released at once.

To his surprise, he subsequently learned that she had been transported to prison in England. Shortly afterwards, he availed of the opportunity to speak with Mrs Shortt, wife of the Chief Secretary, who was attending an entertainment in the Mansion House. He told her of the two sisters he had met at the Bridewell, Mrs Skeffington, whose husband had been killed by a British officer and was now herself being shamefully treated, and Mrs Tom Kettle, whose husband, Professor Tom Kettle, had lost his life in France, and whose house had recently been raided by the police. The Lord Mayor's combined appeal, joined by other influential voices, resulted in the release of Mrs Skeffington.[76]

Back in Dublin, Mrs Skeffington wrote to the Lord Mayor on 21 August:

> I feel much indebted to you for your great personal kindness and
> valuable help. I feel sure but for the protests made that the
> Government would gladly have let me remain interned until
> I was interred.

She went on to express her concern for Mrs Clarke's health and the general health of all the prisoners 'locked away without the slightest charge being made against them'.[77]

Housing the poor and industrial mediation

As Mrs Skeffington was writing, Lord Mayor O'Neill's attention had turned to housing for the poor. "Mr Cowan's Housing Report" had come before the Corporation and had given rise to examination and comment in the press. *The Dublin Saturday Post* in an editorial on the report observed that despite spasmodic efforts on the part of the Corporation the disgraceful housing conditions of the poor of Dublin had become steadily worse. The editor added that it was doubtful if any fault could be found with the Corporation. 'Their powers were limited, their resources were limited, and the difficulties in their way had accumulated through long years of neglect into an almost hopelessly immoveable mass.' In one respect only were they to blame, and this fault they shared with all citizens high and low – They had 'never sufficiently realised the ruinous and demoralising effect of the slum dwellings and the urgency and importance of finding a remedy. Their efforts at reform were consequently spasmodic and half-hearted and did little more than touch the fringe of the evil.'

Laurence O'Neill would probably have agreed with the editor, while, nevertheless, pointing out that little could be done in the absence of Government funds, and that a great amount of time was being taken up in facilitating peace in the city during such tense political times and in calming industrial protagonists and promoting agreement in the work place.

This last was proving critical once more as August drew to a close. A further editorial in the *Dublin Saturday Post*, dated 31 August, observed that 'not for a long time has there been such widespread unrest amongst the labouring population of Dublin as exists at present. There are six or seven actual or potential centres of trouble, and in spite of the strenuous efforts of the Lord Mayor as peace-maker we can hardly hope that all of them will be settled without involving much hardship to the workers affected and much loss to the trade of the city.' The areas in dispute included printers, coachbuilders, butchers, millers, bakers, even the Corporation workers, but 'the most important of the trades affected' was 'the building trade, in which it is said 17,000 men are out'. Here the question seemed to be purely one of wages. 'The two parties', the editor concluded, 'are at present engaged in conference under the mediation of the Lord Mayor, and we can only express our hopes for a speedy and just agreement.'

A week later, on 7 September, the hopes were being met. The editorial acknowledged: 'The strike in the building trade has happily been settled … and many of the other disputes are in a fair way of being settled.' Lord Mayor O'Neill's ability to relate with both sides in a dispute, and his energy, was remarkable. At the fortnightly meeting of the Dublin Trades Council, a motion of thanks to the Lord Mayor was passed unanimously for his work in settling the dispute in the building trade. The secretary, William O'Brien, spoke in flattering terms of the Lord Mayor's action. The men had received an increase of five and a half pence an hour or £1-2shillings-1½ pence per week.[78]

The *Saturday Post* for 14 September, however, had further stories of unrest. The Lord Mayor wrote to the Dublin Trades Council announcing that he was calling a conference between the masters and men with reference to the strike of the packing case-makers. The city, by this, was facing into an infectious strike fever with chemists, hotel workers, the Irish Women Workers Union, the Dublin Cooperative Butchers, and insurance workers, involved in industrial action.

In dealing with industrial relations, O'Neill preferred to be dealing with unionised workers. Thus, when presiding at the inaugural meeting of the National Union of Municipal Officers, he gave it as his view that the municipal workers were doing the right thing in welding themselves into a union. 'After the past two or three years, I have had a rather varied experience of men, masters, and things. And I have had a fairly varied experience of trade unionism, and I have come to the conclusion that trade unionism when properly worked is the *salvation not only of men but also of masters*. It saves the employee from the imperious and slave-driving master, but, on the other hand, it saves the master from the lazy and arrogant employee.'[79] A rather unreal benefit to the employer, especially as the trade union tended to support 'the lazy and arrogant employee'!

Preserving political balance

On 22 August 1918, Ald. O'Neill received a letter from the Irish Recruiting Council regarding the "Inter-Allied Exhibition on the After-Care of Disabled Men". It conveyed 'the unanimous and very warm vote of thanks … in appreciation of the generous hospitality and facilities extended by your Lordship to the Exhibition'. In his acceptance speech in 1917, O'Neill had drawn attention to the serious problem of the after-care of the disabled. Receiving the thanks of the Irish Recruiting Council on 22 August, and two days later informing de Valera that all the Mansion House Committee wished to be remembered to him and hoped he was in good health,[80] provided a cameo of the equilibrium O'Neill brought to the office of Lord Mayor as he sought to make the Mansion House available to all citizens irrespective of creed or politics.

Protests against internment

During September, nearly one hundred people likely to influence opinion or give leadership were cast into prison without charge. The resulting public anger was reflected in a resolution of protest and a requisition, signed by twenty-eight members of the Municipal Council, calling for a special meeting of the Council.[81] Ald. O'Neill convened the meeting on 24 September. He did so, he declared, 'to clear the air'.

He deliberately defused the anger by speaking out vigorously himself in criticism of the Government. He was, he said, heart and mind with the resolution. The Government by their action were enemies not only of this country but of their own country also. 'Their action in arresting, deporting, and interning in English jails so many of our countrymen and women, without any trial, without even any charge being professed against them, constitutes one of the greatest breaches towards the liberty of the subject which any government could be guilty of …'. One of the fundamental principles underlying the British constitution was that every subject was considered innocent of any crime until he or she were proven to be guilty, 'but the people of Ireland, a nation more ancient than England, and one of the oldest in Christendom, are trampled upon by those who clamour that they want to make the world safe for democracy'. The Government hoped to numb the affection of the American people towards Ireland, and to kill the spirit of Ireland's manhood and womanhood and destroy its claim to nationhood, 'but the King's advisers were living in a fool's paradise if they thought they would succeed'.

Many others spoke, some of them vehemently. The only voice against the motion was that of Ald. Quaid, who contended that the supporters of the resolution 'only represented a political party seeking to get the representation of the country...'[82] Sinn Féin, in his view, was behind the entire protest.

The sinking of "The Leinster"

On 10 October, representatives of all sides mourned the sinking of the Irish Mail Boat, "the Leinster", in the Irish Sea. It was struck by two torpedoes with the loss of 587 out of 780 passengers. The Lord Mayor summoned a meeting for the establishment of a fund to assist the families of the deceased. Contributions came from all quarters. Contributors included Lord French, T.M. Healy, and Sir Bryan Mahon, now a commanding officer at the headquarters of the British Expeditionary Force in France. His letter and contribution evoked a warm acknowledgement from O'Neill. 'It was indeed an appalling calamity and, like yourself, I lost some friends and very many acquaintances.' He was very pleased with Mahon's views on the war and hoped that he would be once more 'in a position of trust in this country'. When that time came, he supposed that he (O'Neill), in the natural course of events, would be once more relegated to the position of a private citizen; but even so he would always look back with happy remembrance of his association with him.[83]

The Municipal Council's deepest sympathy with the families and dependants of the victims of this inhuman outrage, was expressed by the Lord Mayor on 18 October.[84] There was considerable unease, however, about the circumstances of the disaster. As a result he further moved 'that this Council if of the opinion that a full and searching inquiry should be held into all the circumstances connected with the loss of "R.M.S. Leinster". The motion was carried. An amendment by P.T. Daly, which was defeated, pinpointed the nature of the unease – 'and, further, we are of the opinion that the practice of carrying armed soldiers on passenger boats should be discontinued'.[85]

Dr Kathleen Lynn and the influenza epidemic

One of the major causes of death during the final years of the Great War, and in its aftermath, was what was known as the "Great Flu" or the Spanish influenza epidemic, which raged in Dublin from mid-1918 until the end of March 1919. During the last quarter of 1918 the death rate in the city soared to 36.1 per thousand. On 25 October, a special meeting of the Dublin Municipal Council passed a proposal that 'in the interests of suffering humanity we demand the release of Dr K. Lynn, and Dr Hayes, Dr Cusack, and Dr McNabb'.

Dr Lynn was well known to Lord Mayor O'Neill from her work among the poor in Dublin. After she was arrested as an active member of Sinn Féin, he intervened on her behalf, taking on himself to assure the authorities that she would not be henceforth involved in politics, and that he was acting solely out of 'a desire to render Dr Lynn free to devote her professional services to the medical work in which she is engaged amongst the poor'. Her deportation order was cancelled and she was free to return to work. She played a vigorous part in fighting the flu epidemic.[86]

Influenza and Prisoners' agitation in Belfast

In Belfast jail the authorities were concerned lest they have on their hands the deaths of political prisoners from influenza. One of the prisoners, Fionán Lynch, recalled that 'warders and prisoners were stricken down. Our cell doors were left open, night and day, so that prisoners who were able to move about could help those who were incapable of doing anything for themselves. Sinn Féin propaganda was highly efficient then, and I think the British Government were much concerned about the publicity that would follow the death of any of us'.[87]

Alderman O'Neill found himself involved as an intermediary between Sinn Féin and the Government in relation to the Belfast prisoners. The Sinn Féin Convention took place at the Round Room in the Mansion House on 29 October. It was sparsely attended because of the many arrests. Sinn Féin sought to keep itself in the public gaze. It planned a public march to Dublin Castle as a protest against the absence of proper treatment for prisoners in Belfast. On this being vetoed by the IRA chief-of-staff, Richard Mulcahy, the convention decided to avail of the Lord Mayor! Harry Boland, secretary of Sinn Féin, came to Ald. O'Neill in his study with the request that he find out at Dublin Castle how matters were in Belfast. O'Neill told him he would not, as it was not a matter arising from the Ashe agreement and, moreover, some of the sub-leaders of Sinn Féin had publicly stated that the Lord Mayor was too fond of going to the Castle. Boland, clearly annoyed at the comments of some of his colleagues, returned to the meeting and came back with the assurance that it was the unanimous wish of the meeting that the Lord Mayor go to Dublin Castle.

Having received what he termed his "passport" from the Convention, O'Neill visited the Castle, met the chairman of the Prison Board, Max Green, and the Medical

Officer, Dr MacCormack, and reported back to the meeting. Dr MacCormack had just returned from Belfast, and he assured the Lord Mayor that most of the ill prisoners were convalescent, and that the epidemic there was very light. He had instructed the medical officer to procure any medical advice and appliances he deemed necessary, and that any prisoner who showed serious signs was to be transferred to the Mater Hospital, Belfast. A vote of thanks to the Lord Mayor was passed by the Convention, and, as he subsequently observed, - 'there was no more croaking about my going to the Castle'.[88]

The Lord Mayor had more immediate contact with the prisoners in Belfast late in December, 1918. A prisoner, named John Doran, from County Down, was awaiting trial by court martial. He was kept apart from the political prisoners. The latter learned that Doran after his trial would be sent to Derry jail as a convicted criminal. Doran had the distinction of having taken part in the Easter Rising. After Mass, they managed to smuggle him to their area in the prison, and to prevent his capture they barricaded themselves in their cells, and wrecked the passage and stairway leading to them. The authorities brought in the army with a view to taking Doran by force. In this state of siege likely to lead to bloodshed, a Sinn Féin deputation waited on Bishop MacRory of Down and Connor on 30 December. The bishop contacted Lord Mayor O'Neill, who said he would communicate with the Chief Secretary before going to Belfast.[89]

Meantime, according to O'Neill's memory of events, an important meeting of the Corporation was interrupted by Harry Boland stating that Sinn Féin wanted the Corporation's assistance in respect of the Belfast prisoners. A deputation was appointed to call on Under Secretary, James McMahon, and through him a letter of permission to visit the prisoners was received from the Chief Secretary. The *Dublin Evening Mail* of 31 December, however, under the headline –"Sinn Féiners Siege in Belfast. Lord Mayor O'Neill going to visit them", reported that O'Neill visited Mr Shortt, the Chief Secretary, and, as he told an *Evening Mail* representative, had a satisfactory interview and was leaving on the 3 o'clock train for Belfast in order to visit the prisoners. Whatever the precise course of events, the important thing was that he had received a letter from the Chief Secretary. In Belfast he met with Bishop MacRory, and together they went to the prison. Armed with his letter, O'Neill and the bishop were courteously received at the prison, and the military were ordered to stand down during their visit. O'Neill managed to meet the leader of the prisoners, his 'old friend', Austin Stack. 'Stack, supported by Ernest Blythe, with his usual foresight and determination, had a set of demands ready.' Doran was to be treated as a political prisoner; all prisoners in the present conflict were to be re-instated as political prisoners and to receive no punishment for the damage they had done; and all political prisoners in Belfast were to be removed to an internment location in Britain.

O'Neill returned to the Governor's office with the demands. MacRory and the deputy-governor were waiting there. He and the bishop agreed that the Chief Secretary should be contacted, even though he was at a Victory Ball celebrating the end of the war. The Lord Mayor read the prisoners' demands to him. The Chief Secretary agreed to them. O'Neill had the deputy-governor take down the details. He then went back to Stack, told him his demands were granted, and bade him and his fellow prisoners good night. As he and Dr MacRory were leaving the prison, however, the deputy-governor rushed after them declaring 'the prisoners will not give up Doran'. The Lord Mayor returned to Stack, who explained they were having 'a little sing-song' (it was now 11.30 p.m. on New Year's Eve) and they wished to have Doran with them. They would hand him over in the morning. This did not satisfy the deputy-governor, who insisted on phoning the Chief Secretary. The latter, discomfited by the interruptions, curtly informed him to leave Doran where he was until the morning.

The Lord Mayor spent the night in Belfast. Next morning, while he and the bishop were at breakfast, the chaplain came to tell them that the prisoners had completely wrecked their cells. When O'Neill visited the prisoners, he found that the entire wing in which they were had been devastated as if hit by a heavy shell. One of the prisoners, Fionán Lynch, explained the convoluted mentality: 'it needed only the slightest excuse for us to create trouble in jail, for in doing so we were creating the elements of some of the strongest propaganda against British rule in Ireland...'.[90] Lord Mayor O'Neill asked Austin Stack what it was all about, but received the evasive answer that they had given Doran a good send off and were now quietly waiting until he and Dr MacRory turned up before evacuating the area.[91]

The extraordinary *denouement* to the saga was chronicled in the *Irish Times* of Thursday, 2 January, 1919. 'About fifty police, fully armed, and about the same number of soldiers, similarly equipped, with officers in command, were present. A number of warders stood quietly by while the prisoners removed the barricades and other obstacles ... The operations concluded, the prisoners, on the command of their leader, Mr Austin Stack, M.P., lined up and then marched down the corridor, each man saluting as he passed the Lord Mayor of Dublin and Most Rev. Dr MacRory. The whole band of prisoners at the same time singing *The Soldiers' Song*. 'They were then brought to a halt, and were addressed by Mr Stack and Most Rev. Dr MacRory. Cheers were then given for the latter and for the Lord Mayor, and the men, on being disbanded, ... immediately repaired to new cells in a building immediately adjoining.'

The *Evening Herald* of 3 January indicated that the prisoners' victory would prove very temporary. There was an Orange outburst against the settlement and great pressure was put on Lord Lieutenant French and on Chief Secretary Shortt. The latter's concessions were soon over-ruled.

Recalling the above event in Belfast Jail, Laurence O'Neill asked the question – Why did the prisoners wish to be transferred to Britain? The most likely answer, he thought, was that the prisoners believed that in Belfast they were sentenced prisoners whereas those interned in Britain were not and were likely to be sooner released.[92]

On 12 November 1918, Harry Boland wrote to the Lord Mayor thanking him for his many 'good turns' to the prisoners, and that when peace was declared in Ireland the prisoners would 'demonstrate their appreciation' of his 'many kindnesses'.[93] Ironically, more than fifty years later, Fionán Lynch was to write:

> I had often felt that, in the records of those times of strife,
> nothing like proper tribute has been paid to the memory
> of Larry O'Neill. He was a most kindly man and was
> unremitting in his efforts to get better conditions for the
> Sinn Féin prisoners of the British. As far as I can remember,
> he did not himself belong to Sinn Féin.[94]

The Bishops and the election in Ulster

O'Neill's reputation, and his ability as a negotiator, led to a further call on him by Dr MacRory. He wished him to negotiate with John Dillon and Sinn Féin to avoid a clash between nationalists and republicans in Ulster in the forthcoming general election. The concern was that such a clash in the forthcoming election could result in a victory for the unionist minority candidate, which would give added strength to the argument for partition.[95] This request to engage in such a delicate and onerous mission was backed by Cardinal Logue. The latter's request, representing the bishops whose dioceses were in the civil, as distinct from the ecclesiastic province of Ulster, was sent to O'Neill on 26 November with the instruction that it be made public when he had undertaken the steps it outlined. The letter was made public in the *Freeman's Journal* and other papers on 30 November.

> The Lord Mayor of Dublin is the first citizen of our country,
> and more than once he has shown how well he can discharge
> heavy responsibilities that have devolved on him in that
> capacity. We, therefore, request him to take in hand and have
> settled the greatest difficulty the election presents …, the
> representation of Nationalist seats in Ulster… Be those seats
> eight or ten in number, we propose that the Lord Mayor, in
> conjunction with Mr John Dillon and Mr de Valera, or, in his
> absence, Mr John McNeill, should divide the representation of
> these seats.

The bishops requested the Lord Mayor to convene these gentlemen 'for a day, not later than next Saturday (30 November), and to have this letter published, on receipt, in the metropolitan and provincial press'.

On being contacted by the cardinal, the Lord Mayor got in touch with Dillon and McNeill. After some correspondence, he felt it necessary to travel to Ballahadereen, County Mayo, to meet Mr Dillon. On 2 December, a conference took place between the Lord Mayor, John Dillon, and John McNeill, at which the two politicians agreed with the bishops that, instead of a contest, the eight seats in question should be equally divided. They left the decision to Cardinal Logue, agreeing to abide by his verdict. The Lord Mayor handed the written consent of the members of the conference to the cardinal, who, on 3 December, accepted the responsibility of allocating the seats.[96] He allocated them as follows: To the Irish Party – South Down, N.E. Tyrone, East Donegal, South Armagh; to Sinn Féin – Derry, East Down, N.W. Tyrone, and South Fermanagh.

Telegrams from Dillon and McNeill to their respective constituencies, however, did not reach them before closing time for nominations, with the result that both parties went ahead and put up candidates for all eight constituencies. This demanded further negotiation between the Lord Mayor, Dillon, McNeill, and the Cardinal to bring about a joint appeal for conformity with the conference's decision and the Cardinal's allocation, and the withdrawal of candidates where required. The signs of a positive response were evident by 11 December, three days before polling in the general election.

Not surprisingly, the northern bishops felt 'under a debt of gratitude' to Lord Mayor O'Neill 'for having undertaken and carried to success so troublesome and laborious work'.[97]

Daily concerns

In referring to O'Neill's many wider involvements, the biographer has constantly to keep in mind that the lord mayor's primary daily concern was the needs of his citizens. Among their chief needs in the final quarter of 1918 was the supply of milk, of coal, and of housing.

At the end of October, the Rural Milk Producers Association ceased their supply of milk to the city. They claimed that they could not produce milk economically at the prices fixed by the Food Control Commission. The Lord Mayor pointed out to representatives of the Association that their decision would have serious consequences and cause great inconvenience to citizens at the present time, with the influenza epidemic raging. He suggested that the milk supply be resumed pending further consideration of the matter by the Food Control Committee. Responding to his appeal, the leading producers agreed to restore supplies next day, Tuesday, and on succeeding days.[98]

He brought his negotiation skills into operation again with respect to the coal shortage, which became acute in the closing months of the year. Through a contact in Britain, O'Neill negotiated an offer of 1,000 tons of coal at 42 shillings and six pence per ton, 'to be stored by the Corporation for the use of the labouring classes and the poor in cases of emergency'. At the Municipal Council Meeting on 4 November the motion was approved. The importance of the acquisition was underlined a fortnight later, when a letter from the Local Government Board was read at the Council Meeting of 18 November, requesting local government authorities to assist the Government by reducing the consumption of coal, gas, and electric light in all undertakings and premises under their control, and to impress upon the public 'the paramount necessity of following this example'.[99]

The 'Housing of the Working Class' in Dublin, as noted frequently, was a pressing problem. Efforts to deal with it were held up by refusal of adequate assistance from the Government. On 20 November, Lord Mayor O'Neill wrote to Prime Minister Lloyd George 'as a last resource' in 'the housing of the working class of the city of Dublin'.

He observed that not withstanding the assurances given in Parliament by Mr Birrell, Mr Duke, and the present Chief Secretary, Mr Shortt, that Ireland was to participate in Government housing grants after the war, the Irish Local Government Board has not, so far, taken any action regarding the financial assistance to be given to this country. The inaction on the part of the Irish Board was in marked contrast to the activities of the English Local Government Board. Appealing to Lloyd George's 'abiding interest in the welfare and social progress of the working classes', O'Neill pointed out that the case of Dublin in that regard was exceptional. 'It is the most densely populated city per acre in Europe, and has been put forward for the last four years as calling for immediate and generous treatment... I would beg of you, therefore, ... at the earliest possible date, give me not alone some assurance – definite and clear – that I can rely on substantial aid from the Treasury to enable the Corporation of Dublin to grapple with the Housing Question within their area, but also to give me some specific information as to the nature and extent of such financial assistance – I have the honour to be, Sir, your obedient servant, ...'[100]

To this frank appeal, Lloyd George replied on 26 November. He apologised for his delay in replying, and assured the Lord Mayor that he was deeply sensible of the great responsibility which attaches to the Government in Ireland, as elsewhere, in connection with this problem of housing. He was 'taking steps to ascertain personally what is the actual position with regard to the progress of schemes for re-housing in Dublin and in other parts of Ireland'. [101] To O'Neill it cannot have seemed other than a hollow evasion.

His *bête noir*

Ald. O'Neill's relations with the members of the Municipal Council was positive, with a very few exceptions. The most striking exception was Ald. Quaid, who, as noted, was capable of fracturing the Lord Mayor's normal equanimity. One particularly notable example was at a meeting of the Dublin Port and Docks Board on 5 December 1918. The chairman, Ald. Moran, who had been in bad health for some time, announced that he would not be at the meeting were it not to counter the vile insinuations made by Ald Quaid at the last meeting of Dublin Corporation. Quaid had stated, among other comments, that Moran was to benefit out of arrangements for the setting up of a dead meat industry in the city by being placed on the board of directors. This, Moran vehemently denied.

The Lord Mayor, clearly incensed, made a vigorous defence of Moran and a remarkable attack on Quaid. He stated that as head of the Corporation for the time being, what concerned him most was that the chairman should come here today, at the risk perhaps of his life, and that he should be agitated – perhaps justly so – at the innuendoes made against his character by a member of the Corporation. All the members of the Corporation, except one, disassociated themselves from the innuendoes made by Ald. Quaid against the chairman, though they hardly considered it necessary to do so. Ald. Quaid by this time was sufficiently well known in the city of Dublin for any honest man to mind what he said. He was one of those peculiar beings who had that sort of diseased mind that when they saw any man wishing to further the interests of the city or of his fellow men... he was considered to be working for the sole purpose of feathering his own nest. On behalf of his colleagues in the Corporation he wished to publicly state that they disassociated that body in its entirety from the foul insinuations made against Alderman Moran. It was unnecessary at that Board to mention all that Ald. Moran had done for the city, and it was but another instance of the kind of gratitude which public representatives got, who were trying to do their best.[102]

Promoting harmony

As well as coping with problems, there were the on-going opportunities to promote harmony and positive developments. Among the benefits Ald. O'Neill brought to city life in the concluding months of 1918 was a further contribution to industrial peace. On 7 December the *Dublin Saturday Post* announced that the engineers in the electricity department of the Corporation had threatened strike, which, if carried out, would leave the city in complete darkness. A week later, however, it reported that the Lord Mayor called a special meeting to deal with the threatened strike, as a result of which the strike was averted. The paper also noted his settlement of the grave-diggers' dispute at Glasnevin cemetery, and of the pork butchers' dispute.

Reflecting on his dealings with "Industrial Strife 1917-1921", Laurence O'Neill admitted that to someone like himself, who had come from a small business, 'it was a difficult task to deal and understand the many complex questions which arose'. 'But', he added, 'the leaders of capital and labour faithfully stood by me, and any suggestion I ever made was never turned down.' In the same optimistic vein, he proudly concluded: 'When other countries were torn asunder by industrial unrest, the trade and commerce of Dublin continued unbroken for three and a half years'. He had to admit, nevertheless, that his attempt to create a conciliation board of masters and men, 'drawn from the reasonable ones on both sides', did not succeed. 'Things were happening so quickly, it had to be shelved.'[103]

Other benefits arising from O'Neill as lord mayor was the promotion of trade and culture. The eleventh annual *Aonach* was opened in the great Round Room of the Mansion House, before a large attendance, on Friday, 8 December. The exhibition of Irish goods was on a larger scale than previous years, and included 'many fine specimens of home manufactured workmanship and art'. The stalls numbered about thirty. The Oak Room was set apart for the Irish Art exhibition. During the evening, what was described as 'an interesting musical programme was rendered by a string band under the direction of Professor O'Dwyer'.[104]

Ald. Tom Kelly, who presided at the opening ceremony, thanked the Lord Mayor for attending (standing in for Madame Markievicz) and added: 'In the history of all the lord mayors, the Mansion House was never more the property of the citizens as a whole than under Alderman O'Neill, who, he could prophecy, would be Lord Mayor for 1919 (applause).' The Lord Mayor, in cheerful mood, 'spoke in praise of the work accomplished by *Aonach* in helping to revive Irish industry, the Irish language, music and dancing. Some people looked upon the *Aonach* as a language gathering, and were a bit delicate about attending it. Others thought it was a kind of arsenal for distributing high explosives, or a country house to distribute German gold, or a sanctuary for "German plots" (laughter). No matter what view might be held, the fact was that the *Aonach* had done, and was doing, good work for Ireland.'[105]

On the wider stage once more

Shortly afterwards, Lord Mayor O'Neill was back on the wider public stage. On 16 December, he proposed a vote of sympathy to the relatives of Richard Coleman, who had been part of the Ashbourne encounter in 1916, and whose death took place in a British jail, where he had been interred without any charge being brought against him. In his speech O'Neill used one of the most emotionally charged contemporary accusations against the English Government, stating 'that young Coleman's case is only a sample of the reign of Prussianism we are going through'. [106]

Richard Coleman had died of influenza in prison in the small Welsh town of Usk. There appears to have been no evidence of medical neglect, but the fact that he died in prison was the important factor. 'A few days ago', O'Neill pronounced graphically, 'there died in an English jail, a village schoolmaster, practically unknown except to a narrow circle of friends. Yesterday, thousands of Dublin citizens followed his remains to Glasnevin Cemetery, and to-night hundreds of thousands of Irishmen, Irish women, and Irish children as they retired to rest would offer up a *Pater* and *Ave* for the salvation of his soul.' 'The Government had flagrantly broken the understanding made at the time of the death of Thomas Ashe as to the treatment of Irish political prisoners.' Now one had the situation where 'young men and women, pure in spirit and upright in character, were compelled to wear prison garb and mix with the dregs of society, often for trivial offences such as singing the songs of their land'.[107]

The Coleman funeral had bordered on an outbreak of violence. O'Neill and the Mansion House, as usual, served as the communication centre for opposing sides. The Commissioner of Police, Colonel Johnston, visited the Lord Mayor and left instructions that no military uniforms were to be worn at the funeral, no arms were to be carried, and that a particular route was to be followed. Shortly afterwards, the militant branch of Sinn Féin, represented by Collins and Boland, called to the Mansion House. They had their own plans for the funeral. The Lord Mayor, seeing his duty as preserving peace and avoiding harm to the citizens, presented them with the police requirements. Collins insisted that they would wear uniforms and would follow their own longer route. O'Neill managed to get agreement on following the shorter route, but made no headway about uniforms. In the event, Collins and Boland marched in Volunteer uniform on either side of the hearse, and all passed off peaceably.

In his speech regarding Richard Coleman, Lord Mayor O'Neill made reference to President Wilson being at Paris for the Peace Conference, and being nearer would be able to learn something first-hand about Ireland's case. His words reflected a strong body of feeling in Ireland that Ireland should make its case for independence at the Peace Conference, and that Wilson's many expositions on the rights of small nations would work in Ireland's favour. From the end of October 1918, O'Neill was under pressure to summon the Mansion House Conference, or a new conference, to deal with the question of self-determination. The meeting of the Labour Congress passed a resolution to that effect, and a deputation called on the Lord Mayor on 4 November. On that date, he informed John Dillon that 'similar representations are being pressed upon me privately by gentlemen of all parties, and of no party, and the press is backing it up'.[108]

As if reassuring Dillon, he explained: 'As I understand the public feeling, the belief is general that a conference of nationalists of all sections can be got to agree upon a simple demand for the right of self-determination, leaving each party free to advocate its own preference as to the form of government that a self-determining people ought to choose. In this manner an almost unanimous expression from nationalist Ireland can be arrived at.' He favoured working through the present conference, but emphasised that something had to be done without delay if the country was to be saved serious trouble. The Mansion House Conference met shortly afterwards but was adjourned in Dillon's absence. The latter wrote a confidential letter to the Lord Mayor on 12 November that a special conference was required to bring about national unity, and that such, in effect, had little prospect of success prior to the general election on 14 December.[109]

Matters remained thus until after polling day. On 18 December, John Sweetman, a recent convert to Sinn Féin, informed the Lord Mayor – 'You are the only man who is in a position to invite all Irish members to meet to consider the best way to present Ireland's case … to the world… There will be no time to be lost when the polls have been declared, and therefore the necessary preliminary steps should be taken without delay.' He added a postscript: 'The above was written before I saw your letter in today's papers, but the two ideas do not clash.'[110]

Invitation to President Wilson

O'Neill had decided to carry out the purpose of a national conference in a more personalised way likely to have unified support: he decided to invite President Wilson to Ireland. On 17 December he took the bold initiative of a letter to the newspapers stating that there was 'evidence of a universal desire on the part of the national public that President Wilson should visit Ireland'. It seemed to him that an invitation to the President should come not from individuals or a group of individuals but 'most fittingly from the Irish Democracy'. He continued:

> I have accordingly decided to call a mass meeting of the
> citizens of Dublin on Sunday, the 22nd inst., and I propose
> that other mass meetings be convoked in every convenient

centre throughout Ireland on the same day, in order that
an invitation may go out from all Ireland to the President.

He trusted that national organisations of every kind, including the labour and women's organisations, would join in issuing the national invitation. As soon as maybe, he hoped to give details to the press of the time, place etc for the meeting in Dublin, and also of the form of the invitation to be proposed for adoption. He requested all provincial papers to publish his letter.[111]

It was an insightful step. There was an enthusiastic response. On 19 December, he wrote to Mrs Hanna Sheehy Skeffington asking her to speak at the invitation meeting to be held in the Round Room of the Mansion House at 3.0 p.m. the following Sunday. He wished to have the meeting and the speakers as representative as possible. She accepted.[112] In response to his invitation, meetings were held throughout Ireland.

On 23 December, the *Irish Independent* described the meeting in the Mansion House as 'enthusiastic and packed to overflowing'. 'An hour before the opening of the meeting the place was practically filled... A remarkable and highly impressive demonstration of enthusiasm took place when the Lord Mayor entered and proceeded to the dais, accompanied by a number of prominent ladies and gentlemen, including two American military officers and several priests. A tremendous cheer burst from the great gathering. It was mentioned by the Lord Mayor on taking the chair, that owing to the overwhelming crowds anxious to take part, overflow meetings would be held in the Supper Room and in the street.

'As his Lordship rose, a voice shouted – "The future President of the Republic". The Lord Mayor said the object for which the meeting had been called was to give the citizens of Dublin, irrespective of individuals or parties, an opportunity of uniting with the country in extending to President Wilson an invitation to visit Ireland. He was 'the only great statesman that the war had produced. He had made many references to small nationalities, and had declared that "nations derive their just power from the consent of the governed". As he had Irish blood in his veins, he must have had Ireland in his mind' in making his statement about the rights of small nationalities.

It was a high moment for Laurence O'Neill as the year drew to an end. A letter signed "Ormond" in the *Irish Independent* captured something of the enthusiasm generated by his invitation to President Wilson. It spoke of O'Neill's 'patriotic foresight' in inviting the President, adding, 'truly the Mayor is a genial and great man, and it is only when he has completed his term in office that the citizens generally will be able to view him at his true worth. His energy is extraordinary.' Over the Christmas period, several American societies sent messages to the Lord Mayor supporting Irish independence.

Portmarnock, August 1914
Front row: Laurence and Anne O'Neill (centre) with two daughters, Annie (left) and Mary
Back row: Son John (on left) with other family members (O'Neill family collection)

Portmarnock, September 1914
Laurence O'Neill (seated) with his son John (left) and a cousin or family friend (O'Neill family collection)

Bridge House, Coast Road, Portmarnock
Laurence O'Neill's family home

THE NEW LORD MAYOR.

(The report of the inauguration of Alderman O'Neill as Lord Mayor will be found on
Page 3.)

Laurence O'Neill on his
inauguration as Lord
Mayor of Dublin.
Cartoon by Frank
Leahy. Dublin Saturday
Post, 24 Feb 1917

Photo.]   [Lafayette.
Dublin's new Lord Mayor and his soldier son.—Alderman L. O'Neill,
an old-time Dublin cyclist and one-time president of the Irish
Cyclists' Association, and Captain W. L. O'Neill, R.A.M.C., who is
now serving in Mesopotamia. Alderman O'Neill goes into office
on Friday next.

Dublin's new Lord Mayor
and his son William.
Photo by Lafayette.
Dublin Saturday Post,
6 March 1917

THE IRISH CYCLISTS' OLD TIMERS' FELLOWSHIP AT THE MANSION HOUSE, DUBLIN, SATURDAY, JUNE 9th, 1917.

Lord Mayor O'Neill (centre, front) with Irish Cyclists' Fellowship.
Photo by Lafayette. From The Irish Cyclist and Motor Cyclist 13 June 1917

Cyclists at the Mansion House.
Cartoon by Gordon Brewster.
The Irish Cyclist and Motor Cyclist, 13 June 1917

Gathering of unemployed outside the Mansion House.
The Evening Telegraph, 27 June 1917

THE CONVENTION: SOME OF ITS MEMBERS

HIS GRACE THE MOST REV. DR. HARTY.   RIGHT REV. JOHN HENRY BERNARD, D.D.   MOST REV. DR. O'DONNELL.   RIGHT REV. DR. CROZIER.   MOST REV. DR. KELLY.   MOST REV. DR. McRORY.   REV. DR. MAHAFFY.   MR. JOHN J. CLANCY, K.C., M.P.

COLONEL CRAIG.   MR. JOSEPH DEVLIN, M.P.   LORD McDONNELL.

RT. HON. SIR HORACE PLUNKETT.   RT. HON. H. E. DUKE, M.P.   ALDERMAN L. O'NEILL, Late Mayor of Dublin.   MR. JOHN E. REDMOND, M.P.   MARQUIS OF LONDONDERRY.

Members of the Convention. Freeman's Journal, 25 July 1917

DELEGATES AT FIFTH SITTING OF THE CONVENTION

THE FIRST AUTHORISED PHOTOGRAPH OF THE CONVENTION.
Taken on the Steps of the Dining Hall, Trinity College, at 3 o'clock yesterday afternoon.
Amongst those in the front row, from left to right, are:—The Most Rev. Dr. O'Donnell, Bishop of Raphoe; Rev. Dr. Irwin, Moderator, Presbyterian Assembly; Hugh Barrie, M.P.; the Most Rev. Dr. Bernard, Protestant Archbishop of Dublin; the Most Rev. Dr. Crozier, Protestant Primate; Mr. Redmond; Dr. Mahaffy, Provost, Trinity College; Sir Horace Plunkett, Chairman of the Convention; the Most Rev. Dr. Harty, Archbishop of Cashel; Most Rev. Dr. Kelly, Bishop of Ross; the Most Rev. Dr. McRory, Bishop of Down and Connor; the Duke of Abercorn, the Marquis of Londonderry, the Earl of Dunraven and Lord MacDonnell.
Photo: Freeman's Journal.

Delegates at Fifth Sitting of the Convention. Freeman's Journal, 22 August 1917

LORD MAYOR & U-BOA
VICTIMS

The Lord Mayor of Dublin (Ald. L. O'Neill
Who presided over a private meeting at th
Mansion House, on Tuesday night, convene
to inaugurate a fund for the dependents o
Irish seamen and firemen and other ship en
ployes who have recently lost their lives a
sea.

Lord Mayor Laurence
O'Neill. Cartoon
by Frank Leahy.
Freeman's Journal,
15 January 1918

THE IRISH PARADOX: WHO SHALL SOLVE THE PUZZLE?

The Lord Mayor of Dublin (Alderman O'Neill) presenting Admiralty cheques to men who rescued the crew of a ship who were overcome by gas fumes after the hatches were battened down. Four lives were lost. Alderman O'Neill, who is to present a No-Conscription petition to President Wilson, himself has an officer son fighting with the British Army. Irish resistance to conscription, he says, is due to England's blundering.—(*Sunday Herald* photograph.)

Lord Mayor O'Neill presents bravery award. Sunday Herald, 5 May 1918

IRELAND AND PRESIDENT WILSON
(An Anticipation).

Cartoon and poem relating to the
proposed meeting of Lord Mayor
O'Neill with U.S. President Woodrow
Wilson at the Peace Conference in
Paris. The Leader, 26 Dec 1918

DEPUTATION TO PARIS
To Be Headed by the Lord Mayor

TO SEE PRESIDENT WILSON

DUBLIN CORPORATION at a special meeting to-day on the motion of the LORD MAYOR, seconded by MR. SEAN T. O'KELLY, M.P., unanimously decided to offer the Freedom of the City to PRESIDENT WILSON on the occasion of his visit to Europe.
ALD. T. KELLY, M.P., moved, and MR. DOYLE seconded, that, in order to give practical effect to the motion, a deputation should go to Paris to offer the compliment to the President in person. Ald. Kelly said the Lord Mayor should head the deputation, and there should be representatives of Sinn Fein, Labour, and the Nationalists.

The Deputation.

After some discussion the following deputation was appointed to wait on President Wilson in Paris to ask him to receive the Freedom of Dublin:—
LORD MAYOR.   HIGH SHERIFF.   SEAN T. O'KELLY, M.P.
ALD. CORRIGAN.   P. T. DALY.   LORCAN SHERLOCK.
THE LORD MAYOR said he had a hope—it might be a slender one—that President Wilson would come to Dublin.

THE MEETING

A special meeting of the Dublin Corporation was held to-day, the Lord Mayor presiding, to consider a motion signed by 58 members, in the following terms :—
We request your lordship to convene a meeting of the Council for the purpose of considering the following notice of mo-
the 10th June, 1918, we (that is, Americans) "are champions of those nations that have not the
MILITARY STANDING
to enable them to compete with the strongest nation, making the world safe for democracy," "the protecti

Dublin City Council voted to send a deputation to the
Paris Conference. Evening Herald, 3 Jan 1919

Irish Peace Delegation in London. Laurence O'Neill stands behind Eamon de Valera

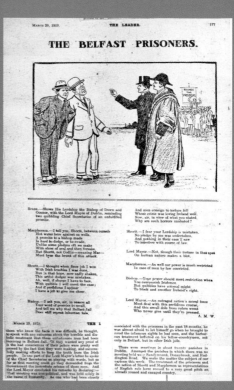

The Belfast Prisoners. Cartoon and poem from The Leader, 29 March 1919

De Valera leaving the Mansion House after his release from prison. Daily Mirror, 29 March 1919

De Valera with O'Neill and the Lord Mayor's two daughters, Annie (left) and Mary. Daily Sketch, 29 March 1919

QUEENSLAND'S PREMIER AND IRELAND.

Mr. Ryan.   Miss O'Niel.   Mrs. Ryan.   The Lord Mayor of Dublin.

Mr. T. J. Ryan, the Premier of Queensland is in Dublin investigating the Irish question first hand. This photograph was taken after a visit to the Lord Mayor of Dublin.—(Daily Sketch.)

Premier of Queensland visits Dublin's Mansion House.
Daily Sketch, 25 April 1919

De Valera with the Lord Mayor.

De Valera paid his first public visit in Dublin since his escape from prison, when he drove to the Mansion House to see the Lord Mayor. There was no public announcement, but the

De Valera at Dublin's Mansion House with Lord
Mayor O'Neill. Daily Sketch, 29 March 1919

DE VALERA AND THE IRISH AMERICAN MISSION.

The Irish-American delegates to the Peace Conference arrived at the Dublin Mansion House from Kingstown in motor-cars flying the American and Irish Republican flags. They were welcomed by De Valera and the Lord Mayor.—(Daily Sketch Exclusive Photograph.)

The Lord Mayor and de Valera
greet the American Delegates
at the Mansion House.
Daily Sketch, 6 May 1919

PENNY PICTORIAL.   10/5/19

De Valera back in Dublin after his escape from Lincoln prison. He is the second figure from the left, while the third is the Lord Mayor of Dublin. The men who have suffered in the cause of the "republic" are now looked upon as heroes and martyrs.

De Valera and Lord Mayor
O'Neill with Arthur Griffith
and Cathal Brugha at a
match in Croke Park.
Penny Pictorial 10 May 1919

World Chess Championship at Mansion House. Lord Mayor O'Neill and Sir Horace Plunkett
with World Chess Champion Jose Raul Capablanca 5 Dec 1919 © RTÉ Stills Library

Sir James McMahon, Under Secretary to three
Chief Secretaries A key support to Lord Mayor
O'Neill re political prisoners © RTÉ Stills Library

Funeral of Tomas MacCurtain, Lord Mayor of Cork O'Neill flanked by Patrick
Meade and Arthur Griffith 22 March 1920 © RTÉ Stills Library

Lord French and Lieutenant-Colonel Johnstone inspecting the Dublin
Police at the Phoenix Park depot 1920 © RTÉ Stills Library

Lord Mayor O'Neill with Archbishop Mannix, of Brisbane, in London 1920

Auxiliaries and Black-and Tans on duty outside the Mansion House 1 Jan 1921 © RTÉ Stills Library

Eamon de Valera, along with O'Neill, bids farewell to
Treaty Plenipotentiaries leaving Dun Laoghaire for London
7 Oct 1921 Courtesy National Library of Ireland

Laurence O'Neill arriving with others for an election meeting at Earlsfort
Terrace June 1922 Courtesy National Library of Ireland

Arthur Griffith, Eamon de Valera, O'Neill and Michael Collins at a
match in Croke Park 1 Jan 1919 © RTÉ Stills Library

(Left to right) Graves of Laurence and Anne O'Neill, that of his parents and those of other
O'Neill families, St. Marnock's Cemetery, Portmarnock. Courtesy M. Mullen

On 3 January 1919, the Lord Mayor and fellow councillors decided on providing President Wilson with a concrete occasion for coming to Ireland. At a special meeting of the Municipal Council, Ald. O'Neill moved, and Clr. Sean T. O'Kelly seconded, that the Freedom of the City of Dublin be conferred on the President of the Unites States of America. The lengthy motion requested the President to secure the application to Ireland of his precept "that the Governments of nations derive their just powers from the consent of the governed", and trusted that he would use his mighty influence in urging the Peace Conference to give a just judgement to Ireland's cause. The Lord Mayor spoke eloquently on Ireland's links with America, on the president's speeches, on "Dark Rosaleen" having been defamed and her people belittled, and requested that the President demand that Ireland be allowed to plead her cause before the Peace Conference. The motion was passed unanimously by those present. Ald. Kelly, M.P., proposed that to give practical effect to the motion, a deputation should go to Paris to offer the compliment to the President in person. This, too, was passed and the following deputation appointed: The Lord Mayor, the High Sheriff, and Sean T. O'Kelly, M.P., Ald Corrigan, Clr. P.T. Daly, and Ald. Lorcan Sherlock.[113]

While there was general support for an invitation to President Wilson and, indeed, for the conferring of the Freedom of the City on him, the wording of the Lord Mayor's motion and his address came in for sharp criticism in a number of unionist newspapers, notably, the *Dublin Daily Express*, the *Irish Daily Mail*, and the *Dublin Evening Mail*. 'It was rather unfortunate', the *Irish Daily Mail* commented, on 4 January 1919, ' that the proposal to confer the Freedom of Dublin on President Wilson should be coupled with the insane desire of a section of the Irish people to set up an independent Republic of Ireland... Very many citizens of Dublin will fail altogether to appreciate what connection the alleged sufferings of "Dark Rosaleen" have with the proposal to confer the Freedom of the City on the distinguished head of the United States of America.' After further criticism, the paper commented that the Lord Mayor was allowing himself to be lectured 'by Sinn Féin on a question which is, and must remain, a matter of private British domestic politics'. Ald. David Quaid, not surprisingly, made it clear that he had not supported the Corporation's address to President Wilson, and pointedly remarked – 'I presume the Deputation will pay its own expenses, or will have them paid out of the Sinn Féin war chest'!

By 9 January 1919, the *Freeman's Journal* was commenting on the 'curious silence'; 'President Wilson's delay in replying', and 'the Deputation still without passports'. On 21 January the *Evening Mail* announced that the passports had arrived, but that there was still no reply from the President. The Lord Mayor had sent the invitation by the American Consul in Ireland, Edward L. Adams, who undertook to transmit it through the American Embassy in London or Paris. O'Neill wrote some eight letters seeking information but got no reply. It was not until 1 April 1919 that he received a response. Then, Mr Adams, the Consul, called to the Mansion House with a typed letter apologising for the delay in replying to his invitation and expressing the President's regrets that it would not be possible for him to visit Dublin 'because of the constant pressure of his engagements'...[114]

Christmas wishes and General Election results

Returning to the final days of 1918, the Lord Mayor sent Christmas wishes to many prisoners, including Arthur Griffith, and de Valera and Cosgrave with whom he corresponded more regularly. Three days after Christmas Day, on 28 December, the results of the general election were published. Sinn Féin had had a sweeping victory: winning 73 seats, compared to six for Dillon's Nationalists, 25 for Unionists, and one seat for Independent Unionists. On New Year's Eve, an elated Arthur Griffith sent his best wishes to the Lord Mayor with the euphoric information that on receiving the election news they had sent a telegram to President Wilson, on behalf of themselves and their constituents, associating themselves with the invitation sent by his Lordship.[115]

A passing assessment

The hopes centred on President Wilson were quite quixotic. Even the 'Irish blood in his veins' that O'Neill spoke of, was orange rather than green. Much of the country was caught up in a fever of nationalism which seemed to obscure clear thinking. The Lord Mayor spoke eloquently of what President Wilson could do, and, given his previously stated principles, would do for Ireland, and yet, when asked by the *Evening Herald* reporter on 3 January 1919, whether he thought the President would accept the invitation, he said –'he had a hope, it might be a slender one, that President Wilson would come to Dublin'. What then of all his exuberant rhetoric? Little wonder that the *Evening Mail* and the *Daily Mail* thought him entrapped in a Sinn Féin delusion! The ineffectiveness of his invitation to President Wilson, however, did not result in any loss of credibility and influence among the majority population, mainly because his critics, individuals and press, were Unionists and hence discounted.

When Arthur Griffith was sending his letter on New Year's Eve, Laurence O'Neill, as related earlier, was seeing out the Old Year in Belfast jail. It was symptomatic of how the job of Lord Mayor took up all his time, and the strain that must have placed on his wife and family. His constant preoccupation and the open door policy of the Mansion House gave little space or time for family life. The pressure may have contributed to the declining health of his very willing and supportive wife, who became progressively ill during 1919.

Notes

1   DCC. Mins. 23 Jan. 1918, no. 76, p. 62; *Dublin Sat. Post*, 26 Jan. 1918. Ald. Quaid was probably correct in his reference to P.T. Daly, who was accused by labour colleagues of similar practices.

2   ONFP. Walsh-O'Neill, 24 Jan. 1918; also INL. O'Neill papers, Ms.35, 294/2

3   INL. O'Neill papers. Ms. 35,294/2. Mahon-O'Neill, 25 Jan. 1918.

4   *Dublin Sat. Post.* "A Citizen's Diary", 5 Jan. 1918

5   DCC Mins. 7 Jan.1918, pp. 2-3

6   Among contributors from Limerick was Rev. W. Hackett, S.J., later to be prominent in social work in Australia, who reported that 200 tons of oatmeal were required to render the people of Limerick famine-proof for a month. This would cost £6,500 and promises to that amount had been received from several merchants. (*Freeman's Journal*, 29 Jan. 1918)

7   T.J. Morrissey. *A Man Called Hughes,* (Dublin 1991), p. 94

8   *Freeman's Journal*, 29 Jan. 1918

9   ONFP. Typed account: "Invitation from Lloyd George"

10   Plunkett-Ld. Mayor,, 29 Jan. 1918. NLI. O'Neill papers. Ms.35,294/2

11   Plunkett-Ld. Mayor, 2 Feb. 1918, idem

12   Idem, 13 Feb. 1918

13   ONFP. Idem.

14   Trevor West. *Horace Plunkett. Cooperation and Politics*, pp. 172-3

15   ONFP. The Convention

16   ONFP. "Mr William Martin Murphy", brief profile

17   NLI. O'Neill papers. J. MacDonagh-Lord Mayor, 5 March 1918. Ms.35,294/2

18   ONFP.

19   ONFP. Lord Mayor-Duke, 5 March 1918.

20   Idem. Duke-Lord Mayor, 6 March 1918

21   ONFP. P.McHugh, Governor, - Lord Mayor, 9 March 1918.

22   ONFP. Sir James O'Connor-Lord Mayor, 20 March 1918

23   Idem. MacSwiney-Stack, 20 March 1918.

24   DCC. Mins. of special meeting, 11 March, no.192, p. 160

25   ONFP. Typed pages- "Political Tragedies".

26   *Dublin Sat. Post*, 30 March 1918

27   ONFP. "Conscription April 1918"

28   DCC. Mins.8 April 1918, no.257, p. 228

29   Trevor West, op. cit., p. 175

30   ONFP. "Conscription Conference"

31   NLI. William O'Brien papers. Ms.7998. Lord Mayor-O'Brien, 13 April 1918

32   NLI. O'Neill papers. Ms. 15,294/15. Messages from Healy and Dillon. Telegrams from Lord Mayor to Healy, 15 April. Wm. O'Brien's Scrap Book, Ms.7998

33   NLI. Curran Ms. 27, 728(2), statement p. 261; in Sean T.O'Kelly papers.

34   NLI. Idem. Also T.J. Morrissey. *William J. Walsh, Archbishop of Dublin*, p. 309; and William O'Brien. *Forth the Banners Go*, pp. 164-5

35   ICD.1919. Record for 1918, 18 April, p. 511

36   ONFP. On the Convention.

37   *Forth the Banners Go*, pp.165-6

38   ONFP. Typed notes. "Arrival at Maynooth".

39   O'Brien. Op. cit., p. 166

40   ONFP. Idem

41   ICD. Op. cit.

42   ONFP. Idem.

43   *Freeman's Journal*, Sat. 27 April 1918

44   Idem

45   NLI. Curran. Ms.27,728, p. 264; and Abp. Walsh's diary for 19 April 1918

46   Curran. Idem, pp.265-66

47   NLI. O'Neill papers. Wm O'Brien-Lord Mayor, 22 April; Ms. 35,294/3

48   ONFP. Printed document: 'Extracts from Official Reports of the National Conference, 18, 19, 24, 29 April and 4 May'.

49   NLI. Curran papers, pp. 266-67

50   Idem, pp.266-7

51   ONFP. Mr Duke was critical of partition and Sir Bryan Mahon opposed conscription according to T.M. Healy to his brother, Maurice, 2 June, 1917; 17, 21 May 1918. T.M. Healy. *Letters and Leaders of My Day*, vol.2, pp.582, pp.598-9.

52   Curran. Op. cit., vol. 2, pp. 262-3, referring to the reaction of his friend, Mr Quinn, Assistant-Commissioner of Police, on the bishops' statement against conscription.

53   NLI. O'Neill papers. B.Mahon-Lord Mayor, 13 May 1918. Ms. 35,294/3

54   T.M. Healy. Op. cit. p.598. Letter to Maurice, 17 May 1918.

55   NLI. O'Neill papers. Ms 35,2924/3. Lord Mayor- Sir Bryan Mahon, 14 May 1918

56   ONFP. "A Speck on the United Horizon"

57   ONFP. and NLI. Ms.35,294/3. Walsh-Ld. Mayor, 24 April 1918

58   ONFP

59   ONFP. Typed notes on the conference.

60   *Dublin Sat. Post,* 25 May 1918

61   ONFP. Extracts from Official Reports of the National Conference. On the American situation: National Archives and Records Administration of the United States (NARA), R.G.65, M580/6, 841,000/76, Wilson-Phillips, 4 May 1918; idem 841,000/71, Lansing to Page, 6 May 1918; cit. Bernadette Whelan. *United States Foreign Policy and Ireland. From Empire to Independence, 1913-1929,* pp. 17—71.

62   Idem

63   T.M. Healy. *Letters and Leaders* …,vol.2, pp.598-9

64   ONFP. Typed notes –"Personal Friction in the Conference".

65   DCC. Mins. 3 June, no, 412, p.328

66   Idem, 10 June, no, 454, p. 355

67   *Dublin Saturday Post*, 29 June

68   NLI. O'Neill papers, Ms. 35, 294/16

69   ONFP. Copy of the document with a covering letter of Lord Mayor, 18 June 1918

70   NLI. O'Neill papers, Ms.35, 294/3, de Valera – Ld. Mayor, 6 June 1918; UCDA. de Valera papers, P 150/612, Ld Mayor-de Valera, 13 June.

71   UCDA. P150/612, O'Neill-de Valera, 3 Aug. 1918

72   NLI. O'Neill papers, Ms. 35,294/3, de Valera, Leicester prison,- Ld. Mayor, 19 Aug. 1918

73   Idem, Cosgrave-Ld Mayor, 19 July 1918

74   ONFP. Typed page "The Lord Lieutenant and Ald. Cosgrave".

75   ONFP. Among some profiles, a typed page on "The Right Hon. James McMahon, Under Secretary"

76   ONFP. "Arrest of Mrs Sheehy Skeffington"

77   NLI. O'Neill papers. Ms. 35,294/3. Hanna Sheehy Skeffington – Ld. Mayor, 21 Aug. 1918

78   *Dublin Sat. Post,* 14 Sept.

79   Idem, Sept.

80   UCDA. De Valera papers. P150/612. L.O'Neill-de Valera, 24 Aug. 1918.

81   DCA. Dublin Corporation Reports, vol.3, pp. 43-4

82   *Irish Independent,* 24 Sept. 1918

83   NLI. O'Neill papers, Ms. 35, 294/3. O'Neill- Sir Bryan Mahon, 23 Oct. 1918

84   DCC Mins., no. 643, p 482

85   Idem, no.645

86   Margaret O Hógartaigh. *Kathleen Lynn. Irishwoman, Patriot, Doctor,* p. 41, and on the impact of the influenza epidemic see P. Yeates. *A City in Wartime. Dublin 1914-1918,* pp. 270-72

87   Fionán Lynch. "Recollections of Jail Riots and Hunger-Strikes – grim times in Mountjoy, Dundalk and Belfast Jails" in *IRA Jailbreaks 1918-1921,* p. 103

88   ONFP. "Sinn Féin Convention. Treatment of Prisoners in Belfast, Oct. 29th, 1918."

89   *Dublin Evening Mail,* 31 Dec. 1918

90   F. Lynch. Art cit. in op. cit., p. 107

91   ONFP Types pages on Prisoners and Belfast Jail

92   Idem

93   NLI. O'Neill papers. Ms 35,294/4: H. Boland- Ld. Mayor, 12 Nov. 1918

94   F. Lynch. Art.cit. in op. cit., p. 106

95   ONFP. Telegram, Cardinal Logue – Ld. Mayor, 3 Dec.

96   Idem. Copy from Sinn Féin office, 6 Harcourt Street, Dublin, 3 Dec 1918, giving Eoin McNeill's account of the basis for the division of seats at the conference; and letter of Cardinal Logue dated 3 Dec.

97   NLI. O'Neill papers, Ms 35,294/4: Cardinal Logue-Ld. Mayor, 6 Dec. 1918.

98   *Dublin Sat. Post,* 2 Nov. 1918

99   DCC. Mins. 18 Nov. 1918, no. 684, p. 529

100   Cit. *Freeman's Journal* 30 Nov. 1918

101   Idem.

102   *Evening Telegraph,* 5 Dec. 1918

103   ONFP. "Industrial Strife 1917-1921".

104   *Irish Independent,* 9 Dec. 1918

105   Idem

106   *Dublin Sat. Post,* 14 Dec. 1918

107   *Evening Telegraph,* 16 Dec. 1918

108   ONFP. O'Neill- Dillon, 4 Nov. 1918.

109   Idem. Dillon-Ld. Mayor, 12 Nov. 1918.

110   NLI. Sweetman papers, Ms. 47,590/6. John Sweetman-Ld. Mayor, 18 Dec 1918

111   *Freeman's Journal*, 17 Dec. 1918

112   NLI. Letters to Hanna Sheehy Skeffington, Ms. 22,685. L.O'Neill, Ld Mayor- Mrs Sheehy Skeffington, 19, 20 Dec. 1918.

113   *Evening Herald*, Friday, 3 Jan. 1919

114   ONFP. Typed letter.

115   ONFP. Griffith-Ld. Mayor, 31 December 1918

9.

1919:

Release of prisoners. Civic reception for de Valera. American Delegates. Prohibitions and constraints. Closure of Mansion House. An independent stand.

As he faced a year in which he was likely to be re-elected as Lord Mayor, O'Neill had among his preoccupations two major concerns: His wife's poor health, and the presence of a new, obdurate Chief Secretary. On his wife's condition, one learns only indirectly, from passing remarks and her absence on public occasions. From such remarks, it would appear that the Lady Mayoress had short periods of improvement or remission. Thus, Bishop MacRory, replying to O'Neill on 5 January 1919, remarked: 'I am delighted to know that the lady Mayoress is better'.[1] As regards the Chief Secretary, Mr Edward Shortt had been appointed Home Secretary, and Mr Ian MacPherson had succeeded him. Against that rather sombre backdrop there were two pleasing comments from very different milieu.

Different sources of approbation

The *Irish Times* correspondent, viewing the display of Union Jacks and Sinn Féin colours at the Mansion House, explained the presence of 'these mingled portents' by asserting that the Mansion House was playing two parts: 'thoroughly loyal in the morning and exceedingly disloyal in the afternoon, or rather it is more fair to say that the Lord Mayor was giving a supreme example of the catholicity with which he puts his fine house at the disposal of all classes of the citizens'. In the morning there was a luncheon for 400 repatriated prisoners of the Royal Dublin Fusiliers, and two hours later, a different room in the same house, 'echoed to the Republican Parliament's declaration of independence'.[2] This last referred to the first meeting of Dail Eireann, minus 36 deputies in prison, which met in the Mansion House on 21 January, adopted a provisional constitution, declared independence, produced a document entitled the "Democratic Programme", and issued an address to the free nations of the world.

The second approbation was of a more exuberant nature. It took the form of a ballad encouraging support for Alderman O'Neill in the 1919 election for Lord Mayor. The short lyric, entitled "Our Good Lord Mayor", by Michael O'Grady, was dated 22 January 1919. Its three stanzas, whatever their poetic quality, reflected much public sentiment. Two of them are sufficient to convey the grounds for the popular esteem.

> The hour is due. Faith to renew in those who've served us
> Well.
> The deeds of one true Irish son, the task be mine to tell.
> Such moment grand when stout hearts band our Freedom to
> Declare
> One name shines forth of peerless worth – our own, our good
> Lord Mayor
>
> ii
>
> In sorrow's hour when demon power had spread its nets
> Around
> To have our sons face Teuton guns on continental ground
> First to oppose those heartless foes who would our youth
> Ensnare
> And give relief was this brave chief, our own, our good
> Lord Mayor

On that day, 22 January, O'Neill was re-elected to the chair of First Citizen; 'the greatest man since Mighty Dan to ornament that chair', as the ballad would have it.[3]

Scarcely had he been elected, than a unwelcomingly familiar problem landed on his desk.

Prisoners in Belfast again

A letter from Richard Mulcahy, commander-in-chief of the Irish Volunteers, informed O'Neill that he had a request from Belfast urging him to ask the Lord Mayor to intervene once more before matters were made worse'.[4] The first act of the new Chief Secretary, in O'Neill's words, 'was to break through the undertaking which his predecessor had given to the Rev. Dr MacRory and myself regarding the Belfast prisoners'.[5]

He and Bishop MacRory exchanged letters on the prisoners' situation. They felt that they had been compromised. The assurance had been given them that the prisoners would be moved to internment camps. The prisoners made peace on the strength of their word. 'The whole system of Irish government', MacRory declared, 'is a tragic and cruel farce… Responsible ministers can give undertakings to-day and run away from them to-morrow.' He had no intention of remaining silent much longer…'[6] On 20 February, the Lord Mayor sent him a copy of a letter he had sent to Mr Shortt, and next day sent the unsatisfactory reply. He proposed that they send a joint letter to the press, 'setting out Shortt's undertaking and the letters which have passed through the new Chief Secretary and myself'.[7] On 25 February, MacRory agreed and sent a version of the joint letter, which he had composed as he had more time than the Lord Mayor was likely to have. He hoped the censor would allow it to appear. He went on to 'heartily hail' O'Neill's formal accession to the third year of office, adding – 'I hope I may see you first President of an Irish Republic. Even very recently a Republic seemed an idle dream … but now I am beginning to hope very strongly.' He concluded his letter by hoping that the Lady Mayoress was well again.[8]

Two days later, on 27 May, both men received a letter from Michael Collins detailing the suffering of the prisoners and impressing on the Lord Mayor and the bishop their responsibility to see that the terms of the agreement were carried out – namely, the prisoners to be removed to an internment camp, and not to be punished for any action taken in relation to the prisoner Dolan. 'Failing the carrying out of the agreement, they owed it to the prisoners to make the facts public so that the Irish people would be able to judge for themselves and (recognise) the only suitable action that is possible against a base and unscrupulous foe.'[9] On the state of the prisoners, he reported that for five weeks they had been continually handcuffed, for lengthy periods with their hands behind their backs. They had been denied facilities for ordinary human cleanliness, so that they now resembled wild beasts rather than civilized beings. 'Above all, they had not been allowed to attend Holy Mass during the period under review…In this connection the prison chaplain cannot be relieved of the responsibility which attaches to his office.' Collins asked Bishop MacRory to visit the prison once again and assure himself that Collins had stated the precise details. MacRory did so, and found Collins to be substantially accurate. The state of affairs was corroborated by a long statement written by Austin Stack and Ernest Blythe.[10] The Lord Mayor was angered and frustrated at his inability to move Government on their behalf.

Confusing reports from the Mansion House

Meantime, events had taken place which complicated matters. On 3 February de Valera had escaped from Lincoln Jail together with Sean Milroy and Sean McGarry. In subsequent weeks there were various 'sightings' as government forces attempted to capture them. At the beginning of March, during the Robert Emmet commemoration concert at the Mansion House, the Lord Mayor was discomfited when one of the escaped prisoners, Sean McGarry, put in a dramatic appearance. According to the *Freeman's Journal* of 5 March, 'Mr McGarry, who wore the uniform of the Irish Volunteers, received a tremendous ovation when he entered the Round Room, accompanied by the Lord Mayor of Dublin, wearing his chain of office, and Mr Sean O' Muirthuille, chairman of the Wolfe Tone Memorial Committee, a pipers' band leading the way. The scene, which was an extraordinary one, lasted for several minutes.' The account continued:

> The Lord Mayor, who was received with enthusiasm, said he stood before the audience in the full adornment of his office out of compliment to the latest fugitive from British injustice (applause).

"I am here", his Lordship proceeded, "for two reasons. The first is to tender a hearty welcome to my colleague, Councillor Sean McGarry (applause), to the Mansion House; and it is within the bounds of possibility his arms may be here and not mine. The second reason for my presence is to show my utter contempt – a contempt which is shared by every liberty-loving man and woman the world over – for a system and a Government which detains in English jails so many of my fellow-countrymen, and one solitary and lonely woman (applause), without any trial and without any charge, and which hits at the fundamental principles of liberty, justice and fair play" (applause).'

'Mr McGarry left the building surrounded by several members of Dail Eireann, and got away before a large police force came up Dawson Street to the Mansion House.'

The Lord Mayor's account of the event, written several years later, omits, or forgets much of the foregoing, but adds some particulars redolent of the time. In his version, he wore the chain of office to honour Robert Emmett and did not expect the arrival of Sean McGarry. He had been asked by the stewards earlier if they might lock the doors because of the pressures of the crowds seeking to come in. It was only later that he realised it was to protect McGarry from the possibility of detectives in the audience alerting the police. He also learned subsequently that the organisers had cut the telephone wires and had surrounded the building with armed men, thereby demonstrating a readiness for shooting and bloodshed. He felt deeply annoyed at this and at his being used by Sinn Féin extremists, and he determined to close the Mansion House to further events. On this last point, there appears to have been a conflation of events.

On Tuesday, 4 March, the date of the above meeting, the *Evening Telegraph* noted that the Lord Mayor had announced that day that at the request of Sir Charles Cameron, the chief medical officer for the city, he had no option but to close the Mansion House to all meetings or entertainments. The flu in Dublin had led to a record total of deaths. 'Yesterday there were 98 burial orders issued. The highest ever in one day.' 'When Sir Charles Cameron considers all danger of contagion is over', the Lord Mayor explained, 'I shall be most happy to place the Mansion House at the disposal of those who are disappointed by its being closed now owing to the epidemic.' No doubt he was happy to close it at this stage, irrespective of the flu.

The prisoners. Campaign for release

In his written notes, O'Neill observed that the Under-Secretary, James McMahon, called to the Mansion House about 8.0 p.m. on 5 February 1919 with a message which O'Neill carefully wrote down: 'The Cabinet will meet tomorrow to consider the unanimous request of the Irish Government to release all the political prisoners in Britain, but there is hope in the highest quarters that the men may be out to night. Lord French has travelled to London.' McMahon was so sure, he informed O'Neill that he might acquaint the relatives of the prisoners. The Lord Mayor did so, and, as a result, the Mansion House was crowded with anxious relatives into the early hours and the following day. But the next day passed and succeeding days without information. There was extensive public criticism of the Castle authorities, and some was directed at the Lord Mayor.[11] On 6 March, however, following the death of Sinn Féin prisoner, Pierce McCann, M.P., of influenza at Gloucester Prison, the British parliament announced the release of Irish prisoners in Britain.[12] The release, unfortunately, was not applied to the Belfast prisoners for several weeks. On 10 March, in proposing a vote of sympathy to the McCann family, the Lord Mayor criticised the policy of the Government and declared that Pierce McCann was dead 'owing to the delay of his release. The English Prime Minister was warned a month ago of the deplorable result which would follow the detention of these men'.[13]

Following the funeral, O'Neill directed his focus on conditions in Belfast Jail and on the release of the prisoners there. He embarked on a campaign to win the support of the Catholic hierarchy for meetings across the parishes of Ireland protesting against conditions in Belfast. Motors were hired to bring a deputation from the Municipal Council to meet Cardinal Logue at Armagh, Archbishops Harty and Gilmartin in Thurles and Tuam, and Archbishop Walsh in Dublin.[14] The bishops were horrified at the conditions endured by the prisoners, but some pointed out that they were forbidden by canonical legislation against treating of political matters from church pulpits or having political meetings within church grounds. Dr Walsh pointed out, also, that rather than have all the meetings on St Patrick's Day, as originally planned, they should be spaced through subsequent days. On 19 March a circular letter was sent by O'Neill to every parish in the country. It ran to five A.4 printed pages. It had a nation-wide impact. He introduced the document with an explanation of the contents. The "facts" that he gave regarding the treatment and condition of the prisoners made harrowing reading. He elaborated on the outline provided to him and Dr MacRory by Michael Collins, and added: 'This state of things was a result of a breach of the undertaking given to the Lord Mayor of Dublin, and Dr. MacRory, Bishop of Down and Connor, by Chief Secretary, Right Hon. E. Shortt, on behalf of the Government, which was –"That within a reasonable time the proposal to have the political prisoners removed to an internment camp would be sympathetically considered".'

Attached to the Lord Mayor's document were two letters: one from Mr Ian MacPherson dated 11 March, which denied that Mr Shortt made a definite pledge to remove prisoners to England and, that, besides, it would be illegal to do so and would not receive permission from parliament; the second signed by the Lord Mayor and Dr MacRory recalled the circumstances leading up to Mr Shortt's undertaking to them and accused MacPherson of playing with words; and as to the transfer of the prisoners being "illegal", why not solve the problem by releasing the prisoners? Had they not suffered enough already?[15]

On Sunday, 23 March, mass meetings of the population of several parishes in Dublin City, and in parishes across the country, were held adjacent to the churches for the purpose of hearing the statement issued by the Lord Mayor, on behalf of the Corporation. At a large meeting in Marlborough Street, near the Pro-Cathedral, the Lord Mayor was in attendance. There was also read the joint letter of Bishop MacRory and the Lord Mayor to the Chief Secretary. Called on to speak, Ald. O'Neill, according to the *Irish Times* of 24 March, declared: 'the question was whether the Bishop and himself were telling lies or not. He felt it his solemn duty to attend the meeting, and to take whatever risk – and there were risks now for anyone assembled in the streets of Dublin – might be attached to it. He had never asked anyone to accept a risk which he was not prepared to take himself. He was almost afraid to let himself go on the subject of the infamous sights he had seen, and the barbarous treatment inflicted upon his fellow countrymen, not only in Belfast, but in every jail in Ireland at the present day.'

A Civic Reception for de Valera?

Events piled on each other in those days and weeks. Eager to intensify pressure on the Government and magnify popular pressure, Michael Collins had Harry Boland call on the Lord Mayor to enquire -'If a reception were given to Mr De Valera on his return from England, would he publicly receive him?' O'Neill replied: 'Certainly, as Mr de

Valera was a member of the Mansion House Anti-Conscription Conference'.[16] Soon after, a letter appeared in the press signed by the joint secretaries of Sinn Féin, Harry Boland and Tom Kelly, stating that The Right Hon. the Lord Mayor would publicly receive Mr de Valera on his return from England at the gates of the city, and escort him to the Mansion House.[17] The *Evening Telegraph*, of 22 March, wrote of 'A State Entry into the City on Wednesday next (and) procession to the Mansion House'. This was too much for Chief Secretary MacPherson, who instructed Lieutenant-General, Sir Frederick Shaw to issue a proclamation forbidding the reception for Mr de Valera. The *Irish Independent* carried the prohibition on Tuesday, 25 March.

The same day the Lord Mayor issued his own proclamation. The *Evening Herald* announced that evening that it was unable to publish his proclamation 'owing to circumstances over which we have no control'. Expecting this, O'Neill had a number of copies made, large poster size, and placed in various locations. In large print, the poster declared that the Lord Mayor understood that 'the Competent Military Authorities' feared that a reception given to Mr de Valera would give rise to grave disorder and place undue demands upon the police and military forces. He, however, as 'the one charged more directly with the peace and order of the city', dissented wholly from the view that grave disorder was pending. Nevertheless, 'having as Chief Magistrate done not a little to keep the peace and good order of this city for the past two years', he now respectfully requested his fellow-citizens, in his capacity as Lord Mayor and charged with the responsibilities of that office, to follow his advice and give no opportunity for provocative action, which might cloud the prospects of the Nation during the Peace Conference.[18] The message to his fellow-citizens to avoid provocative action was well directed, as there was, as he knew, an extreme section of Sinn Féin that wanted to defy the Government's prohibition and viewed failure to do so as being on par with Daniel O'Connell's capitulation in calling off his mass meeting at Clontarf in 1843. The Government, for its part, was disrespectful of the Lord Mayor's appeal. The police were instructed to tear down his posters.

De Valera thought it wiser to call off the reception. His judicious decision was conveyed to the Lord Mayor on 27 March. He thanked his Lordship for the great honour he had proposed doing him, and went on:

> Your love of peace and order are known to all who have met you or even
> heard of you. Were I to be received by you in the public manner proposed,
> surrounded in the public streets by all the marks of popular approval, the
> devices of deportation, *lettres de cachet* etc., by which English oligarchs
> get rid of those who represent the public will in Ireland, would be exposed
> … That is, of course, precisely why the forces in occupation "proclaimed"

it. A peaceful orderly demonstration would be too powerful indictment of England's oligarchic militarism – an orgy of blood under the pretext of quelling a riot or some similar pretext would suit exactly their purpose and their propaganda.

'I am sure you will agree with me that in these circumstances it would be an injury to Ireland no less than an act of cruelty towards the citizens to proceed. I have called the Sinn Féin organisation to abandon the reception, and I beg to thank you again for an act and an intention which I am certain was promoted by a desire to serve your country.'[19] De Valera already viewed himself as the embodiment of the country.

The following day, de Valera walked unnoticed through the streets of Dublin and made his way to the Mansion House. The *Daily Sketch* of Saturday, 29 March, carried photographs of him walking through the city, leaving the Mansion House in company with the Lord Mayor, of crowds gathering to see him drive away, and finally a larger picture of de Valera, the Lord Mayor and his two daughters, probably taken in the garden of the Mansion House. Significantly, the Lady Mayoress was absent.

Although the official reception was cancelled, probably to his relief, the Lord Mayor remained angry at the manner in which the posters carrying his proclamation had been torn down by the police, and the premises of the printer raided. He wrote a carefully modulated letter to the Chief Secretary on 28 March, asking by what authority or for what reason the proclamation was torn down. Having been censored in the press, the poster was the only means of reaching the public and advising them to 'give no opportunity for provocation'. Outside of the indignity which it cast upon him as Lord Mayor, he thought that as one who had the peace and good order of the city as much at heart as any other authority, it was due to him that he should know where his proclamation was wrong. Ian MacPherson replied bluntly the same day, taking full responsibility for removing the posters. In his view, the proclamation was an attempt, under cover of advice to the public to keep the peace, to justify a previous proposal of the Lord Mayor of an unconstitutional nature which had been prohibited by the Government. The proclamation was designed 'to disregard and to bring into contempt lawfully constituted authority'. O'Neill answered next day, asking for an explanation in what way a proposal of his was 'clearly of an unconstitutional nature'. Not surprisingly, MacPherson replied that it was evident that it was O'Neill's intention, 'as Lord Mayor and Chief Magistrate of the City of Dublin to receive as his Majesty alone should be received, at the gates of the City of Dublin, a man who claims unlawfully to be president of an Irish Republic'. He had no objection to their correspondence being published, but he could not sanction the publication of the proclamation.

Unable to answer in MacPherson's terms, the Lord Mayor launched into a succession of rhetorically charged questions, which indicated that he, though Chief Magistrate, no longer viewed Britain as the legitimate authority in Ireland: 'Was it unconstitutional for me to receive Mr de Valera on his return to the city at any given point in the city I wished? Was it a crime for the inhabitants of this city to receive one of their countrymen who had been interned for close on ten months in an English jail, without any charge, or without any trial, an act which was condemned even by the Lord Lieutenant of the period, and an act, which, in my humble judgement, hits at the very root of Justice, of Liberty, and Fair Play? Was it anti-constitutional for me to receive a colleague of the Mansion House Anti-Conscription Committee, which had sent its message to President Wilson and to the world?' O'Neill then added words with which Mr MacPherson might heartily concur!

> I am afraid Chief Secretary, it will take you a long time to learn, or to understand the Irish temperament, or what is bred in the Irish bone, namely, our hatred of oppression and injustice.

As to the publication of their correspondence, the Lord Mayor thought it would be incomplete without the proclamation, which he trusted the Chief Secretary would allow to be published in Ireland now that it had been published already in England. He concluded with a defiant challenge – 'I accept full responsibility for the proclamation in every detail, composition, printing, publishing, pasting up etc'.[20] This time the Chief Secretary did not reply.

As a bizarre post-script to the detention of Irish political prisoners in England for almost a month after their release was announced by the British Parliament, Lord Mayor O'Neill was given an explanation three years later during a visit to the United States of America. He was introduced to a Captain Moore, a particular friend of Lord French, who had been with him in London three years previously. French had told Moore that he was over about the release of Irish political prisoners. He then took suddenly ill and during his illness his whole trouble was, 'What will the Lord Mayor think of me for breaking my word?' When he was convalescent the prisoners were released. 'What a reflection this was', O'Neill commented, 'on the way the affairs of this country were managed; when we find owing to the sudden illness of one man, hundreds of our people were detained for … a month in jail.'[21]

A challenge and enjoyment

The very busy month of March continued on its sombre way with a notice of strike by the nurses and attendants at Portrane Asylum against the Corporation's scheme for a 56 hour week. The Lord Mayor moved quickly as he sought to impress on the public that the strike was 'wholly unwarranted and unjustifiable'. The *Evening Herald* reported on 31 March that the Trades Council had disclaimed emphatically any sympathy with the strike and that Ald. O'Neill had directed that the relatives of the patients should be notified. He was confident that no sympathy would be given to a strike which imperilled the lives and health of a large number of human beings.[22]The problem dragged on for many days. On 18 and 19 April, however, the *Freeman's Journal*, referring to the monthly Corporation meeting, reported that Clrs Lawlor and P.T. Daly had been interviewing nurses and attendants and that the strike had been averted.

April turned out to be a more relaxed and enjoyable month in many ways. O'Neill was pleasantly surprised on 5 April by an article in the *Leader* newspaper on Dublin Corporation, which contained more praise than criticism. It suggested that the Corporation's bad name might be largely due to the fact that it was a nationalist body. It had, no doubt, many faults, but was the old ascendancy Corporation one to boast of ? 'Dublin is a non-progressive city,' the article continued, 'and English government is mainly responsible for that. Dublin Corporation has to manage the affairs of the capital of an enslaved and handcuffed nation. Had Ireland been free twenty-five years ago – to go no further back – the slum problem of Dublin would not exist as it does today.' Following this supportive, if somewhat fanciful note, the author conceded that the present rates were 'staggering and a drag on the city', but that this was 'partly due to the war with its inflation of prices and consequently wages'. He added pointedly that the *Irish Times* 'has no indignation for the awful over-taxation of Ireland, it keeps it all for the rates of Dublin'; while Murphy's *Independent* would be more credible 'if, in addition to its horror of the Dublin rates, it expressed indignation at the exorbitant and cruel rates of Murphy's Dublin trams'.

The unaccustomed support from an organ of the press added to O'Neill's enjoyment as he attended two different football codes. The *Irish Independent* of Monday, 7 April, carried a photograph of the Lord Mayor, with his friend Lord Justice O'Connor, who started the match, and the captains of Blackrock College and Old St Mary's, who met in the final of the O'Connor Rugby Cup at Lansdowne Road on Saturday, 5 April; and on Tuesday, 8 April, the *Daily Sketch* had the celebrated photograph of Laurence O'Neill sharing a bench with Michael Collins, Eamon de Valera and Arthur Griffith, all in jovial mood, at a Gaelic football match between Wexford and Tipperary, which was played at Croke Park before an attendance of 20,000 people. De Valera threw in the ball, and Harry Boland, M.P., was referee!

On 16 April the Lord Mayor announced that Thursday, 1 May, would be observed as "Labour Day", and the markets would be closed on that day.[23] On 20 April, Easter

Sunday, O'Neill and many members of the City Council, as was the custom, attended in full robes at High Mass in the Pro-Cathedral.[24] Subsequently, during Easter Week, he was host at the Mansion House to the Premier and Attorney-General of Queensland, Mr J.T. Ryan, together with his wife, and the secretary to the Premier, Mr J.W. O'Hagan, and the Crown Solicitor of Queensland, Mr W.F. Webb. The *Evening Telegraph*, on Wednesday 23 April, carried a photograph of the group together with the Lord Mayor and one of his daughters. Once more, the Lady Mayoress was absent.

Closing of Mansion House Conference

With conscription long past, the disposal of the National Defence Fund remained to be decided. The Conference members appointed O'Neill to a small sub-committee charged with the task. On 26 April, William O'Brien, M.P. (Mallow) wrote that, in his view, 'the first call' on the fund should be 'the dependents of the large number of political prisoners still incarcerated in Irish jails under conditions of injustice and barbarity'. He went on to pay a major compliment to O'Neill:

> Pray let me offer my respectful congratulations to your Lordship on the courteous and tolerant spirit in which you invariably preside over the meetings of the Conference.[25]

Laurence O'Neill had been chairing meetings for much of his adult life, but the words of the celebrated old parliamentarian must have been especially gratifying.

Hosting the American delegates

On Saturday, 3 May, three Irish-American delegates to the Peace Conference arrived in Ireland. They came as part of their brief to present the case for Irish independence to the Conference. They received an enthusiastic welcome, much to the embarrassment of the Government. On their arrival at Kingstown (Dun Laoghaire) they travelled to the Mansion House, by now the focal point for many visitors and for both local and national events. They journeyed 'in motor-cars flying the American and the Irish Republican flags. At their arrival, there was already a large crowd around the House, where they were welcomed by the Lord Mayor and de Valera.[26] A photograph shows the delegates with 'their hosts'. The Americans were Messrs Edward F. Dunne, Michael J. Ryan, Frank P. Walsh, and the 'their hosts' were some of those who had come to the forefront in making the case for Irish independence: Count Plunkett, Eamon de Valera, Arthur Griffith, William Cosgrave, Lord Mayor O'Neill, and Fr. Michael O'Flanagan.[27]

On 9 May, at a special session of Dail Eireann, de Valera formally welcomed the delegates in the name of the Republic. Subsequently, they experienced a demonstration of the Government's heavy-handedness when they were stopped by military on their way to the Mansion House, and found their destination surrounded by army lorries and military searching the premises for Michael Collins and Robert Barton.[28] The Lord Mayor organised a special reception and concert in their honour on 16 May. It was a prominent social occasion. It was marred, however, by a raid by Government forces. While it was on, the Lord Mayor, according to the "Talk of the Town", a supercilious column in the *Irish Times*, 'strutted up and down Dawson Street like a hen on a hot griddle wearing a dinner jacket over a lounge suit waistcoat'. "They haven't suppressed the reception", he said to me, "but now don't you think it looks very much like they wanted to".'

In their brief visit to Ireland, the delegates had received a bad, even exaggerated impression of the outrages being practised in Ireland, and this was reflected in the report they submitted to the Peace Conference in Paris on 3 June 1919. They appealed to the Conference to give a hearing to the people of Ireland; and on 6 June the Senate of the United States requested the American Peace Commission at Versailles to endeavour to secure a hearing at the Conference for an Irish delegation. President Wilson, however, when he eventually met the Irish American delegates, Edward F. Dunne and Frank P. Walsh (Michael J. Ryan having returned to the United States), on 11 June, confessed that he had rendered himself impotent in that the Committee of the Four Major Nations had made an agreement that no small nation should appear before it without the unanimous consent of the whole Committee; which allowed Britain a veto on the hearing of Ireland's claim.[29]

An independent spirit

Lord Mayor O'Neill had been so supportive of Sinn Féin on a number of occasions that some thought him either a member of Sinn Féin or deluded by Sinn Féin. In fact, he was not afraid to court unpopularity at times by opposing Sinn Féin demands. One such occasion related to the Paris Peace Conference. A circular, issued in the name of Count Plunkett, requested all public bodies to issue "A Demand for Representation at the Peace Conference". The Lord Mayor ruled it out of order at the Corporation meeting. He did so, he later explained, 'not out of disrespect for Count Plunkett or Sinn Féin, but because

> there was a crisis in the city, groups of unemployed were marching about,
> food supplies were running short, negotiations were going on for a large
> grant for housing, the rates of the city were going up, and I considered the

Corporation had enough to do without being involved in a political controversy.

He added: 'Sinn Féin was very angry with me. My friend Alderman Tom Kelly gave me a very bad quarter of an hour. My friend, Councillor Willie Cosgrave, was not too well pleased, and the *Irishman*, a weekly Sinn Féin paper, referred to me as 'a high-handed national degenerate'.[30]

Industrial relations and high salaries

The Lord Mayor's reference to unsettled conditions was reflected on 16 May by his effort to get both parties in the hotel dispute to meet;[31] and some days later, 24 May, the *Irish Independent* noted his involvement in the setting up of an arbitration court to settle a threatened bakers' strike. A further factor adding to the social unease was what the *Evening Herald*, of 22 May, termed 'an orgy of salary raising', and in that regard O'Neill's Corporation seems to have made itself a ready target for complaint. The satirical correspondent claimed that, in a time of financial difficulties and restraints, 'those excellent guardians of the poor … who manage the affairs of the Dublin Union' had given most of their 300 officials a generous increase in salary; and it was rather similar with Dublin Corporation, whose swollen salary list testifies to the solicitude of our worthy City Fathers for the material interests of their army of officials'.

Prohibitions and confrontations

As summer commenced, the clash between Sinn Féin and the Government became more marked, and some of the effects were experienced by the Lord Mayor at his official residence. On 3 June, Dermot O'Hegarty, on behalf of Sinn Féin, requested the use of the Mansion House for a private session of the Dail on Tuesday, 17th inst. and subsequent dates. The Lord Mayor agreed that the Mansion House would be available on those dates.[32] On the day he replied to O'Hegarty, 6 June, O'Neill received a letter from the Chief Commissioner of the Police, W. Edgeworth Johnstone, informing him that the Government would not in future 'permit meetings in the Mansion House of Dail Eireann or of any councils or committees connected therewith'.[33]

The Lord Mayor did not acknowledge Commissioner Johnstone's letter. On 17 June, Johnstone visited him and asked if the Dail was meeting that day. On being told that it was, he reminded the Lord Mayor that the Chief Secretary had forbidden such a meeting to be held. The Lord Mayor argued that the prohibition did not make sense as other Dail

Eireann meetings had been held in the Mansion House without any objection from the authorities, and Dail Eireann had a better right than anyone else to meet in the Mansion House as its members were the elected representatives of the people, and the Dail, itself, so far as he was aware, was a properly constituted and legal organisation. He refused, therefore, to deny Dail Eireann admission to the Mansion House.[34]

Confrontation occurred once more on 12 July, when the Chief Commissioner informed the Lord Mayor that the advertised lecture by Arthur Griffith would not take place in the Mansion House.[35] O'Neill replied that as he had given a room in the Mansion House for a lecture by Mr Griffith, 'on no consideration' could 'he see his way to withdraw that permission'.[36] On the evening of the lecture, the Mansion House was surrounded by police with batons and revolvers, and Griffith was refused entrance. His lecture was delivered instead at the Sinn Féin headquarters, 6 Harcourt Street, and was fully reported in the press the following day. At the time, Arthur Griffith was acting President of Dail Eireann, in the absence of de Valera, who had gone secretly to the United States in the second half of June to win support for Irish independence.

Facets of war

By the end of the summer the struggle for independence had taken on an increasingly militant aspect. The Irish Volunteers viewed themselves as the armed force of the legitimately elected Irish government. In August the Dail required deputies, officials, and the Volunteers to swear allegiance to Dail Eireann as the government of the Irish Republic, and in keeping with that claim, land courts were set up to settle disputes and bypass the regular courts. The Government, as indicated, responded by increasing curtailments of liberty and free expression, including widespread arrests and detention without charge. Already by the end of June 1919, soldiers with fixed bayonets were a regular feature on the streets, and the *Freeman's Journal* told of Dublin's quays being 'jammed with tanks, armoured cars, guns, motor lorries and thousands of troops, as if the port was a base of a formidable expeditionary force'.[37]

Michael Collins

During this summer, Michael Collins established himself as a key figure. He was not only Minister of Finance in the Dail, he was director of organisation in the Irish Republican Army (a new name for the Irish Volunteers) and was Director of Intelligence. In this last, it was his task to counter the highly effective Dublin Castle system of information and espionage. He was remarkably successful in establishing contacts all over the country, even in Dublin Castle, the army and the civil service. Laurence O'Neill had personal experience of Collins's intelligence network in an unusual way.

A gentleman farmer from 'down the country', with whom he had dealings from time to time, called to see him at the Mansion House and reported that his motor car had been taken by the republicans, and that fourteen days after he had purchased a new car that too had been taken. He asked the Lord Mayor's assistance to have either of them restored to him. On the face of his story, O'Neill called on Michael Collins, who, as O'Neill acknowledged, 'at all times, whether in danger or safety, never refused to see me', and told him the story of the man and his cars. 'Without uttering a word', Collins 'took some letters out of his pocket, which, he told me, had, with many others, been raided in the post. He produced one, which I recognised bore the hand-writing of the man who had called on me. This man, under his own hand, was giving information to Dublin Castle that republicans were hiding in the vicinity of his house. In fact, said Collins, we are going to deal with this and some others this evening. I knew what this meant, and although this man had not been straight with me, I pleaded with Collins not to be too severe. The man had to leave the country.'

'It often occurred to me', O'Neill added, 'that some acts committed in the name of the Republic were severe, but from this on, I did not interfere except I was absolutely certain of my facts.'[38]

The Last Straw

On 10 September 1919, Dail Eireann was declared a dangerous association and was prohibited.[39] Then, on 15 October, the impingement of Dublin Castle on activities in the Mansion House reached a new level. Police Commissioner Johnstone informed the Lord Mayor that the Government had issued an order prohibiting and suppressing the Sinn Féin organisation, Sinn Féin clubs, the Irish Volunteers, Cumann na mBan, and the Gaelic League. Any meeting of these was illegal and would be prevented, and the same applied to the *Árd-Fheis* of Sinn Féin, which it was proposed to hold in the Mansion House on 16 October. The final straw, where Lord Mayor O'Neill was concerned, occurred on 11 December, when a letter from Johnstone informed him, at very short notice, that 'the *Aonach* arranged to commence at the Mansion House this evening will not be permitted'.[40]

The manner in which the prohibition was carried out by the authorities faced O'Neill with a difficult decision. On 17 December, he wrote to Michael Collins:

A few days ago the *Aonach na Nollag*, which had been held here every year since 1906 for the sale and exhibition of Irish industries and Irish works of art, was prevented from being held by the Authorities at the last moment, and at the point of the bayonet, 150 police and over 500 soldiers taking part in the operation ... Therefore, in view of what has taken place, and what may happen at any moment,... I feel compelled to close down the Mansion House, as I do not desire to have any conflict between the citizens and the soldiers which might end in bloodshed.[41]

On the same day O'Neill availed of the *Evening Telegraph* to explain his decision to a wider public. When he was elected lord mayor nearly three years ago, he had promised he would endeavour to be 'lord mayor of this city, and of its people as a whole'. Consequently, 'any of the citizens who applied for the use of the rooms in the Mansion House for meetings, lectures, fairs, sale of work, dances etc, had their request willingly granted.' He then described the last minute cancellation of the *Aonach na Nollag* (Christmas Fair), even though the day and hour of opening had been published for weeks, and its prevention from being held 'at the point of a bayonet, and over 500 soldiers fully equipped'. In view of the action of the Authorities on this occasion, he envisaged what might happen in the near future, at for example, the Fancy Dress Ball for children, due to be held on 30 December. He imagined it banned at the last moment by the Authorities, and the little children, their friends and mothers, prevented from entering by soldiers and police, 'and some unthinking mother pushing forward might draw down the wrath of these gentlemen'. Who would guarantee that the slaughter of these innocents would not take place? Nothing was impossible so far as the present rulers of this country were concerned. He regretted having to take this action, and its inconvenience and expense to promoters, as the Mansion House had been 'booked up every night from now until the middle of February 1920'.[42]

Attempted assassination and intimidation

Despite his anger at the actions of the Authorities, O'Neill was deeply upset by the attempt to assassinate the Lord Lieutenant, Viscount French, on that same date, 17 December. Commenting some years later, after Dan Breen in his *Fight for Irish Freedom* had dealt with the attempt to kill the Lord Lieutenant, his disappointment at its failure, and his subsequent statement that he was glad now that Lord French had escaped, O'Neill remarked that if Dan Breen had declared that he was glad the Lord Lieutenant had escaped 'a week, a month, a year or two years afterwards, what a fate would have overtaken him! When moderate men of the time said what Mr Breen took years to make up his mind to say, their lives were threatened.'

The ambush against the Lord Lieutenant's party was carried out by Dan Breen, Sean Tracy, Martin Savage, and eight other members of the Irish Republican Army, at Ashtown, near to the Phoenix Park, Dublin. In the encounter Savage was killed. Four days later, 21 December, an IRA group raided the offices of the *Irish Independent* and demolished its production plant, because the newspaper had the temerity to describe Savage as a would-be assassin. The Lord Mayor was not immune from similar intimidatory tactics.

At a meeting of the Port and Docks Board, a mild resolution was carried with the support of Lord Mayor O'Neill: "That the Port and Docks Board expressed their thankfulness at the failure of the recent attempt upon the life of Lord French." His support of the resolution caught the public attention. The *Evening Herald* paid him a remarkable compliment on 23 December 1919. He cherished the tribute.

'On several occasions during the past three years', the paper commented, the Lord Mayor 'felt compelled in his official capacity to denounce crime and murder.

> It did not matter where the murder or crime was hatched, whether in high or lowly places. It did not matter, as far as he was concerned, whether the attempt was made in the case of a peer or peasant. It did not matter, as far as he was concerned, what individual or individuals committed the crime or murder, whether it was out of personal spite or political revenge, whether it was committed by a Catholic or a Protestant, by a Nationalist or a Unionist, and no matter what organisation took part in it, whether it was Sinn Féin, Hibernianism, or Free Masonry, the Church to which he belonged having told him – Thou shall not kill – his conscience told him it was wrong to kill, and so far as he was concerned he believed that crime or murder such as was mentioned in the resolution, hit at the fundamental principles of his religion, and retarded the regeneration of this country.

'That night', O'Neill recalled, 'two young men called to the Mansion House and explained that they had been sent by their Company' to warn him that if he were not more careful in his language they would "plug" him. 'Having received up to this', O'Neill observed, 'over twenty threatening letters with hieroglyphics of a gruesome character, and many verbal threats as well, and not being prepared to stultify my conscience at the bidding of these two young men, I did not lose my nerve or temper.' Subsequently, he often tried to visualise what was in their minds. Was it that they had themselves 'tuned up to such a pitch that they honestly believed they were doing it in their country's interest', or 'was it fear, that if they did not carry out the orders of the leaders of their oath-bound society they would be "plugged" themselves ?'

In his regard, there seems to have been a re-consideration of his case, and he was left live as a kind of necessary evil. Soliloquising many years later, in the context of Mr Breen's book, he noted that Breen gave the names of the eleven men who took part in the ambush to kill Lord French, and he observed sadly – 'In a few years those of the eleven who were left were in opposite camps, using the same weapons, adopting the same means to kill each other, as those adopted in the attempt on Lord French's life, but with far more devilish instinct and bitterness.' 'What a lesson', he added, 'for the younger generation now, and in the years to come; avoid those who have the lust for blood, avoid secret societies in which, according to the oath you take, you are compelled to do things which you will find repugnant to your better feelings.'[43]

Positive response to need

While dramatic and harrowing happenings such as these were becoming part of life in the city and county, the ordinary needs of people continued or were magnified. As Christmas drew near, concern for the poor of the city was very much to the forefront. The Lord Mayor led the annual appeal on behalf of the 'Mansion House Coal Fund'. In a printed leaflet he called on his fellow citizens for a prompt and generous response so that the committee associated with the Fund would be able to make substantial grants of coal for distribution amongst the very poor of our city during the present winter season. He reminded his readers that the work of the committee was carried on free of any expenses, save for postage and printing, 'so that the poor receive the full value of every penny subscribed'. The names of the committee were given, to whom subscriptions might be forwarded. It was noticeable that they included both Catholics and Protestants, united in a common cause. It was some sign of hope in a country becoming increasingly divided.

Notes

1   ONFP. MacRory-Ld Mayor, 5 Jan. 19

2   *Irish Times,* 21 Jan. 1919

3   ONFP. "Our Good Lord Mayor" by Michael O'Grady

4   Idem, and INL. Ms 35,294/7. R.J. Mulcahy-Ld. Mayor, 28 Jan. 1919.

5   ONFP. Note entitled "Belfast Again".

6   Idem. MacRory-Ld. Mayor, 5 Feb. 1919

7   Idem. Ld. Mayor-MacRory, 21 Feb. 1919

8   Idem. MacRory-Ld. Mayor, 25 Feb. 1919

9   Idem. Ml. Collins- Dr MacRory, and the Lord Mayor, 27 Feb. 1919.

10   Idem. Material on Prisoners in Belfast

11   ONFP. Typed pages without title.

12   D. Macardle. *The Irish Republic* (1968 ed.), ch. 28, p. 262

13   *Irish Independent,* 11 March 1919.

14   ONFP. An extant bill from Louis J. Lemass & Co., automobile and general engineers, 6 April 1919, charging £19 for 'hire of a car to Tuam' on 12 March.

15   NFP. The Document to the Parishes and letters.

16   Idem. Typed notes, "Reception to Mr Eamon de Valera".

17   Idem

18   Idem. "A Proclamation".

19   Idem. De Valera-Ld. Mayor, 27 March.

20   ONFP and see *Evening Telegraph* and *Evening Mail*, Wed. 16 April 1919.

21   ONFP. Typed pages on political prisoners, but not headed.

22   *Evening Herald*, 31 March 1919. "Asylum Workers"

23   *Dublin Saturday Post,* 19 April

24   *Freeman's Journal* of Tuesday, 22 April 1919

25   ONFP. Notes on William O'Brien, M.P. and on Mansion House Conference.

26   *Daily Sketch*, London, Tues. 6 May

27   Photograph, idem.

28   D. Macardel. *The Irish Republic,* p. 273. The account is somewhat garbled. It is not clear that the Dail meeting and the delegates being stopped by the military took place on the same date.

29   Idem, pp. 273-75

30   ONFP. Typed page, "My popularity is waning"

31   *Evening Herald,* 16 May 1919

32   ONFP. "Dublin Castle and Dail Eireann": O'Hegarty-Ld.Mayor, 3 June; Ld.Mayor-O'Hegarty, 6 June

33   Idem. Johnstone-Ld.Mayor, 6 June 1919

34   ONFP. Note taken by Miss O'Sullivan, secretary to the Lord Mayor, who was present at the interview between Johnstone and the Lord Mayor on 17 June 1919.

35   ONFP. Johnstone-Ld. Mayor, 12 July

36   Idem. "Lecture by Arthur Griffith"

37   *Freeman's Journal,* 10 June, cit. Macardle, op.cit., p. 277

38   ONFP. Typed page entitled "Foolishness"

39   Macardle, op. cit. pp. 283-4

40   NLI. O'Neill papers. Calendar of prohibitions issued by the police: W.E. Johnstone-Ld.Mayor, 11 Dec. 1919

41   NLI. Ml. Collins papers, Ms. 10,723. L.O'Neill-Ml. Collins, 17 Dec. 1919

42   NLI. F.S. Bourke Collection, Ms. 10,723/12. Ld.Mayor- Editor of *Evening Telegraph,* 17 Dec. 1919

43   ONFP. Typed pages: "The Attempt on the life of the Lord Lieutenant, Lord French, Dec. 1919".

Laurence O'Neill, 1864-1943
Lord Mayor of Dublin, 1917-1924
Patriot and Man of Peace

10.

1920:

A Year of Violence, Intimidation, Reprisals, and the deaths of Terence MacSwiney and Kevin Barry

By the close of 1919 the activity of IRA columns in many country areas had resulted in the burning of local police barracks and the retreat of the police to larger towns. Early in January 1920, the Royal Irish Constabulary (RIC) enrolled the first of several thousand British recruits, later dubbed "Black and Tans" because of the uniform they wore. The Black and Tans were an ill-disciplined and ruthless body of men, who became associated with many atrocities as they sought to win back areas lost and to cow the population. Significantly, Sir J. Byrne, a senior figure in charge of the RIC, resigned his position in February 1920 because the force no longer had a civilian character but had become a branch of the army service under the commander-in-chief.[1]

The arrival of this body in Ireland signalled a more ruthless government policy, which terminated the ease of relations reflected in the Lord Lieutenant's invitation to O'Neill, on 8 January 1920, to luncheon at the Vice-Regal Lodge to discuss 'the conditions affecting the employment of demobilised soldiers in Ireland'.[2] The contrast presented by the Black and Tans when they raided the Mansion House could not have been starker. They made a very negative impression, exhibiting 'nothing but vulgarity, rushing through the house, using language most vile, pilfering where they could and wilfully destroying, and as an amusement kicking the coachman's hat through the yard'. This last incident greatly irked Laurence O'Neill, and he was in the act of writing to the their superiors in the Castle, when James MacNeill, brother of Eoin MacNeill, counselled against writing about such a trivial matter. He took the advice, though what really annoyed him, he remarked in recollection, was not so much the destruction of a few old hats, but that 'here was a gang within a few hundred yards of Dublin Castle, in broad daylight on the premises of the Lord Mayor, the Chief Magistrate of the City, using language most obnoxious', and he pictured to himself what would happen, and did happen, to defenceless men and women, who had no redress 'when this gang of ruffians were let loose on the country'.[3]

Corporation elections and Ald. Kelly

The municipal and urban council elections, held every three years, took place on 15 January. The result in the Municipal Council of Dublin was a majority of Sinn Féin councillors. One of the best known and respected was Ald. Tom Kelly, who topped the poll in Area 3 of Dublin, comprising Fitzwilliam Square, the Mansion House, the Royal Exchange and South City Wards. The vote was doubtless influenced by the fact that Ald. Kelly was currently imprisoned in England. Sinn Féin saw his election as Lord Mayor as an embarrassment for the Government and as a possible means of securing his release. By 19 January, it was widely rumoured that he would be the next Lord Mayor.[4] On 30 January, Ald. Laurence O'Neill chaired the meeting to elect the Lord Mayor for the year 23 February 1920-23 February 1921. Accepting the political reality, and, as a friend of Tom Kelly, he proposed him to fill the office of Lord Mayor. Nobody asked Tom Kelly for his approval. He was a very sick man, and subsequently wrote to his sister that had he been asked he would have refused the position.[5]

In his proposal speech, Lord Mayor O'Neill spoke of Kelly's straightness and of his outstanding work in the Corporation for many years. He also spoke of the long history of the Mayoralty, and of the problems at the present time. His position as Chief Magistrate had been undermined by the Government to the extent that 'the soldiers of the King break his windows, hammer at his hall door with trench tools; his official residence is raided at the whim of some under-strapper who pulls the wires at Dublin Castle' (applause). 'But outside of all that', he continued, 'the Lord Mayor of Dublin is in an independent position if he maintains it (hear, hear): he signs no pledge, he takes no oath, he owes no allegiance to any power or authority except the people who return him and to you who elect him to the position.' Pursuing this paean to independence, at a time when oath-bound groupings were prominent, and reflecting his own values, he added: 'Consequently, it is a position which the most fastidious may occupy without his conscience being annoyed, without his morals being corrupted, or his principles being interfered with in any way. Therefore, to fill such a position, it is my pride and privilege to propose the name of Alderman Thomas Kelly.' [6]

Many of his listeners may have been struck by the ambiguity between his view of Lord Mayor as one who 'owes no allegiance to any power or authority' and Tom Kelly who was strongly committed to Sinn Féin; but O'Neill apparently placed his trust in what he termed Ald. Kelly's 'straightness' and the other members of the Corporation had no doubt about his fitness for office. Even Dr McWalter, who regretted that Ald. O'Neill did not allow his name to go forward, and described the Sinn Féin movement as the most infamous tyranny Ireland ever suffered, even worse than Orangeism and Carsonism, yet stated that he could not vote against Tom Kelly because of his record in the Corporation.[7]

When the date of inauguration arrived on 23 February, Ald. Kelly was still in prison and in poor health, and it appeared that he had not signed the declaration of acceptance of the mayoralty. The Town Clerk, Henry Campbell, announced that Kelly's installation would have to be deferred, and the City Law Agent, Ignatius Rice, announced that the present Lord Mayor would continue in office until his successor was installed.[8] At the meeting on 23 February, O'Neill announced that he would visit Ald. Kelly at the earliest opportunity, but that there was no option but to defer the installation for the present. 'Whatever action I take', he stated, 'is not to please anyone, is not for my own peace of mind, is not for the sake of popularity, but solely for the sake of Tom Kelly for whom I have more than a passing affection.'[9] Meanwhile, Ald. Kelly had left prison but was in a nursing home in England requiring constant medical attention. When he was eventually allowed home on 29 April 1920, his health was such that it was clear that he could not fulfil the office of Lord Mayor. O'Neill, however, at the Corporation meeting on 30 April, extended a welcome home to Ald. Kelly on behalf of all the members, and expressed the hope the he would soon be restored to health and able to take his place once more amongst them, above all in the position to which they had elected him, 'that of Lord Mayor of this city'.[10] In effect, O'Neill was to carry on as Lord Mayor throughout 1920.

Conflict with the Town Clerk

At the meeting to elect the Lord Mayor on 30 January, there were other happenings which attracted much publicity. Mrs Wyse-Power, recently elected to the Corporation, signed in Irish her declaration accepting office. The Town Clerk, Mr Campbell, informed the meeting that, on counsel's advice, such a signature was invalid and that, as a result, Mrs Wyse-Power was disqualified from attending. Ald. O'Brien proposed that the counsel's opinion be ignored and that the Town Clerk be instructed to put Mrs Wyse-Power's name on the division list. This was seconded. The Lord Mayor then announced that he would discard the counsel's opinion, that he was going to burn his boats and see that Mrs Wyse-Power's constituents were not disfranchised. The proposal was passed unanimously. At which the Town Clerk declared – 'I decline to recognise your resolution'. Mr O'Brien then moved the suspension of the Town Clerk because he had refused to carry out the declared intention of the meeting. After heated debate, it was pointed out that a motion on a matter not on the agenda was out of order. The Lord Mayor, accordingly, declared Mr O'Brien's motion out of order. When asked by Ald. McGarry, however, if Mrs Wyse-Power would continue as a member of the Corporation, the Lord Mayor answered 'Yes', but the Town Clerk declared 'I say No'.[11]

Before the year was out, the Town Clerk was in further conflict with the Municipal Council: he refused to record in the minutes speeches made in Irish, and he refused to obey the order of Council not to submit the books of the Corporation for audit to the British Local Government. The Council appointed another clerk, Mr Walsh, to carry out the duties of Town Clerk. [12]Towards the end of the year, Mr Campbell eventually resigned. He wrote an accusatory letter to the Lord Mayor, stating that his attitude had ensured that he could no longer remain in office. He referred to 'the illegalities, irregularities and indecencies perpetrated or attempted to be perpetrated by the Council in reference to his position as Town Clerk and the duties and obligations therewith which had forced him to conclude that he would best serve the citizens of Dublin... by severing his connection with the Municipal Council'.[13] Not content, however, to allow him the initiative, Ald. O'Brien pushed for Mr Campbell's dismissal at a full meeting of the Corporation. As a result, his resignation was refused and he was declared dismissed. Despite the dismissal, Campbell, who had served the Corporation with distinction for many years, was honourably employed by the Local Government Board and was later knighted as Sir Henry Campbell.[14]

Housing, Tom Kelly, and Inspector's report

Tom Kelly's absence from the Corporation was felt particularly in the Housing Committee of which he was chairman. On 2 January, 1920, the Local Government Board had convened an inquiry concerning the major housing scheme for Marino on the north side of the city. It was the first such scheme under the new Housing Act which became law in August 1919. Under this legislation, each local authority was required to submit to the Local Government Board a survey of the housing needs of their districts within three months of the passing of the Act, specifying the number and nature of the houses to be erected, the approximate quantity of land to be acquired, and the average number of houses proposed per acre, together with an estimate of the time required to carry out the development. The Lord Mayor sent a telegram to the Lord Lieutenant asking for Kelly's release in view of his importance as a witness and an adviser. The extent of Kelly's illness was not known at this stage. The Chief Secretary replied, stating that the request could not be granted. The Lord Mayor, after consultation with the Corporation, decided to cooperate fully with the inquiry. In the event, the inspector described the Corporation's scheme as ideal. It had been prepared with up-to-date planning principles: apart from standard accommodation, each house was to be provided with a scullery, larder, bath and toilet. The chief architect and his staff had prepared well. As a result, a more constructive relationship developed between the Corporation and the Local Government Board. Plans were submitted by the city architect and the Housing Committee for further housing schemes and were accepted by the Local Government Board in July 1920.[15]

Living with harassment and fear

Even as the installation of Ald. Kelly was postponed on 23 February, the Government imposed a curfew on the city. No one was to be out of doors between midnight and 5.0 a.m. without a permit. The Corporation reacted by decreeing that no employee was to seek a permit, that municipal work was to cease from 11.30 p.m. to 5.0 a.m., and that the city's lights were to be extinguished at 11.30 p.m. Ald. O'Neill also deplored and criticised the Government forces treatment of him as Lord Mayor and Chief Magistrate.

The harassment of nationalists by military, police, and the Black and Tans intensified from then on. During March, O'Neill found himself under increased pressure. The situation bordered on the ludicrous at times. On one occasion, as he and Ald. Cosgrave were walking down Dame Street after a Corporation meeting at City Hall, a friendly member of the Metropolitan Police whispered as he passed them – 'You are being watched'. Next day the friendly policeman called to the Mansion House and told O'Neill that he and Ald. Cosgrave were watched the previous night by detectives. "G-Men" (as they were called), who were watched in turn 'by secret service men of another branch of Dublin Castle, as some of the detectives were under suspicion of being friendly with the republican leaders', and, in the rear, watching all these were 'some members of Collins's intelligence department'.[16]

On 20 March, Tomás MacCurtain, Lord Mayor of Cork, was shot dead by Government forces in front of his wife and children. Dublin City Council adjourned for a week as a mark of respect, and the Lord Mayor and Mrs Wyse-Power attended the funeral. Ald. William O'Brien had been arrested and deported to Wormwood Scrubs Prison, where he went on hunger strike and by 24 March was reported seriously ill. The following day, Ald. Cosgrave, T.D., was detained in the Bridewell in Dublin and deported, and on 26 March Joseph MacDonagh was arrested and sent to Wormwood Scrubs. That same day, Alan Ball, a magistrate investigating Sinn Féin and Dail Eireann funds, was taken off a tramcar at Ballsbridge, Dublin, and shot dead on the order of Michael Collins. Accommodation was offered in Dublin Castle to officers of the military for their own protection.[17]

The Lord Mayor was used to receiving death threats, but a particularly gruesome one arrived on Dublin Castle notepaper after Bell's murder:

> O'Neill
> Your time has come
> Your life for Allen Bells
> Avenger

It was accompanied by a drawing of a dagger dripping with red ink, and a coffin, drawn in black, with his name on the breastplate.

O'Neill claimed that he threw it into a drawer and did not let it trouble him further. But a few nights later he had an experience which demonstrated how tense he was. Walking home at night to the Mansion House from City Hall, as he passed through St. Anne's Street, which 'was dark and lonely', he heard voices behind him saying "There he is". He half turned and noticed two young men coming behind him. Their footsteps came nearer and nearer, and the threat of a few mornings before flashed before his mind, but there was no means of escape. They closed up on him, and passed by, joining up with a young girl who was standing at the corner. What they must have said was -"There she is". It became unwise, thereafter, to have night meetings of the Corporation.

Correspondence with Lloyd George

Exasperated by the disruption to his work and that of the Corporation by Government forces, Lord Mayor O'Neill decided to explain his difficulties to the Prime Minister, himself, whom he had met briefly as a member of the National Convention. He wrote in a personal, reasonable style which induced a response. The style was the man in many ways. The letter was dated 26 March 1920. It ran:

Dear Sir,

When one is in a dilemma as to the proper authority to approach, it is a very safe procedure to adopt to approach those who are in authority overall.

For three years I have been Lord Mayor of Dublin. When my term of office expired on the 23rd of February last, my successor, Alderman Thomas Kelly, was unable to take my place, owing to being in a very precarious state of health as a result of having been interned in an English prison. The duty still rests upon my shoulders to carry out the duties of Lord Mayor.

At the recent Municipal Elections, carried out under the new scheme of Proportional Representation, the citizens of Dublin returned as their representatives to the Corporation, a majority consisting of members of the Sinn Féin party. The different committees were selected to carry out corporate work, and corporate work only. On these committees, Sinn Féin members were in many cases placed in high positions by their colleagues of different degrees of thought in the Corporation.

The Dublin Castle Authorities, since the Municipal Elections were held in the middle of January, have been picking off one by one members of the Sinn Féin party in the Corporation, which leaves the work of the Corporation practically at a standstill for want of quorums. For instance, the Estates and Finance Committee, the most important committee of the Corporation; its numbers have been for some time depleted by three of its most useful members, and to-day a climax was reached when the chairman of that committee, Alderman William Cosgrave, a man who has given a wonderful amount of time and thought to the finances of the Corporation, was arrested also; and like his colleagues – deported to an English jail, detained without any charge being made against him, and no trial whatever, and the irony of his arrest is, that the Council meeting of the Corporation for the consideration and striking of the Rates and the adoption of the Financial Report, which bears his name, is to be held on next Wednesday.

Consequently, it has occurred to me to write to you to let you know what is going on in Dublin in reference to Corporation affairs, as I am certain you must be somewhat in the dark, as it is hardly possible, although time creates many changes, that you the democrat of other days, would be a party to arresting men but recently elected under the new Proportional Representation scheme, and a party to having these representatives deported to another country, away from friends and relatives, detained without any charge, without any trial whatever. Thereby, in my humble judgement, hitting at one of the fundamental principles of British Law: - 'That every subject is considered or at any rate looked upon as being innocent, until he or she is proved guilty'.

And therefore the deporting of these men has undoubtedly held up Corporation work, Housing, Public Health etc in which you have always taken such a lively interest.

Now, I have been wondering can you help me in this matter or can you give me any advice as to how Corporation work is to be continued if my colleagues are carried off and detained in prison.

Although I am in a very, very minor position compared to you, Sir, I put it to you this way. If the members of your Government were picked off one by one and say deported to Ireland or America, detained in prison, away from friends, relatives, and admirers, without any charge, and without any trial, how would they and you feel? And how would you carry on the Government of your Kingdom? That is the position I find myself in at the moment. In my endeavour to carry out the work of my little kingdom (and, after all, every man, woman and child in this world has a kingdom of their own) I find I cannot do so if my colleagues are taken from me.

Will you please give this whole matter your serious consideration, and oblige one whom you invited to act as a member of the ill-fated Convention you set up, and who accepted in good faith that invitation.

Yours respectfully,
LO'N.

That Lloyd George took the trouble to respond in some detail was probably due to the above letter carefully acknowledging and appealing to his Liberal ideals, and also requesting his advice, and all so dispassionately. Most likely, too, it was considered wise to keep the reasonable Lord Mayor of Dublin reasonably disposed towards British authority by responding to him in a 'reasonable' manner. The Prime Minister replied on 31 March. The main weight of his response was in the first paragraph:

My dear Lord Mayor,

I deeply sympathise with you in the dilemma in which you are placed, but I appreciate also the difficulty from the other side. Ireland to-day is menaced by a formidable organisation which seeks to promote its ends by terrorising public officials and the Irish people by the weapons of murder and assassination. This campaign has attained such proportions that it is impossible to obtain evidence in the ordinary way which will lead either to the arrest or the conviction of the murderers and assassins. In these circumstances the Executive which is responsible for the maintenance of government and the protection of the life, liberty, and property of the individual citizens is placed under great difficulties. They certainly do not wish to arrest the guiltless. On the other hand, their first and imperative duty is to leave no stone unturned to enable them to lay their hands upon those who are terrorising society, and they may at times have no option, if they are to grapple with the problem of organised murder, but to dislocate in some degree the normal life of the community.

He went on to decry the Sinn Féin campaign as making impossible 'a settlement of the Irish question by reason and goodwill', it depended upon 'violence in opinion and violence in action'. Its policy would never lead to a united Ireland, and it would 'never achieve its avowed object, an Irish Republic'. The letter concluded on a more moderate, if unconvincing note:

The Government, however, is most anxious to make as easy as possible the task of those who are endeavouring to carry on the administration of the country on reasonable lines. And if there are any means by which moderate men can be helped and encouraged to withstand and oppose the present campaign of intimidation and so bring nearer a settlement of the Irish question, I will gladly co-operate in bringing them into effect.

Ever Sincerely,
D. Lloyd George.[18]

Whatever hope the Lord Mayor had of some concession from the Prime Minister, the latter's letter offered little comfort. There was no acknowledgement of faults and atrocities on the part of the Black and Tans and other forces of the Government, and 'moderate men' were described as those prepared 'to withstand and oppose the present campaign'. All criticism was reserved for Sinn Féin, but with no acknowledgement of that party's overwhelming support in national and local elections.

Plight of prisoners in Mountjoy

Within a short time of his correspondence with the Prime Minister, Lord Mayor O'Neill was involved once more with the problems of Sinn Féin members in Irish prisons. Lord Mayors, and Mayors, were barred from visiting Irish prisons towards the end of 1919. As a result, the general public were unaware of what was happening in them from October 1919 to April 1920. Mountjoy Prison, in Dublin, became the focus of public concern in April 1920, following the decision by political prisoners there, on 5 April, to go on hunger strike until all had 'been given prisoner-of-war treatment or all released'.

As the days went by, and the men were getting weaker, and the government showing no signs of any amelioration, the standing committee of the Catholic bishops issued a statement: declaring that in almost every civilized country, political prisoners received the treatment of political prisoners, and that in Ireland at the present time 'these canons of civilization' were 'trampled under foot'. If a disaster ensued from this insensitive course, unspeakable harm would be done and the responsibility would rest with the Government that substituted cruelty, vengeance and gross injustice 'for the equity, moderation, and fair play which should ever accompany the exercise of repressive law'. 'The cry we utter to-day', the bishops proclaimed, 'is the cry of humanity.' Questions were raised in the House of Commons, but to all the entreaties, the response of Mr Bonar Law, on behalf of the Government, was – 'No relaxation of prison rules would take place'. Crowds assembled near the prison. The Government feared some daring venture by the IRA to release the prisoners. In anticipation of trouble, Mountjoy was surrounded by military with machine guns.

On 12 April, the *Evening Telegraph* told of a situation which could have been disastrous were it not for the Lord Mayor's intervention. A large crowd waited outside the prison anxious for news of those on hunger strike. Their mood became more menacing about one o'clock. Major Wallace, in charge of the military, came to the front of the huge crowd and addressed them through a megaphone. 'The military did not wish to have any collision with the crowd, but if anybody attempted to rush the cordons of soldiers they would have to take measures for their own protection.' At this 'there was considerable excitement … and great tension prevailed for half an hour. The anxiety was somewhat relieved when Lord Mayor, Alderman Laurence O'Neill, appeared in front of the crowd, having come through the cordons from the Drumcondra direction. His Lordship mounted a stone which formed part of a barricade, and removing his hat addressed the crowd in tones of great earnestness.' 'The occasion was too sorrowful', he declared, 'for any untoward incident', and he reminded the people that they must not come into collision with the military forces. And 'turning in a friendly way to the line of troops, he said: 'These men are simply doing their duty, and we must not interfere with them'.

The correspondent observed that 'the Lord Mayor's words had a visible effect on the crowd, which thinned and thinned, until at two o'clock it was reduced to comparatively small numbers'.

The Lord Mayor called to the prison but was not allowed to see the prisoners. He learned that they were very weak. He sent a telegram to the Lord Lieutenant telling of his visit, and called on him to give the men immediate release or political treatment such as had been agreed between Mr Duke and himself. The Lord Lieutenant replied that under the rules made the previous November there was no room for providing political treatment, and all prisoners on hunger strike had been forewarned as to the consequence of persisting in their conduct.[19]

At a meeting of the Corporation it was decided to send a further telegram to the Lord Lieutenant asking him to meet the Lord Mayor and the High Sheriff, Dr McWalter. The Lord Lieutenant referred them to the statement made in House of Commons by Mr Bonar Law. They then sought an interview with Bonar Law, conveying 'the terrible risk to the peace of this city should any of the men die' and requesting that he release those prisoners on hunger-strike whose health had been impaired. Bonar Law's secretary replied, on 13 April, refusing an interview and referring them to Bonar Law's response to questions in parliament, namely, that 'the decision had been taken by his Majesty's Government and he did not see any chance of altering it.[20]

The Executive of the Trades Union Congress called for a stoppage of all work throughout the country on 13 April in protest at the treatment of the prisoners on hunger strike. On 12 April, Dublin Corporation adjourned for a week in sympathy with the prisoners. Lord Mayor O'Neill felt despondent. The Government seemed unyielding. Moreover, he had heard of a secret order issued to the military, 'if provoked not to spare the people'. He wondered did the Government wish to provoke the country into open rebellion?

On the morning of 14 April, O'Neill was in Mountjoy, but not allowed to see the prisoners, when his secretary, Miss Mary O'Sullivan, fought her way through the crowds and the cordons of military and police to bring him a message from the Vice-Regal Lodge, that the Lord Lieutenant wished to see him at once. In haste, the Lord Mayor got back to the Mansion House by borrowing a bicycle and then securing a ride on a milk cart. At the Mansion House he availed of a motor car to bring him to the Phoenix Park. At the Vice-Regal Lodge he was greeted with respect by the sentries and brought to meet Lord French, who was accompanied by Mr Wylie, law adviser to Dublin Castle (Later Justice Wylie under the Free State Government). Wylie, in O'Neill's estimation, was 'the only sane man connected with the Castle at the time'.

It soon became apparent from their demeanour that they were anxious for a settlement. Eventually, after much discussion, the Lord Mayor suggested – 'Why not adopt the line of least resistance like Mr Duke when he released all the hunger-strikers from Dundalk in November 1917 at my suggestion.' Mr Wylie, as O'Neill recalled, rose to the occasion by shifting the responsibility for the men's release from the Government to the prison doctor. He drew up the order: 'The doctor to get unlimited authority and to use his discretion as to the release of the prisoners on hunger strike in Mountjoy, who in his opinion are in any danger.' O'Neill could scarcely believe it after Bonar Law's "no relaxation" in the House of Commons the previous day. He asked for a copy of the order. A courier was to bring the order to the prison.

The Lord Mayor drove his car with reckless speed to Mountjoy. He was allowed to see the prisoners, who were overjoyed. The doctor ordered ambulances to take the first batch of prisoners to hospital. The order arrived for the Governor. It differed from the one the Lord Mayor had received. It required the men to sign a parole docket. To O'Neill it appeared that officials at the Castle had their way and were saving face. The men refused to sign parole dockets and were prepared to go back on hunger strike. When the vast crowd outside heard there was a hitch, their indignation was palpable. Among them was Arthur Griffith. O'Neill explained the situation to him. He told O'Neill to tell the men to stand firm. In the stalemate, the Lord Mayor headed back to the Vice-Regal Lodge. He arrived at 8.30 p.m. uninvited. The Lord Lieutenant lost his temper and asserted: 'I find there are some of these men in prison for very grave offences, and I'll be damned if I allow any of them out.' A military man, who was in the room, was then introduced as General Sir Neville Macready. As Lord French cooled down, the Lord Mayor pointed out that these men were on hunger strike for a principle. Now after the order for their release, of which he the Lord Mayor had a copy in his pocket, if they were detained and any of them died, his Excellency would be arraigned for murder. At this outrageous scenario, Lord French seemed nonplussed, but Macready came to his rescue. 'Chief, the Lord Mayor is right, these men must be released, as mistakes have been made, and we will deal with those who have made them, and we shall place the blame on someone.' Then Macready said to the Lord Mayor: 'You may take it, this is the last time hunger strikers will be released'. O'Neill went back to Mountjoy with the latest news. Within twelve hours all the men were released unconditionally.[21] At the Municipal Council meeting on 19 April, Ald. Byrne moved, and Clr. Medlar seconded, a vote of thanks to the Lord Mayor 'for the great services he has rendered the City during the past week'.[22] The members placed on record their appreciation of his efforts on behalf of the prisoners.

The foregoing account regarding the hunger-strikers and their eventual release is largely that of Laurence O'Neill, committed to writing some years later. Sir Neville Macready, in his book *Annals of an Active Life* [vol.2, pp.446-48], attributed blame for the final debacle to Sir J. Taylor, the Assistant Under Secretary, and the Castle organisation which he described as in a state of chaos. Quoting from the book, O'Neill also recorded the reply from Taylor, given in the *Morning Post* on 8 January 1925. Taylor pointed out that Macready skipped lightly over the events of 14 March 1920 and sought to show that "the terms of release" were to apply only to persons arrested under the Defence of the Realm Regulations, whereas, in fact over 70 hunger-strikers (convicted and unconvicted in about equal proportions) 'were released and, with one exception, unconditionally'. 'The conclusion fairly to be drawn from all this', Taylor stated, 'is that the Lord Mayor, whom Sir Neville in his book affects to despise, proved himself more than a match for the latter...'[23]

Relations with British representatives

O'Neill appears to have acted on the belief that there are good, likeable qualities in everyone. He approached others with this positive approach, which disarmed opponents, who often responded positively in return. Thus, General Macready, subsequent to their meeting at the Vice-Regal Lodge, arranged to meet him again to acquaint himself with the true state of affairs in the country. They met both at the Vice-Regal Lodge and at Lord Justice O'Connor's house on Herbert Avenue. Before accepting the invitation, O'Neill consulted some bishops and Arthur Griffith, who was a frequent visitor to the Mansion House. All he consulted approved of his action. Of course, not everyone did.

It appeared in the press that he had interviews with Macready. One night about 11 p.m., after a very tiring day, two Sinn Féin colleagues in the Corporation called on him, Ald. McGarry and Ald. McGuirke. They came to tell him not to go near Macready any more. Annoyed, O'Neill expressed his dislike of their dictation and presumption. As they were colleagues, however, to ease their minds he told them that he had visited Macready with the full concurrence of Arthur Griffith. At which they drew themselves up and said in harmony – "Arthur Griffith is not our leader!" They did not say who was, and O'Neill did not ask. He told Griffith next day of their visit and their remark concerning him, and Griffith remarked rather sadly, 'Everything must be done by the gun now'. [24]

Macready, in his book, was cynical at O'Neill's expense: "Larry O'Neill's sole object was to get every concession possible without giving anything in return"; he was "a master of Irish blarney"; and "a very shifty gentleman" and so on. Yet O'Neill's observation was: 'I found him not at all a bad fellow, and to his credit he was very adverse to the brutal methods of the Black and Tans; but, like a great many leaders of the time, he had not the courage to condemn the action of their subordinates… All in all, I am grateful to Sir Neville Macready for his kindness and forbearance with me in granting many favours, not personal ones, but favours through me to 'republicans and mothers-in-law' (permitting one prisoner to be visited by his mother-in-law). 'In the end I believe he was glad when the truce and the treaty came along, as it prevented him from being retired, like so many of his predecessors, in disgrace.'[25] Despite Macready's later dismissive treatment of O'Neill in his autobiography, he sent a pleasant note to him on the establishment of the Irish Free State wishing him every success.

Lord Mayor O'Neill's relationship with Lord French was stormier but warmer. He had no illusions about the many unacceptable events that took place during French's regime as Lord Lieutenant, including his notorious comment on 6 July 1918 that "They should stamp on any form of rebel as they would on a poisonous insect". But, as O'Neill observed, 'I always like to deal with people as I find them'. In the course of many meetings with Lord French he found him a bluff soldier, 'a gentleman true to his word, and no small ways about him, but owing to his position as Lord Lieutenant in which he was in many ways only a figure-head, he had to act very often in carrying out duties he disliked'.

French sought O'Neill's advice on occasion, as when he did not know how to proceed about a man in Limerick Jail who had committed a heinous crime, was sentenced to five years, and had now gone on hunger strike and was calling out "Up the Republic". O'Neill commented that if this man was as bad as French had represented him he had probably gone on hunger strike in the hope of being released from prison. He was very different from the hundreds of young men who went on hunger strike for a principle. In his view, when the pangs of hunger really get to the Limerick prisoner, he will forget the republic. It turned out as he predicted.[26]

In conversation, O'Neill felt able to ask him personal questions. As, for example, 'how it was that he, a soldier of distinction, a cavalry officer of renown, commander-in-chief of the forces at the front, accepted a position which had at the time neither honour, dignity, or credit attached to it. He simply answered, "I was needy".' And when O'Neill spoke to him 'about the action of the Ulster Volunteers, backed up by the civil heads, he admitted their action was the cause of most of the trouble in Ireland, and as to General Gough of Curragh Mutiny fame, the response was – "I would have shot him".' And in his final analysis of Field Marshal, Lord French, Lord Lieutenant of Ireland, O'Neill commented: 'When one man saves the life of another, it is the greatest test of sincerity, and I am satisfied Lord French saved my life...' Unfortunately, the next page in O'Neill's account is missing!

The Corporation takes sides

On 3 May, Dublin Corporation abandoned any pretext of neutrality and pledged its allegiance to Dail Eireann.[27] This gave rise to many problems. The Corporation refused to present its books for audit to the Local Government Board. In accordance with an order from the Dail, no income tax was paid by the Corporation or its officials to the British authorities. The Government, in response, withheld funds that were necessary for the running of city services. As O'Neill subsequently observed: 'A great deal of the confusion which subsequently arose over Corporation finance was caused by orders from Dail Eireann.' 'In fact', he continued soberly, 'during those years law abiding citizens did not know where they stood. If they disobeyed the order of the British Government, they ran the risk of being imprisoned. If they disobeyed the order of Dail Eireann, they ran the risk of being what was known in republican circles as "plugged".'[28]

Violence and dislocation

May and June witnessed numerous scenes of violence and defiance. Among the more publicised events were: disturbances in Derry resulting in eighteen deaths; a "munitions strike" in Kingstown (Dun Laoghaire), which spread to most of the country, and resulted in the refusal to carry munitions in trains, a ban later extended to the transporting of armed troops; a police mutiny at Listowal, Co. Kerry, on 16 June; and ten days later a British general and colonel were kidnapped by the IRA while fishing near Fermoy, Co. Cork. Of more political significance was the election in June to county councils, rural district councils and boards of guardians, in which Sinn Féin was highly successful.

And as if to testify to the dislocation of the time and the desire for social justice, a soviet was established at the central creamery, Knocklong, County Limerick, from 16-19 May, 1920.

Food shortage

Against such a countrywide background of disruption, the threat to food supplies to the capital became a major concern for Dublin Corporation. On 29 June, the Lord Mayor presided over a Food Emergency Committee composed of R. Mulcahy, T.D., M. Staines, Mrs Wyse-Power, R. McKee, J. MacDonagh, and three Labour/trade union members, Tom Johnson, Tom Foran, and William O'Brien. The committee set itself four objectives: '1. Find out what food was in the shops and in warehouses; 2. Where supplies of food can be procured; 3. What means of transport is available to convey it to the city, and the organisation of the same; 4. Ascertain numbers and devise rationing system for the population of the city.' Various areas were allocated to the members and some others: Milk – Mrs Wyse-Power; provisions – Clr. Farren; transport– Mulcahy and McKee; canals – Farren; supplies of coal – O'Brien and Foran; meat – Staines and a Mr O'Reilly; and bacon- Johnson. Area committees were instructed to take a census of each area in terms of food and prices. The Lord Mayor was to contact bakers and to arrange the despatch of flour by canal as soon as possible. Shopkeepers were to be recommended to lay in stocks of certain non-perishable foods, including condensed milk. In the prevailing disturbances the transport of cattle to the capital was difficult. The potato crop was likely to be poor. Flour supplies were not sufficient. The tasks of the committee seemed endless.[29]

Accelerated violence, the Auxiliaries, Terence MacSwiney

During July and August 1920, the atmosphere of murderous violence became even more pronounced. Lieutenant-Colonel G.B.F. Smyth, divisional commander of the RIC in Munster, was shot dead in Cork by the IRA. A native of Banbridge, County Down, his death led to the expulsion of Catholics from there and from nearby Dromore. In Belfast, Catholics were expelled from the shipyards, and there was rioting and over a dozen deaths. On 27 July a new injection of ferocity was added with the inauguration of a para-military force, later called the Auxiliary Division of the RIC. Its members were said to be ex-officers of the British army. They proved an effective fighting unit, but were feared and hated for their ruthlessness. On 13 August, the Lord Mayor of Cork, Terence MacSwiney was arrested and deported to Brixton Prison. He went on hunger strike the day of his arrest.

Meantime, there was word that Archbishop Mannix of Melbourne, a staunch supporter of Irish independence, was coming to Ireland. On 5 August, at a special meeting of the Municipal Council, it was decided to confer Freedom of the City on the archbishop, and a deputation, led by the Lord Mayor, was appointed to meet his Grace at whatever port he landed. Government intervention, however, prevented a meeting. Dr Mannix was not permitted to land in Ireland. He disembarked in England. Bishop Fogarty, of Killaloe, went to London to greet him. Particularly concerned at this stage for the health of Lord Mayor MacSwiney, O'Neill sent a telegram to Bishop Fogarty asking for news. Fogarty replied on 21 August:

> Today we are trying for permits to see the Lord Mayor of Cork, who is dangerously weak. His sister is here, and is told by the Home Office that this Government will on no account consent to his release even with the certainty of his dying. But they have said such things before.[30]

MacSwiney's condition was attracting attention in Europe and America. Arthur Griffith, during his frequent visits to the Mansion House, discussed with the Lord Mayor how MacSwiney might be saved. O'Neill felt sure that that the authorities would not yield on this occasion. He recalled General Macready's warning – 'This is the last time hunger strikers will be released'. He suggested to Griffith that he, O'Neill, should visit MacSwiney and represent to him that it was the wish of the "Republican Executive" that he give up the hunger strike; that is if the Executive permitted him to do so. If the Executive wished to keep the permission secret, O'Neill was prepared to take the blame on himself for MacSwiney going off hunger strike. Griffith put the matter to the republican leadership and came back to Lord Mayor O'Neill with the message – 'They have decided MacSwiney must die if the Government do not give in'. He gave O'Neill to understand that some of MacSwiney's relatives were strongest in that respect. On 6 September, the Dublin Municipal Council adjourned for a week at the Lord Mayor's proposal of protest 'against the slow murder of the Lord Mayor of Cork and his colleagues which is now being committed by the British Government in Brixton and Cork jails'.[31]

During the long weeks of MacSwiney's painful struggle, the warfare between the IRA and the Auxiliaries and Black and Tans continued north and south. A district inspector of police, O.R. Swanzy, was murdered at Lisburn by the IRA on 22 August. In reprisal, Catholics were driven from their homes, and in Belfast some thirty people were killed. Lord Mayor O'Neill set up a fund to assist refugees from the Belfast pogrom. On 20 September, the Black and Tans sacked the town of Balbriggan, County Dublin; and in Mallow, on 28 September, in the aftermath of an IRA raid on a police barrack, British soldiers sacked the town. One act of terrorism led to another even more savage. Even sporting events suffered.

The IRA and Golf

As the plight of the Lord Mayor of Cork was receiving international publicity, an international golfing championship, involving Irish, Scottish and English players, was taking place at Portmarnock Golf Course, in O'Neill's home area. After the first day's play a republican flag was hoisted over the club house, and the intimation was conveyed that if the championships continued the greens would be dug up. The secretary and a member of the committee made a hurried visit to the Mansion House requesting the Lord Mayor to intervene. He learned that his old acquaintance, Austin Stack, was in charge of this branch of republican activity under Cathal Brugha. He met with Stack. They had a forthright discussion during which Stack declared – 'Why shouldn't we make ourselves felt when they are killing MacSwiney'. After some time he gave way. The championships could continue, but on no account was the republican flag to be removed. The games were played to a close under a republican flag, which remained flying until the winter winds displaced it.[32]

The All-Ireland hurling final, on the other hand, went ahead at Croke Park without interference. And, as a celebrated photograph testifies, Griffith, de Valera, the Lord Mayor, and Collins were in attendance and in jovial mood.

The death and funeral of Terence MacSwiney

Terence MacSwiney, Lord Mayor of Cork and commandant of the 1st Cork brigade of the IRA, died at Brixton Prison on 25 October, the seventy-fourth day of his hunger strike. His remains were brought to the Catholic cathedral at Southwark. The bishop, Dr Amigo, gave permission for the body to remain there until arrangements were finalised to bring it home. Lord Mayor O'Neill went to Southwark, and was greatly impressed by the respect shown by the English population as MacSwiney's remains passed through the streets of London to Euston Station, *en route* to Cork, *via* Dublin. 'On the night mail to Holyhead', O'Neill recalled, 'an ugly rumour reached us that soldiers were assembled and gun-boats were standing by' at Holyhead. On arrival, the rumours were confirmed. Moreover, a phone message from his secretary informed him of a communication handed in at the Mansion House, 8.30 p.m., announcing that the remains of the late Lord Mayor of Cork would not be conveyed *via* Dublin, but would be brought by steamer from Holyhead to Queenstown (Cobh).

The Government were determined to avoid a massive Sinn Féin funeral demonstration in Dublin, followed by a virtual funeral procession all the way to Cork city. To O'Neill, and MacSwiney's relatives and friends, who expected to take charge of the coffin at Holyhead, the rough behaviour of the British soldiers seemed quite unacceptable, all the more so as relatives were not permitted to accompany the body by boat.

In Dublin, despite the absence of the coffin, the arranged procession took place after Mass in the Pro-Cathedral, at which Archbishop Walsh presided. The very large cortege was led by a hearse, followed by some 50 priests walking, the archbishop in his car, and a long line of carriages carrying the brothers and sisters of MacSwiney, the Lord Mayor of Dublin and his chaplain, the Deputy Lord Mayor of Cork, mayors of a number of cities, chairmen of urban councils, leaders of the Labour Party, members of Dublin Corporation, Cork Corporation, and representatives of numerous organisations. A body of Volunteers marched ahead of the hearse, which was filled with floral tributes. Thousands lined the footpaths and all business premises were closed. There was no music. It was an impressive silent demonstration.

It was accompanied by feelings of tension and anxiety as to how the authorities might react. As the procession passed O'Connell Bridge, two lorries filled with armed police Auxiliaries took up station at Eden Quay. In the account provided by the *Dublin Evening Mail*, 29 October, all passed quietly. The Lord Mayor of Dublin's memory of the final stage of the procession, however, was anything but peaceful. When near King's Bridge, where the train for Cork waited, 'motor lorries filled with soldiers and Black and Tans, accompanied by an armoured car, swooped down upon the procession…The hate of these villainous ruffians was let loose, lorries of them scattering the pedestrians in all directions, and rushing those in vehicles into side-streets, and for the first time in my life a thrill of genuine fear took possession of me as to what might happen, as the armoured car circled around our carriage, with eyes like demons peering through the port-holes … They rushed us over the bridge, down the northern line of the quays, surrounding us all the time as far as Grattan Bridge. This line of conduct prevailed about this quarter of the city until the train had left for Cork.' Although writing some years after the event, the Lord Mayor's sense of outrage remained vivid: 'of all the degrading and provocative acts committed towards us which adorn the English escutcheon, this was one of the most wanton'.[33]

A large representative group took the train to Cork for the funeral. The *Dublin Evening Mail,* of 29 October, noted that 'members of Dublin Corporation and County Council, of Dail Eireann, the Labour Party, the Trades Council, together with various Sinn Féin representatives, travelled in the special train, which left the station at 2.0 p.m.'. A notable absentee was the Lord Mayor of Dublin. He was unable to attend the funeral because he was deeply engaged, together with Archbishop Walsh, in efforts to save the life of Kevin Barry.

Kevin Barry, the Lord Mayor and Lloyd George

Kevin Barry was an eighteen year old medical student, who had been condemned to death for the murder of a soldier on 20 September, even though the evidence that he fired the fatal shot was doubtful.[34] On Lord Mayor O'Neill's efforts to save his life, the *Irish Times* correspondent, "Quid Nunc", wrote shortly after O'Neill's own death. 'After the death sentence was pronounced', the Lord Mayor 'forwarded personal appeals to all the members of the British Cabinet and to several ex-ministers who were known to disapprove of General Macready's measures. In most instances the replies were simply formal, and, when he found that his letter to Prime Minister, Lloyd George, brought only an official acknowledgement from his private secretary, he at once set off for Downing Street bent on pressing his appeal for commutation of Barry's sentence.' On arrival in London, 'he learned that the Prime Minister was at Caernarvon'. When O'Neill reached there, he learned that Lloyd George had left for Swansea a few hours earlier. That day of disappointment was followed by two more days of failure to overtake the elusive Prime Minister, and, 'when at last he came to quarters with him at Chequers, it was approaching the day of Barry's execution'.[35]

O'Neill appears to have received an assurance from Lloyd George that he would do all he could, and he returned to Dublin with some hope. The *Dublin Evening Mail* of Saturday, 30 October 1920, carried the heading – "Shall Kevin Barry Die? Hopes of Reprieve". Efforts to secure the reprieve continued into Sunday, 31 October. At midnight, 'Lord Mayor O'Neill was told by Mr Lloyd George on the telephone that the Government could not grant a reprieve'.[36] Next morning, 1 November, Kevin Barry was hanged; the first execution since May 1916. The large crowd gathered outside the prison praying for him were shocked by the news of the hanging. On that day, 'scores of his fellow-students at the university enrolled in the IRA'.[37] Many English people were also disturbed at the execution, and J.H. Thomas spoke of it with indignation in the House of Commons.[38]

Although opposition was growing in England to the Government's Irish campaign, its cost and the methods being employed, the Government continued with its policy. 'We have murder by the throat', Lloyd George trumpeted at the Lord Mayor's Banquet in London on 9 November. The Government received a serious setback on 21 November, however, when IRA groups, on Collins's orders, shot dead 14 suspected secret service agents in Dublin. In response, Auxiliaries killed two senior IRA members of the Dublin Brigade, and the Black-and-Tans opened fire on the crowd and players during a football match in Croke Park, killing 12 people. In that month of horror and mourning, the IRA retaliated, in turn, by arson attacks in Liverpool on 27 November, and on the following day, at Kilmichael, County Cork, a patrol of eighteen Auxiliaries were ambushed and mercilessly slaughtered by a brigade of the IRA. On 10 December, Lord French imposed martial law on the counties of Cork, Kerry, Limerick, and Tipperary, the main areas of resistance. Unauthorised possession of arms, and aiding, harbouring or abetting rebels became a capital offence. The following day, Auxiliaries and Black and Tans set fire to the city of Cork, causing over £2½ millions of damage.

The Lord Mayor and the Auxiliaries

The Auxiliaries were feared and loathed by a large section of the population, but even of them the Lord Mayor of Dublin found good things to say. Without wishing 'to mitigate the dreadful deeds they committed in the city', he gave two examples 'of their better natures' that he had experienced. One party that raided the Mansion House was under the control of an Auxiliary, a former captain in the Grenadier Guards, who sought 'to cause as little annoyance as possible'. Subsequently, in mufti, the same man insisted on joining O'Neill in a train journey from Holyhead to London, and told him that following the raid on the Mansion House, he had been ordered to raid a house in Merrion Square, and there he noticed in the drawing room the photograph of a soldier comrade who had been killed in the Great War. It made him so ashamed of the kind of work he was compelled to do in Ireland, that on his return to barracks he resigned his position and was now returning home to his wife and children in Derbyshire.

The other instance was more dramatic. It concerned another raid on the Mansion House. As O'Neill described it: 'At this time, the Mansion House was the channel of communication with most of the republican leaders. Letters, when handed in, were carefully stowed away by Miss O'Sullivan, my son, or myself. When the raid commenced, two Auxiliaries took on the examination of the upper portion of the dwelling part of the house; one was very officious, the other calmly observant. They went into my son's room and insisted on having some locked drawers opened. The Auxiliary, who was not the officious one, stood by. When the drawers were opened by my son, letters for Austin Stack, Michael Collins, and de Valera were on view. "Close it up at once. Don't let the other fellow see it", the Auxiliary remarked.' After the raid, O'Neill never saw 'the good Samaritan again'. 'By degrees', he remarked, 'all the decent ones left Ireland, and nothing but the dross remained.'

The kind of unsettling methods sometimes used by Auxiliaries was displayed shortly after this raid, when O'Neill found a letter in the mail-box addressed to the Lord Mayor:

Your Worship,

I have very good information I could give Michael Collins.
I could be waiting for him at your house at seven o'clock Tuesday evening.
Dare not give my name.

(Signed) A True Friend of the Cause.

'The thing was so stupid', O'Neill saw through it at once. Soon after there was an early morning raid. The captain in charge very significantly asked for the key of the letter-box, and when nothing was found the raid was called off.[39]

The status and impact of Collins

In the height of the "troubles", one of the main ambitions of the government forces was to capture Michael Collins. A large reward was on his head, but he remained elusive, taking chances bordering on rashness. One particular occasion was etched in O'Neill's memory.

It was believed by the Castle authorities that republican leaders on many occasions escaped by the city's sewers. The Black and Tans raided the Engineers Department of the Corporation and took away the plans of the sewers of the city. Soon afterwards, Government agents, or "watchers", as they were called, reported that Collins was in the Mountjoy area in the north of the city. Straightway, the area was 'entirely surrounded by soldiers, Black and Tans, barbed wire fencing, with all war accoutrements even to cooking kitchens, evidently prepared for a long stay'. As British officers went down manholes in the streets, Michael Collins passed O'Neill on the south side of the River Liffey, 'leisurely cycling down Westmoreland Street... and passing by Trinity College (was) saluted by a big policeman on point duty'. 'It occurred to me at the time', O'Neill wrote later, 'here was a man, a huge reward offered for his capture, surrounded by hundreds of young fellows, none of them blessed with very much of the world's goods,' yet 'there were no informers; and when the history of these times come to be dealt with in full, this in itself will stand out to the character of the young men of that period.'[40]

Life goes on

Day after day, newspaper headlines were taken up with raids, shootings and killings. Nevertheless, while so many fearful things were happening, basic employment issues required attention. Dublin building trades workers ceased work on 4 October. Some 8,000 men were involved. The Lord Mayor was called on. The *Dublin Evening Mail* announced that he 'has worked indefatigably to bring about a settlement. It is to be hoped his sincere efforts, which, in spite of numerous difficulties, he continues, will meet with the success which they undoubtedly deserve'.[41] Ordinary citizens, meanwhile, endeavoured to carry on with their accustomed work and engagements. Among the last mentioned, was the well established annual conference of the Catholic Truth Society of Ireland, with its public lectures and reports. It was held at the Mansion House on 22 October. The *Daily Sketch* of 23 October carried a photograph of the Lord Mayor on one knee about to kiss the ring of the aged Cardinal Logue on his arrival at the Mansion House. Later in the day, his Eminence paid a tribute to Lord Mayor O'Neill which went way beyond conventional social courtesies:

> The Lord Mayor has said a great many things and said them well. He could
> tell them … the Lord Mayor was there when there was any useful work to
> be done, when there was any national need to be met. Whenever the interests
> of the country had to be protected, the Lord Mayor of Dublin was forthcoming.
> He was a man of modesty, without any pretensions whatever, but he could tell
> them, he was a man of merit.

The cardinal concluded – 'He worked hard and never spared himself, and never minded when he had a good cause to carry forward whether he found favour with those in authority or with the people.'

The following month, another instance of resilience in face of tumult and danger, was supported by the Lord Mayor. Early in November, 1920, Maude Gonne MacBride wrote to W.B. Yeats: 'I am very busy with Mrs Erskine Childers getting up an "All Ireland Relief for the Devastated Areas Committee". The Lord Mayor will take the lead in it. Something must be done to help the thousands who are homeless and starving as a result of military depravation – Something to show the solidarity of the Nation before common terror, is necessary.'[42]

The Corporation's problems and dilemmas

The "common terror" invaded the Corporation on 6 December, when its proceedings were interrupted by the entrance of armed forces, who arrested Ald. Staines, Ald. Thomas Lawlor, and Clrs. Clarke, Lawless, Brennan and Lynch.[43] A week later the Municipal Council faced a host of other problems. The dispute regarding the Town Clerk came to a head with his resignation; and there were major financial issues – the treatment of tuberculosis was being halted as operations were deferred and hospitals were closing, there was a shortage of money to pay wages, staff were not being replaced, requests from the Technical Education Committee were not being met, there was difficulty about awarding scholarships, and road improvements were delayed - all because the necessary financial aid was not forthcoming from the Government following the Corporation's open declaration for Dail Eireann and its refusal to cooperate with government departments.

On 20 December the serious effect of its independent policy came to a head. The Lord Chief Justice, Mr Justice Gibson, in the case of the Local Government Board against the Corporation, 'made an order that a peremptory writ of *mandamus* should issue directing the production of such books, accounts and vouchers as are in the possession, power or procurement of the Corporation, and giving costs against the Corporation ...'. He warned that if it became necessary for the Court 'to use its full powers and enforce compliance... the result might be financial ruin to the city and untold misery to many of the citizens'. Urging the Corporation to seriously consider the consequence of disobedience, the Chief Justice observed:

> However strong the opinions of the Corporation might be, they represented the whole body of the citizens at large, and they should realise that the contest should not be carried on by sacrificing the interests of the local community, and at the expense of the poor and the sick as well as of labour and the well-to-do. That was the problem that the defendants now had to face.[44]

For Lord Mayor O'Neill, however strong his national feeling, the judge's words must have cut to the bone. He had prided himself on being the mayor 'of all the people', and he had a strong commitment to the poor and the disabled, yet he now found himself restricted in the Corporation by the dominance of the Sinn Féin majority. He was caught between two fires. He was reputed to be competent at gauging the mood of a meeting, and indeed of the city and country, sensitive to the differences between his fellow members on the council, and sure in his management of the council, quite firm when needed. Ald. Cosgrave had acknowledged that he had steered the council into calmer waters so that 'more cordial relations existed than formerly', but as a practical politician he realised that he could only lead if the majority were prepared to follow. It helped that he agreed with many of Sinn Féin's views, and that many of his close friends were Sinn Féiners. All was easy when his own preferences coincided with theirs, as in the case of the Town Clerk, even if it meant that illegalities were countenanced and the official concerned was undermined. But on the political issue of allegiance to Dail Eireann and its instructions, however unreasonable, Sinn Féin remained obdurate.

The 20 December also brought a more immediate structural shock. That morning, 'the military authorities, in accordance with previous notice served on the Corporation, took complete possession of the City Hall, City Treasurer's office, and other Corporation buildings'. The municipal flagstaff was removed from the roof, and 'during the day a large crowd of military were engaged erecting barbed wire entanglements. Their activities attracted a large concourse of people, who curiously gazed on at their manoeuvres'.[45] The Government was making it brutally clear that the Corporation, by allying itself with the republican rebels, could no longer be regarded as a reliable administrator of the needs of all the citizens. The Corporation, henceforth, held its meetings in the Mansion House.[46]

On 15 November, with a railway crisis pending and its harmful effects on industry and employment, the Corporation called on the Lord Mayor to bring about 'a cessation of all …industrial disputes in the city'.[47] It was a tall order, and this time he was not successful. On 29 November the railway strike took place.[48] It upset business not just in the city but across the provinces. Hence, when de Valera left the acclaim and publicity of the United States, he returned, on 23 December, to a country in disarray both politically and economically. There was little in the way of Christmas cheer and good will. Indeed, the editorial in the *Dublin Evening Mail* of 31 December, entitled "*Vale* 1920", judged that

> It is doubtful whether any previous year in its (Ireland's) history
> has witnessed so many tragedies, such widespread misery, and
> so parlous an industrial outlook.

Laurence O'Neill, characteristically, spent part of Christmas Day visiting prisoners in Mountjoy Jail, and, almost inevitably, found himself with a prisoner problem. Two young fellows, who had been sent up from the country the night before, had gone on hunger strike. He spoke to them. They had no complaint of ill-treatment. Their sole reason for going on strike was to gain release from prison. He spoke to some of the senior republican prisoners, but they were reluctant to get involved. O'Neill then explained that because the Ashe Agreement had not been broken by the authorities, he did not feel justified in intervening. At that, one prisoner, John O'Mahony, agreed to see what he could do. O'Neill arranged for him to meet the young fellows and, fortunately, they took his advice and ended their hunger strike.[49] The Lord Mayor may have been able to spend the rest of the day with his family. During this troubled year and subsequent years, he and his family, especially his daughter Annie who lived at home, were worried about his wife Anne's continued serious illness, the nature of which is not mentioned; while he was also concerned about his business and the pressure on his son, John, to maintain it.

Notes

1   *Dublin Saturday Post,* 17 Feb. 1920

2   ONFP. Edward Sanderson, private secretary,-Ld. Mayor, 8 Jan. 1920

3   Idem. "Raids on the Mansion House"

4   Sheila Carden. *The Alderman. Alderman Tom Kelly,1868-1942,* and Dublin Corporation, p. 166

5   Cit. Carden, p.169

6   DCC. Mins. no.8, p.25

7   Carden, p. 175. *Irish Independent,* 1 Jan. 1920

8   Carden, p. 176

9   *Evening Telegraph,* 24 Feb. 1920

10 Idem. 30 April 1920

11 *Irish Independent,* 31 Jan. 1920

12 DCC. 4,8 Nov., no.7436, pp.517-21, 536

13 Carden, op.cit. pp.182-3

14 T.J. Morrissey. *William O'Brien, 1881-1968,* p. 184

15 Carden, pp. 173, 180

16 ONFP. "A String of Detectives"

17 *Evening Herald,* 26 March 1920

18 NLI. O'Neill papers. Ld.Mayor – Rt Hon. D. Lloyd George, 26 March; Lloyd George- Ld. Mayor, 31 March 1920. Ms.35, 294/10

19 ONFP. "Release of Hunger Strikers"

20 NLI. O'Neill papers. Ld. Mayor & High Sheriff- Bonar Law, 12 April 1920. Ms. 35,294/11; P.D. Waterhouse-Ld.Mayor, 13 April, Ms. Idem.; and Oral Answered Record of House of Commons, 13 April, pp. 1508-1511, in O'Neill papers, idem.

21 ONFP. "Release of Hunger Strikers"

22 DCC Mins., 19 April, n. 264, p. 217; and *Dublin Sat. Post,* 24 April 1920

23 ONFP. "Release of Hunger Strikers"

24 ONFP. "General Sir Neville Macready. Seeking Light".

25 Idem. "General Sir Neville Macready and Mothers-in-Law"

26 Idem. "Lord French and a 'Up the Republic' prisoner in Limerick Jail"

27 DCC Mins. 3 May, n. 424, p.307. Despite the advice of the Law Agent, the vote was carried, 38 votes to 5. The Lord Mayor is not recorded as voting.

28 ONFP. "The Dublin Corporation and Dail Eireann"

29 NLI. Wm. O'Brien papers, Ms. 15,704 (9). See DCC. Mins. 28 June, no. 509, and Report of Emergency Committee, 16 July, no. 561, pp. 390-93

30 NLI. O'Neill papers. Ms. 35,294/12. Bp. Fogarty-Ld. Mayor, 21 Aug. 1920

31 DCC. 6 Sept. 1920, no. 639, p. 441

32 ONFP. "Fear of Republicanism"

33 Idem. "Death of the Rt. Hon. Terence MacSwiney, Lord Mayor of Cork"

34 Macardle. *Irish Republic,* p. 360

35 *Irish Times,* the "Irishman's Diary", 29 July 1943

36 *Dublin Evening Mail,* 1 Nov. 1920

37 Macardle, op. cit., p. 361

38 Idem

39   ONFP. "Raids on the Mansion House".

40   Idem. "Michael Collins (rashness)"

41   *Dublin Evening Mail,* 4 Oct. 1920

42   A. MacBride White and A. Norman Jeffares (eds.). *Always Your Friend. The Gonne-Yeats Letters, 1893-1938. p.417*

43   DCC. Mins., 6 Dec. Special Meeting, no. 832, p.576

44   *Dublin Evening Mail,* 20 Dec. 1920

45   Idem., 22 Dec. 1920

46   DCC. Mins., pp. 608-11

47   Idem., no.790. p. 552

48   *Dublin Evening Mail,* 29 Nov. 1920

49   ONFP. Typed pages without a title, commencing "On Christmas Day…"

11.

1921:
Through Carnage to Peace

The New Year was to bring unexpected developments, contacts, travel, and sadness for Lord Mayor O'Neill.

The White Cross

On 8 January 1921 he received a letter from Eamon de Valera stating that he had set up an Irish Relief Committee when he was in the United States. He wished to set up a similar body in Ireland to be known as the Irish White Cross. It would liaise with the American body and be the vehicle of funding from America 'for the relief of those suffering as a result of the present British campaign'. Also in January, James G. Douglas, an Irish Quaker, was chosen by the American Committee for Relief in Ireland (ACRI) - a non-political body founded by a Dr William Maloney and strongly supported by the Society of Friends - as their means of sending relief. He contacted the Lord Mayor, who told him he would discuss the matter with de Valera. The overall result was the setting up of a special organisation termed the 'Irish White Cross'. De Valera made it clear that the new body would have to appeal to all shades of opinion in the Unites States, and, hence, must be representative of all ranges of political and religious persuasion. The Lord Mayor would see, de Valera observed, 'that he would be the proper person to launch it in public'. Dr Fogarty of Killaloe would call on him to explain it further.

In his letter, de Valera indicated the spread of people he would envisage on the National Committee of the Irish White Cross. Cardinal Logue would, he hoped 'act as head', and O'Neill had 'more influence with him than anybody' de Valera knew. Also on the Committee would be the mayors of the principal cities, representatives of Dail Eireann, of Cumann na mBan, the Vincent de Paul Society, the Society of Friends, representatives of Labour, and of the Co-operative Movement. He suggested an active organising committee including Mrs Erskine Childers, Tom Johnson (Labour), and James Douglas assisted by four or five energetic ladies. Douglas received a personal letter from de Valera. He was a key link with the American organisation. De Valera also suggested names for a Board of National Trustees, which included, as well as some of the foregoing, the Archbishop of Dublin, Arthur Griffith, T.D., William Cosgrave, T.D., and Michael Collins, T.D. These prominent Sinn Féin personalities would not take an active part. They were present to give assurance to Sinn Féin members concerning the Irish White Cross, which would be a non-political organisation and its funds, as stipulated by the American Committee for Relief, would be used on a strict non-political basis and solely for the relief of suffering.[1]

O'Neill replied on 10 January, commencing the letter with 'My dear Friend' because of censorship. Outside the great compliment paid to him, it would give him the greatest pleasure to have de Valera's wishes carried out. He would get in contact with all those de Valera had named.[2] Four days later, he wrote again. The election for Lord Mayor would take place in 12 days time. He had determined not to seek re-election but de Valera's letter of 8 January had altered his mind. 'What I feel now', he continued, 'if I am not Lord Mayor (please don't take this as egotism) I would have very little weight and less influence in launching the scheme as suggested by you, and moreover some of those whose names you have mentioned in your letter (particularly the ecclesiastics) would do for me as Lord Mayor what one could not expect them to do if I were a private individual. Therefore, the point I would respectfully ask you to consider – Is it your wish that I should seek re-election as Lord Mayor? With the object of helping to the best of my ability to make the Relief Scheme a success.'[3] O'Neill was aware that Sinn Féin members had one of their own members in mind for Lord Mayor. To his mixture of concern and realpolitik, de Valera responded next day that he had not had the forthcoming election in mind when he asked him to undertake the work for the Relief Movement, but he did not think there was anyone in his own party 'who could at present, even as Lord Mayor, secure such a general co-operation from all parties as your Lordship can.' If asked privately for his counsel, he would give it in support of O'Neill, but his Lordship would understand that it would scarcely be advisable for him to go further than that.[4] On 27 January, having learned from a further letter of O'Neill that he was going forward for re-election, de Valera explained that he had had a number of interviews with influential members of the party and that, as the coming year was likely to be a critical one in the fortunes of Ireland and the Republic, the republican members of the Corporation were very anxious to have a Lord Mayor who would not compromise the republican position. He went on with almost tortuous delicacy

> Your Lordship's views are thought not to be out and out republican with the result that if you were elected there is a fear that at a critical time … you might possibly with your views as to the best interests of Ireland act in a way which would be detrimental to the Republic, which means detrimental to Ireland according to republican views as to Ireland's best interests.

He went on to state more plainly that he had been promised that if he , de Valera, could give a personal guarantee that in political matters regarding relations with England and England's agents, in which O'Neill was called upon to act as lord mayor, O'Neill would 'take counsel with and be advised by the responsible political representatives of the vast majority of the Irish people', then O'Neill would be proposed as Lord Mayor by a member of Sinn Féin, which would probably lead to his unanimous election. An honour, de Valera assured him, which he certainly deserved and which he hoped would be conferred upon him. A favourable line from O'Neill on the foregoing would finally settle the whole question.[5]

O'Neill's cherished independence and his claim to represent all the citizens was being compromised. On the other hand, the reality was that the Sinn Féin majority controlled the Municipal Council and as Lord Mayor he had had to live with that. Consequently, on that evening, 27 January, he sent a strictly private and confidential reply, stating that his action as Lord Mayor this year if elected would 'be on the lines suggested' in de Valera's letter, and he quoted the requirements 'that in matters of a political character' and so on he would 'take council and be advised by the responsible political representatives of the vast majority of the Irish people'.[6]

At the Corporation meeting to elect the Lord Mayor, Ald. Laurence O'Neill was proposed by Clr. Forrestal and seconded by Mrs Sheehy Skeffington. The election, however, was not unanimous. His long-time supporter, Clr. Captain McWalter, M.D., who strongly disapproved of Sinn Féin, and apparently deemed O'Neill to be sacrificing his independence in order to retain office, proposed a unionist candidate, Ald. Sir Andrew Beattie, P.C., D.L., J.P.. At the latter's request, however, the amendment was withdrawn and the main motion was put and carried.[7] On 1 February, de Valera was pleased to congratulate O'Neill 'on breaking the record for the Dublin mayoralty'. He hoped he might 'be privileged to add the further record of being our capital's first Lord Mayor in a once more independent Ireland'.[8] Also on that date, there was a letter from Archbishop Walsh which, perhaps, occasioned some discomfort. He congratulated O'Neill on his unanimous re-election to an office, 'the naturally exacting character of which' he 'had added a hundred fold' by his 'high sense of public duty' and his 'readiness to devote' himself 'to the interests of every citizen of Dublin'.[9]

In the same letter, Dr Walsh expressed his willingness to assist the White Cross but made it clear that he would be unable to attend meetings because of ill health. Cardinal Logue had already agreed to give every assistance to the White Cross to help those who had been left destitute by the murder of those on whom they depended, or ruined by the destruction of their property'.[10]

O'Neill had sent out a number of carefully worded letters inviting chosen people to join the Executive Committee of the White Cross. Among them were two well known women, the Hon. Mary Spring-Rice, Mount Trenchard, Foynes[11], and his colleague on the Corporation, Mrs Tom Clarke. The manner of his invitation to Mrs Clarke indicates why so many people responded positively to his invitation.

> Dear Mrs Clarke,
>
> It has been suggested to me to take in hands the forming of a "White Cross" to act in co-operation with the "White Cross" already formed in America for the relief of our suffering people. With that object an Executive Committee will be required to work out the scheme, and I would feel deeply complimented if you would act on the Committee, as of course, it will not be narrowed in its construction by any sectional differences. The duty of the Committee will be to act in conjunction with the smaller committees that will be set up throughout the country, for the consideration and distribution of funds.[12]

Meantime, de Valera continued to emphasise the urgency of developing the White Cross throughout the country. On 11 February, he observed that representatives of the American Committee for Relief in Ireland had arrived in London, and he suggested that the Irish White Cross should get in touch with them at once, either through Mr Douglas or the secretary.[13] On 15 February, O'Neill informed de Valera that the Executive Committee of the White Cross had appointed an organising sub-committee which had been doing all the actual work since. It was composed of L. Smith-Gordon (chairman of the Executive Committee), Douglas (Hon. Treasurer), J. McNeill (Hon. Sec.), Mrs T. Clarke, T.Foran (Labour), E. Childers, and Mrs McBride (Maud Gonne). 'We have met very frequently in connection with parish organisation… and numerous other things', but the most important matter was the arrival last Saturday of the American delegation, Messrs France, McCoy, Price, Furness, Spice and another. 'We met them at lunch on Saturday to make acquaintance, and McNeill, Douglas, Smith-Gordon and I spent five hours with them on Sunday afternoon in a close and frank conference.' Five of the seven delegates were Quakers. The three who counted most were France, McCoy and Spicer, and they were very supportive of the Irish White Cross. France had contacted the Irish Office in London and visited Dublin Castle in order to give no grounds for interference. He was told in the Castle that no relief was to be given to the areas under martial law.[14]

This last presented a real problem as many of the deprived areas and suffering people were in districts under martial law, and the American Consul was very reluctant to approve of anything that might displease the government. General Macready sought to obtain the acquiescence of the delegates to a proposal that the Castle should nominate a committee to redistribute the funds. Faced with this 'monstrous proposal' and general stalemate, de Valera, by 24 March, was determined to get in touch with the people in America in whom he had confidence before the whole thing blew sky high.[15] Representatives would have to be sent to the United States to explain the situation. Meantime, the one bright spot in relation to American aid was the funds being collected by American bishops and sent via Cardinal Logue to the Lord Mayor. On 25 March, Logue enclosed 'a monster cheque' from Philadelphia for £22,665, 17 shillings and one penny'.[16]

On 30 March 1921, Mr C.J. France reported to the Executive Committee in the United States that, due to the opposition of General Macready, the American Consul was against sending any aid. Macready described the White Cross as a vehicle of the IRA, and he laid down conditions as to who should receive aid. De Valera would prefer to receive no aid rather than comply with conditions laid down by the Castle. He wished all aid to come directly through the White Cross by which relief would be given on non-party lines. France urged the American Executive Committee to make no decisions against the Irish White Cross until Lord Mayor O'Neill, R.A. Anderson (Secretary of Irish Co-operative Society), and James Douglas, arrived in the United States.[17] France wrote directly to O'Neill, on 2 April, that he had supported the idea of a delegation from the beginning, and even then it had occurred to him that O'Neill, better than any other person connected with the White Cross, would be able to present the case in such a way that the American Executive Committee would appreciate the position of the Irish White Cross and give it their whole-hearted support. It was his, France's, duty to impartially put before the Executive Committee the views of all the parties, but having done that he had urged the Executive to make its choice on the side of the Irish White Cross.[18]

All the members of the Executive Committee of the Irish White Cross were far from convinced of the usefulness of sending the Lord Mayor and Mr R.A. Anderson to America. Smith-Gordon, chairman of the Standing Committee, expressed this view to de Valera and received a strong rebuttal. On 6 April, de Valera disagreed that the visit of the Lord Mayor and Mr Anderson will be "useless". I know, he stated, that the visit of the Lord Mayor and Mr Anderson can make such a case for the White Cross position that there would be no misunderstanding it. [19] In preparation for his journey, de Valera informed O'Neill, on 16 April, that he had asked the 'Publicity Department' of Sinn Féin to prepare for him 'some of the facts setting forth the amount of destruction etc', and he referred him to some useful information in this respect in yesterday's *Independent.* [20]

Lord Mayor O'Neill left no record of his visit to the United States of America with Messrs Anderson and Douglas. The fact that they belonged to three different religious bodies – O'Neill a Catholic, Anderson a Church of Ireland Protestant, and Douglas of the Society of Friends - was in itself an affirmation that the Irish White Cross aimed to be of assistance to everyone, regardless of political or religious affiliation. The Lord Mayor's sincerity and eloquence, and the fact that Douglas was treasurer, helped to assure the members of the American Executive Committee that General Macready's denigration of the Irish White Cross could be discounted. Thereafter, the American Committee for Relief in Ireland (ACRI) sent funds directly to Douglas, although the State Department accepted the British view that the White Cross was an agency of the IRA.[21] Ironically, the man who most smoothed difficulties in Douglas's way and supported him in keeping the White Cross out of politics, was Michael Collins.[22]

While they were in the United States, O'Neill made sure to contact the other major source of funds, the American Catholic bishops. The support of many of them was symbolised by Archbishop Moeller, who, acting as Hon. Chairman of the Cincinnati Committee of ACRI, announced that 'these gentlemen may take back to that stricken land that the people of Cincinnati and its archbishop are behind them and help them'.[23] Cardinal Logue, on 15 June, was glad that the Lord Mayor was safe home again and that his 'mission to the United States was so successful'. He was forwarding to him £904 sent by Dr Russell, Bishop of Charlestown, for the relief of distress in Ireland.[24] The benefits collected through the White Cross, and distributed through parish organisations, amounted by 31 August 1921 to £1, 374, 795.[25] The organisation continued its work for the suffering people and areas into the subsequent troubled years.

Accelerated mayhem and murder

The White Cross launch and development took place during a period of intensified warfare and brutality. In the month of March expressions of condolence and sympathy in response to executions and murders became a frequent feature at Corporation meetings. On 7 March condolence was expressed to the relatives of Messrs Alan, O'Brien, O'Callaghan, Lyons, McCarthy, and O'Mahony, who were executed by the military authorities in Cork prison. The Corporation begged to place on record their 'admiration for the heroic fortitude with which they met their deaths'.[26] The Municipal Council made no reference, however, to the relatives of the six British soldiers, prisoners of the IRA, who were shot in retaliation.

On the very day of the Corporation meeting, there was a double murder by the Black and Tans of the Mayor of Limerick, George Clancy, and a former mayor, Michael O'Callaghan. At a Municipal Council meeting, Lord Mayor O'Neill moved, and Mrs Wyse Power seconded, 'that as a mark of respect at the awful calamity which has overtaken Limerick… this council do now adjourn until this day week …and that a delegation be appointed to attend the funeral. Those appointed were Clrs. Forrestal, Daly, Wyse Power, 'together with the Rt. Hon. the Lord Mayor'. The vast funeral at Limerick – with mayors and members of corporations, from Waterford, Cork, Derry, Wexford and Clonmel, the Bishops of Limerick and Killaloe, 100 clergy, and Volunteers guarding all approaches to the cathedral – passed off peaceably as thousands lined the streets. The turn out from Dublin was deeply appreciated. On 12 March, the Bishop of Limerick, Dr Hallinan, wrote to O'Neill: 'I have many things to thank you for. It was so kind and characteristic of you to come and console me by your presence in our deep affliction, and then to write such a thoughtful letter…'[27]

On yet another occasion, just two days later, 14 March, the Lord Mayor moved a motion of condolence to the relations 'of the six men executed in Mountjoy Gaol this morning' – Thomas Whelan, Patrick Moran, Thomas Bryan, Patrick Doyle, Frank Flood, Bernard Ryan - and placed on record the Corporation's admiration 'of the heroic fortitude with which they met their deaths for Ireland'. As a mark of respect the meeting adjourned until 16 March.[28] Six British prisoners were shot in retaliation. The original number to be executed at Mountjoy was eight. Deputations led by Lord Mayor O'Neill called on General Macready. The evidence against two prisoners, Conway and Potter, was so flimsy that they were released at once. Efforts to release two others, Moran and Whelan, failed, even though the evidence suggested they were innocent. The night before the executions, O'Neill visited Moran in Mountjoy. He had known him previously. He was deeply impressed by the young man's faith and peace of mind. 'My parting with Moran so affected me that I could not brace up courage to see the others. When parting he gave me a little souvenir, a card of St. Christopher with the words written: "Good-bye Ireland and you. Mountjoy Prison, March 1921, to Lord Mayor, Alderman O'Neill. Paddy Moran".'

Next morning, hours after the executions, the Lord Mayor received by first post, a letter from Thomas Whelan, which intensely moved him:

> Your Honour,
>
> Will you permit me to thank you for your kindness to my Mother during her stay in Dublin. This is the 14th, it has come at last to find us ready… I am in the best of spirits, now as ever an Irishman's honour is a great pledge, so like men we shall meet our doom in the morning. It is now 4.40 a.m. so I have not long. I wish to thank you again and all the citizens of Dublin for their kindness to me.[29]

Condolences extended into May, as Dublin Municipal Council became a voice for the whole country. Thomas Traynor, 'recently hanged in our city', was mourned together with Maurice Moore, Patrick Ronayne, Thomas Mulcahy, and Patrick O'Sullivan 'recently shot in Cork Detention Barracks',[30] and on 6 June sympathy was extended to the family and relatives of 'Thomas Keane, who was executed at Limerick last Saturday'.

Two major losses by natural death

In addition to this grim litany, which stirred both compassion and anger, there were two natural deaths in the early months of 1921 which left Laurence O'Neill deeply bereft. The first was of his old mentor and friend in the Corporation, a man with a deep sense of social justice, Clr. Dr McWalter, M.A., B.L. In a tribute, Ald. W.T. Cosgrave expressed the views of probably most members when he observed: 'The City has lost a brilliant son, the Corporation a gifted colleague, the medical profession an able and generous practitioner, and we have lost a friend.[31]' The second death was even more deeply felt by Laurence O'Neill, and widely felt not only in Dublin but in many parts of the country, that of Dr William Walsh, Archbishop of Dublin.

The Corporation assembled in a special meeting on 13 April to record their deep regret at the death and the loss it entailed 'to the Church, the cause of education, and the welfare of our country generally'. Clr. Forrestal moved, and Clr. Thomas Foran seconded, a resolution authorising the Lord Mayor's unusual decision to close 'municipal services on Thursday, 14 instant, from the hour of 12.o'clock, noon, in order to afford an opportunity to staff to attend the funeral of the late Archbishop; and requesting the citizens to observe general mourning from 12.o'clock to 3.0 p.m.' The motion was put and carried.[32]

In the death of Archbishop Walsh, Laurence O'Neill felt he had lost a friend and a strong father-figure. Reflecting some years later, his expression of his loss extended to three typed pages. Another, with not dissimilar feelings was Eamon de Valera, who voiced his sense of deprivation in a revealing letter to the Lord Mayor. As he was unable to attend the funeral, he had asked Sean O'Ceallaig (Sceilg) to represent Dail Eireann and himself officially, and he was asking Mrs de Valera to be present. He asked O'Neill to take care of her 'as she would be rather shy'. He continued with a personal expression of his regard for the late archbishop:

> Although I hadn't met His Grace so very often, I felt for him something
> of the intimate personal affection of a son for a father. You can scarcely
> realise what confidence it gave to me, a novice, during the three or four
> years I have been in public life to feel that there was always one at hand

on whom I could rely for ripe counsel and wisdom in any hour of need.

Besides, his presence as a member of the hierarchy was always for us a surety that the enemy would not succeed in impinging upon the Christian kindness and goodness of heart which lays our bishops so open to the wiles of the English.

I am sad, as I am sure you are, and every other lover of our country. May God quickly raise to us such another champion.

He had not sent any message, he added, either to the Auxiliary Bishop, or to the Vicar-General. Anything he could say publicly would so poorly represent his feeling that he preferred to leave it unsaid. Perhaps his Lordship would be good enough to convey to them verbally an expression of his sorrow. As soon as possible he would call on them himself.[33]

From death tolls to stirrings for peace

The extent of the daily conflict and carnage during the first six months of 1921 was suggested by the weekly review from Dublin Castle on 1 April. In the previous week there had been 22 ambushes and 46 people killed (one more than on the previous week). Twenty-seven were killed by the military, and nineteen police were killed. Between January and June 1921, the number of republicans killed while in custody was estimated at 131, and people killed by indiscriminate firing amounted to 38, including 17 children.[34]

The bitterness of the struggle, with almost every death begetting retaliation, inevitably gave rise to desires for and moves towards a truce and peace. On 2 February 1921, the Lord Mayor received an unexpected *ballon d'essai* from General Macready congratulating him on his re-election, conveying 'a pleasant remembrance' of the occasion on which they had met, and wishing for him that during his term of office he might experience 'a return to peace and normal conditions in the City', and this, he added, was the wish, not only of himself, but of all the ranks in the military profession.[35] Around the same time, A.W. Cope, Assistant Under Secretary for Ireland, was charged by the British Government to explore unofficially lines of negotiation. One of the people he consulted was Lord Mayor O'Neill. Both men became friends and availed of their contacts to promote peace.

On-going events, nevertheless, appeared to offer little prospect of 'a return to peace and normal conditions'. On 25 May an attack by the IRA on the Dublin Custom House had serious consequences for both sides. The British Administration suffered the destruction of the files of two major taxing departments and all the records of the Local Government Board. The IRA had a number of casualties, together with some 100 members of the Dublin Brigade captured.[36]

On 14 June, however, de Valera informed Art O'Brien, in London, that the British were trying to get in touch, through intermediaries, and intended availing of General Smuts in that role. On the suggestion of Art O'Brien, Tom Casement (brother of Roger Casement) was delegated to contact Smuts. The latter expressed interest, and discussed the Irish situation with the Prime Minister and King George.[37] Casement returned to Dublin to report to de Valera, but was at a loss as to where he would find him. He happened to meet P. S. O'Hegarty who brought him to the Mansion House. O'Hegarty's subsequent account of what then happened reflected the atmosphere of the time.

He knocked at the door. There was no answer for a considerable time. 'Then Buckley (butler, and a distinctive presence in the Mansion House) opened the door about six inches', and O'Hegarty said: 'We want to see Mr de Valera'. Buckley responded: 'We don't know anything about Mr de Valera here' and he made to shut the door. Whereupon, O'Hegarty interjected: 'We are not detectives and it is very important that we see Mr de Valera. Tell the Lord Mayor.' Buckley went away, leaving them outside. 'Then Alderman O'Neill came and I explained. He brought us to Mr de Valera and I introduced Tom and left them together.'[38]

On 22 June, King George visited Ireland for the formal opening of the Northern Parliament. His speech on the occasion proved significant. He had discussed its tenor with Smuts and revised his original text. Towards the conclusion of the address, in Belfast on 22 June, he declared:

> I speak with a full heart when I pray that my coming to
> Ireland today may prove to be the first step towards the end of
> strife among her people, whatever the race or creed.[39]

It proved a definite first step. On 24 June, Lloyd George invited President de Valera to a conference, stating that the British Government were deeply anxious that, so far as they could assure it, the King's appeal for reconciliation in Ireland should not have been made in vain.[40]

De Valera replied four days later that he was in consultation 'with such of the principal representatives of our nation as are available'. He desired lasting peace between the two islands, but it depended on Ireland's essential unity being recognised and the principle of national self-determination. Before replying more fully, he was seeking a conference 'with certain representatives of the political minority in this country'.[41]

That same day he sent an invitation to five representative Unionists to meet him at the Mansion House on Monday, 4 July. The five were: Sir James Craig (prime minister in the Belfast parliament), the Earl of Midleton, Sir Maurice Dockrell, Sir Robert H. Woods, and Mr Andrew Jameson. Craig refused the invitation, the others accepted. On 4 July, American Independence Day, the American flag and the Dublin City flag fluttered above the Mansion House as the assembled crowds cheered the arrival of de Valera, Griffith, and each of the Unionists. The Lord Mayor welcomed them at the portals of the Mansion House. The *Irish Times* followed events in some detail. 'The drawing-room, the scene of many notable conferences, including that called to resist conscription, is just beyond the entrance hall. A small round table was placed in the centre of the spacious apartment, six chairs were placed around it – the same table, the same chairs, even the same inkbottle as were used in the Anti-Conscription Conference.' While the members of the Conference were sitting in the drawing-room, the Lord Mayor was busy receiving many callers, including American visitors. The crowd outside thinned but swelled again around 2.0 p.m., expecting to see the break for lunch. The Unionists came out, shook hands with the Lord Mayor, and were cheered by the crowd. De Valera and Griffith stayed in the Mansion House where they were photographed and filmed with the Lord Mayor. The latter delivered a brief, official report on the talks to the crowd, informing them that the Conference would resume on Friday.[42]

In the context of later events, this Conference was a small, preparatory affair, but to O'Neill at the time it was a major historical occasion. He said as much to the Corporation at their meeting that evening: - 'I am breaking no confidence in telling you that during the past three or four hours in the drawing-room close by, one of the most delicate and most momentous conferences that has ever been held in this country has taken place – I have great hopes that a great deal of good will come out of this.'[43]

The next day, General Smuts arrived at Kingstown (Dun Laoghaire). A small army of press men awaited him. There was no sign of him and the rumour circulated that he was not on board. In fact, he remained on the boat until the Lord Mayor and other prominent citizens arrived to greet him. The Lord Mayor held a consultation with him before they travelled by motor car to the Mansion House, where the General was the Lord Mayor's guest. Subsequently, as planned, Smuts met with de Valera and Griffith, and had conversation with other members of Sinn Féin.[44]

A Truce

On 8 July, the Conference with the Southern Unionists was resumed. Again, a large crowd greeted the participants, and an element of hope and expectancy was evident. During the negotiations, the crowd joined in the rosary and other prayers for the success of the peace negotiations.[45] In the wake of the Conference, news of a truce and the end of the curfew was announced on 11 July. General Macready faced de Valera across the table in the Mansion House. The principles governing the truce were agreed and liaison officers were appointed to work out the details. The *Dublin Evening Mail* of 9 July commented on the widespread joy at the news of a truce and negotiation. General Macready found himself cheered by the Dublin crowd as he entered the Mansion House.

The *London Morning Post*, however, viewed the developments with a jaundiced eye. It pointed out that in the eleven days since the Prime Minister's letter to de Valera there had been in Ireland – '50 murders, 13 ambushes, 32 residences burned, 21 unsuccessful attacks on police, 36 police and military wounded, and 5 attacks on trains'. These outrages, the paper suggested, may be planned from outside Ireland. 'De Valera himself is not an Irishman.' The author of the article was sure that the Government had proof in their possession 'of the complicity of de Valera in the murders and outrages'. A more balanced and neutral observation occurred elsewhere in the *Morning Post* in the column on "Dublin Day by Day". It noted that 'the heatwave continues to hold the city in its merciless grip', but with 'the Truce feeling' in the air 'its electrical effects are perceptible in the faces of city men and women… Everyone looks brighter and cheerier than they have looked for many a long day in Dublin'.[46]

While events of major significance were taking place in his official residence, and to which he was host, Alderman O'Neill was also dealing with industrial relations problems. At the Corporation meeting on 4 July, Ald. William O'Brien moved, and Clr. Michael Moran seconded, that 'This Council expresses appreciation of the action of the Rt. Hon. the Lord Mayor during the past few days in connection with the threatened dispute in the drapery trade'.[47] A week later, on Monday 11 July, when the Municipal Council was considering the Paving Committee Report, Alderman O'Neill twice left the meeting, vacating the chair to Ald. Cosgrave, T.D.[48] The 11 July was Truce Day marked by celebration and many demands on the Lord Mayor. There were 'many bonfires, and songs and dances in the street' and people wished to see him. It is not unlikely, moreover, that he was involved in preparations for the departure of the Irish negotiation party for London.

With the Negotiation Party in London

Next evening, 12 July, the *Dublin Evening Mail* carried the heading: 'Mr de Valera leaves for London. Count Plunkett and the Lord Mayor accompany Peace Delegates. Michael Collins remains in Dublin'. It was mentioned that there were also several ladies in the party and a secretarial staff. The party left from Kingstown. Mr de Valera made the journey to the boat in the Lord Mayor's open touring car from his home in Blackrock, and Mr Griffith was also in the car. The latter had come earlier to the Mansion House from his home in Clontarf, where he took a seat in Alderman O'Neill's car, and thence to Blackrock. The delegates were said to have been chosen after long deliberation, and to represent different sections of the Sinn Féin organisation.

On 13 July the Irish party settled in at the Grosvenor Hotel in London. Crowds gathered to welcome them and to see de Valera, but he stayed elsewhere with Dr and Mrs Farnan. The de Valera papers carry a photograph of the party taken in the London hotel, which appeared in a French publication, L'Illustration.[49] The front row depicts 'Eamon de Valera and Arthur Griffith; back row, left to right, Count Plunkett, Mr Childers, the Lord Mayor of Dublin, Mrs Farnan, Miss O'Brennan, Robert Barton, and Miss O'Connell (de Valera's secretary). At the Grosvenor Hotel there awaited them messages from Australia, the United States, New Zealand, Isle of Man, and Scotland, expressing support and wishing them success.[50]

On 14 July 1921, de Valera was accompanied to Downing Street by Art O'Brien of the Irish Determination League in London, and Robert Barton. There, de Valera met Lloyd George alone at 4.30 p.m., and again next morning 15 July at 10.0 a.m., while the others waited in an anti-room.[51] On 15 July, de Valera left Downing Street for the day at 1.0 p.m. and was cheered by supporters outside.[52] The negotiators were to meet again on Monday. On 16 July, the editorial in the *Dublin Evening Mail* observed that there were no obvious grounds for optimism being exhibited beyond the fact that negotiations had not broken down, as it was feared they might at the first meeting on some question of status. What role did Alderman Laurence O'Neill perform? It seems to have been a mixture of public relations and catering for the welfare of all the members of the party. The *Star's* political correspondent indicated something of that nature:

> I had a word or two with Mr Larry O'Neill, the picturesque Lord Mayor of Dublin. He is "the good fellow" of the party, and is in charge of all the members of the delegation., 'I am amazed', he said, 'to find every shade of political opinion in England is anxious for a settlement. We had not been led to believe in Dublin that you were all for peace. And don't forget, we in Ireland are for peace too'.[53]

At 10 o'clock on Sunday morning, 17 July, de Valera and the Catholic members of the Irish delegation attended High Mass at St George's Cathedral, Southwark, where the body of Terence MacSwiney had been received. The Church of Ireland members attended Matins at St Paul's Cathedral. In the afternoon, President de Valera and his party motored out of London, stopping en-route at St. Anthony's Hospital, Sutton, where the Lord Mayor of Dublin's son was resident surgeon. They received an enthusiastic reception from the staff, and were entertained to tea.[54] On another occasion, they visited Nazareth House, Hammersmith, where Archbishop Mannix had resided during the whole of his stay in London, and were received by the Mother General and the nuns. Then, after lunch at the Grosvenor Hotel, the President visited Oxford by motor car.[55] The delegation received numerous letters inviting them to houses and meals. But they refused nearly all of them because of the pressure of business, the difficulty of planning free time, and so on.[56]

On 19 July, de Valera and Lloyd George met with Sir James Craig, who remained immoveable on partition. Two days later, de Valera had his final meeting with the British Prime Minister. The Irish party, 'in good humour', prepared to return home. A press editorial on 22 July observed that de Valera returned to Ireland with the final offer from the British Government of a basis on which a conference to settle the details might be held. He was to discuss it with his colleagues, but it seemed clear that the basis for a formal conference had not yet been found.[57] The Irish party were scheduled to arrive at Kingstown at 5.30 p.m. on 23 July, and from there travel to the Mansion House where they would be entertained. After their twelve days absence, large crowds waited at the Mansion House to welcome them home. After they had entered, there was an insistent demand for re-appearance and a speech. 'Mr de Valera, the Lord Mayor, Ald. Cosgrave, and Mr Griffith appeared at the door of the Mansion House, and de Valera gave a brief address, during which he remarked soberly that 'in Ireland for the last few years the Irish people have learned the lesson that it is by acts not talk that a nation will achieve its freedom'.[58]

During the next week, Alderman O'Neill was host to de Valera as he consulted colleagues, the Sinn Féin organisation, and the Dail Eireann cabinet. On 29 July conflicting views were emerging as to the progress of the deliberations.[59] On 6 August, all interned and imprisoned members of the Dail were released. On 16 August the Second Dail assembled in the Round Room of the Mansion House. After two public sessions and a private session, the terms offered by Lloyd George were rejected. The Prime Minister, on being informed, requested de Valera and his colleagues to meet him to see how far the Government's considerations could be reconciled with Sinn Féin's aspirations.[60] After communications over and back, Dail Eireann agreed to participate in such a conference and, on 14 September, chose five delegates to negotiate with the British Government. Those appointed were Arthur Griffith, Michael Collins, Robert Barton, E.J. Duggan, and G. Gavan-Duffy. On 11 October, the delegates arrived in Downing Street. Scenes of enthusiasm greeted their arrival at no. 10. People sang hymns and songs, and many knelt as the rosary was recited. The intensity of feeling was palpable.[61]

The City's affairs

The incidence of violence and murder in the first six months of 1921 and the excitement and expectation thereafter, occupied the attention of the press. Corporation business received little publicity. Yet important decisions were taken. A special committee was established to investigate the problem of unemployment and to take steps to secure funds to alleviate the problem.[62] On 16 March, the Lord Mayor appointed Ald. Mrs Kathleen Clarke to be his deputy as president of the Court of Conscience for the year.[63] The court dealt with smaller claims. The appointment was a further example of O'Neill's support for women in public life. In May, the Municipal Council, looking ahead to winter, set up a committee to plan the city's coal supply and to examine if coal could be purchased in the USA or on the Continent;[64] this was in accordance with the policy of the Local Government Department of Dail Eireann which issued orders against the purchase of British goods – from British made ploughs to soap and margarine. At a busy meeting on 6 June, the emphasis was on examining the best means to secure a pure supply of milk at a reasonable price for the citizens, while condolence was expressed on the death of Lady Gilbert.[65] In her will she handed over to the Corporation the books, manuscripts, and note books of her distinguished husband and scholar, Sir John Gilbert, and arranged that the Corporation might negotiate for the purchase of his pictures and engravings. During August an unexpected occurrence threatened city business and the enjoyment of the citizens. Once again the Dublin Horse Show was involved.

The Lord Mayor copes with delicate situations

With the truce in operation, some 25,000 visitors were expected for that year's Horse Show. The Dublin hotels and shop-keepers looked forward to a busy week after the lean years, when raids from the Black and Tans disturbed events and frightened people. Then, consternation, as an order was issued that the Show was not to take place, and any attempt to do so would be broken up by force. The ultimatum came not from British military, but from a section of the IRA. Mr Bohan, the secretary of the Royal Dublin Society, together with a prominent member of the Society, called to the Mansion House in distress. The Lord Mayor promised to do what he could to help. He contacted

President de Valera and Arthur Griffith. Both were against the ultimatum 'but had to be very careful not to give offence to the army'. O'Neill suggested that a short statement should be issued, with which the Show Committee could comply and which would not compromise de Valera or Griffith with their followers. The Lord Mayor drew up a statement, which both men signed, and which he witnessed. It announced the conditions under which the Dublin Horse Show of August 1921 would be held:

1. No bunting of any description except the Society's official flag

2. No ceremony or reception of the Lord Lieutenant

3. No bands, no anthem of any description

4. The only music, Irish pipers in the main hall.

The Show went ahead. The Lord Mayor visited, in company with Arthur Griffith, and both were satisfied that the conditions were carried out. Concluding his recollection of the occasion, O'Neill observed – 'Of the many thousands, few took any interest as to what band played, or flag floated'.[66]

Towards the end of the month, he was faced with another delicate situation. In keeping with the spirit of the truce, his own vision of the mayoralty, and irrespective of any hostile views from the IRA and the more extreme supporters of Sinn Féin, he hosted in the Mansion House the "Carnation Carnival Fete on behalf of the friends of the Comrades of the Great War". Fortunately, it passed off quietly and successfully. So much so that Lord Aberdeen wrote to congratulate the Lord Mayor on 31 August. 'The opening proceedings as reported in Irish papers were evidently of a highly gratifying and also most significant character; thus, for example, the fact that your Lordship was introduced by Lord Holmpatrick, D.S.O., the esteemed head of a well-known family, always identified with unionist doctrines, was in itself a most favourable feature.

> Your Lordship's own address (if I may be allowed to express
> an opinion) was a masterpiece; because, while in no way ignoring
> or glossing over your own convictions as to affairs, you succeeded
> in avoiding any expression that could cause a jar in the varied
> assemblage which you were addressing.

'That this was the case', he continued, 'is sufficiently indicated by the fact that Lady Arnott, D.B.E (who would necessarily be regarded as speaking in a representative sense) alluded to your oration as "magnificent".'[67]

Aberdeen concluded with a mild warning, aware of the uncertain negotiations between de Valera and Lloyd George and of the extreme attitudes of some republicans. The fact that he made it to O'Neill indicated that he saw him as in a position to pass on his view to key figures in Sinn Féin. 'One of the arguments in favour of that peace which we all so ardently desire', he said, would consist in Ireland, given control of her own destinies, aiming steadfastly at the most friendly relations with Britain. This was important not only from the commercial point of view, but also so that Irish statesmen would not be entangled with any power hostile to Britain. Should this last occur, it would be an 'immediate occasion for Britain to take such defensive measures as Ireland would always most ardently wish to avoid'.[68]

On 5 September, the Lord Mayor, following a long tradition, proposed, and Ald. Cosgrave seconded, at a special meeting of the Municipal Council, that the Council present an address of congratulations to his Grace, the Most Rev. Dr Byrne, on his appointment as Archbishop of Dublin. The motion was put and carried.[69] A week later, as has been seen, after much interchange between Lloyd George and de Valera, the Dail agreed to enter into conference with the British Government, and on 11 October the Irish delegation arrived at Downing Street.

Towards a Treaty

From that date the negotiations seemed to go on interminably. By 31 October, the *Dublin Evening Mail* was expressing 'grave fears regarding the possibility of breakdown'. The delegates returned to Dublin at regular intervals to report to the cabinet. The conference continued into November despite violence against Catholics in Belfast. At the start of December there was an atmosphere of gloom in Dublin about the conference, and then on 6 December came the news that an agreement had been reached, which each delegation had agreed to recommend to their respective parliaments. As word of the terms circulated, there was, according to the Dublin evening press, 'happiness abroad'.[70] On 8 December, amidst cheering crowds at the Mansion House, the delegates arrived separately and were met in the vestibule by the Lord Mayor.[71]

Laurence O'Neill on negotiations, the Treaty, and the split

O'Neill was friendly with key members on both sides in the eventual split over the treaty, and had watched the impact of the protracted negotiations on members of the Irish delegation. Some nine years afterwards he put some of his memories on paper. Like many historical accounts written years afterwards, happenings sometimes get telescoped in memory, and when not speaking from personal experience his account is dependent on what he learnt from newspapers or/and witnesses, but when relating his own personal experience of people and events his cameos add insight and poignancy to the tragic denouement of four years of united endeavour.

'There was one thing certain. The people wanted no more blood-shed, no more war... Many consultations took place between de Valera and his lieutenants, all taking place in the Mansion House. Many letters passed between de Valera and Lloyd George. Poor Dev., between the devil and the deep. George on the one side, the extremists on the other. He took refuge in tumbling the English language upside down, inside out, to coin some phrase which would satisfy himself to meet George on the plain of an "Irish Republic". George was willing to negotiate on anything and everything except an "independent" Ireland. De Valera in desperation sent a letter by special messenger to George, who was staying at Inverness, Scotland, in which he stated negotiations must be on the lines of an "independent" constitution. George, on receipt of this letter, wired Cope, Under-Secretary in Dublin Castle, who had been taking a very active part towards a settlement for some time.' Lloyd George held over de Valera's letter, and meantime instructed Cope 'to use all the influence he could secure on de Valera to either withdraw or modify his letter, otherwise all negotiations must cease'.

'Cope, whom I had met on many occasions, motored down very late at night, accompanied by the late Fr John O'Reilly, to my home at Portmarnock. He detailed George's message, and pleaded with me to see de Valera and use my influence with him to withdraw or modify his letter. A very large and delicate request. I saw de Valera next morning as he was passing into his office in the Mansion House, and told him of Cope's visit. That day, at a great gathering of all the essential parts of the republican movement, every room in the Mansion House being occupied, de Valera's letter to Lloyd George was modified, and the way paved for the plenipotentiaries to proceed to London... The opinion of the Dail Eireann Cabinet was that de Valera should stay at home.'

'For months the plenipotentiaries were coming from and going to London. As usual, all meetings were in the Mansion House. On many occasions, coming from the mail-boat, Collins had breakfast with me; and from "the boy" he was when going to London first, he was gradually becoming a man of the world, losing that boyishness and good humour which had always characterised him. As the long weary months of negotiation were beginning to tell, Collins on more than one occasion complained bitterly to me that the plenipotentiaries could not come to a decision on trivial points until, as he put it, "like a pack of school-boys we brought them back to the Executive to be torn asunder". One could plainly see the growing spirit of unrest in Collins, and I felt that very soon he would assert himself.'

Signing the Treaty

'The night came, which had turned into morning, when George and his colleagues fired at the head of the plenipotentiaries – "the threat of immediate and terrible war, and that a gun-boat was in readiness to leave for Belfast with the news, Treaty on or off". Why a gun-boat? Why Belfast (bluff)? At an early hour in the morning, after hours of pressure, the plenipotentiaries signed the "Treaty". Griffith and Collins well knowing the risks they were running personally and to their reputations, but as Collins stated – "The Treaty was signed as a stepping-stone to greater freedom".'

'That morning (6 December), James MacMahon, the Under Secretary, phoned me that a treaty had been signed, but no particulars were to hand. There was no enthusiasm in the city, no flags, no bells, everyone looked solemn instead of gay, a cloud appeared to have spread over the spirits of the people. All day callers came to the Mansion House for news. De Valera was away in the country reviewing Volunteers, but he returned that evening to preside over a lecture given by Count Plunkett on Dante. I met him previous to going to the lecture. He said: "Surely they have not signed a treaty without taking it back to be dealt with by the cabinet; that was the solemn undertaking given by Griffith on behalf of the plenipotentiaries". At this early stage, before the plenipotentiaries had returned from London, men and women were taking sides. One man during the lecture, a technical official, created a scene by loudly shouting "Collins is a traitor". I was sitting besides de Valera and he seemed like a man in a dream, paying little attention to what was going on around him …'

'A meeting of the Executive was held on the return of the plenipotentiaries from London. What a change in a few days, no cheerful meetings, no handshakes, dead silence as they passed each other going in, and if the drawing-room could speak, what a story it would unfold of broken friendships. De Valera still hoped to pull a majority of the cabinet with him, seven in all: three had already signed for the Treaty, Griffith, Collins, Barton; three had declared against it, de Valera, Brugha, and Stack; and Cosgrave was wavering. De Valera hoped to have him on his side.'

'The memory of that night is as fresh before me, now as I write, now over nine years ago, as if it were but yesterday. The fierceness of their language could be heard outside. The pent up animosity of Brugha towards Collins was let loose. De Valera was pleading, and Cosgrave made many visits to the study, where the Lord Mayor of Cork (Donald O'Callaghan) and I were. Cosgrave was battling with his conscience, and speaking to himself – "I cannot leave Dev. He stood by me when others wanted me turned down. My oath to the Republic haunts me", and many other ejaculations. Never again do I wish to see a human being struggling so much between love and duty. He asked my advice when he was almost in despair. I said, "Willie, I am in a different position to you by being for the Treaty (and because) I have never taken an oath to be true to the Republic". And putting my hand on his shoulder, and knowing the deeply religious man he was, I said to him – "If I were you I would be guided entirely by prayer". All this time, the Lord Mayor of Cork was in the same position of doubt. Cosgrave went to the other side of the room, and came back in a few minutes looking very much relieved. He returned to the drawing-room and declared for the Treaty.'

'It is not my object in mentioning these facts,' O'Neill concluded, 'to pillory these men in any way, who were for or against the Treaty, but I am endeavouring to show the agony of mind they were passing through before determining their action.'[72]

A pleasing interlude

On 8 December, Laurence O'Neill had a welcome intermission in the form of a letter from General Bryan Mahon, now living at Mullaboden, Ballymore Eustace, County Kildare. 'How glad I am', he said, 'that a settlement has been arrived at, and I sincerely hope it may bring peace and prosperity to our country. There is no man, in my opinion, to whom Irishmen and Ireland, no matter what their politics or opinions are, owe a greater debt of gratitude than to yourself. You have had a most difficult and responsible position and have come through it all as an honourable and straightforward man and have proved yourself deserving of the respect of all.' He hoped to see O'Neill soon. He signed himself simply 'Bryan Mahon'.[73]

A winter of the spirit

On 13 December, Dail Eireann met, not in the Mansion House, but in University College Dublin, Earlsfort Terrace. It began a debate on the Anglo-Irish Treaty which was to rumble on until the Christmas Break. It was noted that Messrs Griffith and Collins arrived at the College looking very cheerful, while de Valera, in contrast, seemed exceedingly grave and preoccupied. The quality of the debate was of a poor school-boy standard at times. Overall, it was confused, stormy, with moments of good argument as well as of personalised, spitefully vitriolic point-scoring. It dragged on and on. A frustrated crowd gathered outside University College on 21 December shouting "Ratify, Ratify".[74] The following day, Mrs Jenny Wyse Power wrote to Sighle (Humphreys): 'Last evening at the Dail was so terrible that I had not the courage to go to-day...The sorrow here today is intense as all have now given up hope of uniting the country.' [75] That day, 22 December, on the motion of Michael Collins, the Dail adjourned to 3 January 1922.

Thus, Christmas 1921, and the close of the year, were characterised by divided families, as anxiety and fear in the face of "immediate and terrible war" if the Treaty was rejected, vied with loyalty to the Republic and bitterness and anger against those who betrayed it; and through it all, as Wyse Power remarked, there was an intense sorrow.

Notes

1   UCDA. De Valera papers. P.150/1418. De Valera-Ld.Mayor, 8 Jan. 1921. See J.A. Gaughan (ed.) *Memoirs of James G. Douglas,* p. 61

2   UCDA. Idem, P. 150/1418, 10 Jan. 1921

3   UCDA., idem, Ld. Mayor-de Valera, 14 Jan. 1921

4   Idem, de Valera-Ld. Mayor, 15 Jan. 1921

5   Idem, de Valera- Ld. Mayor, 27 Jan. 1921

6   Idem, P 150/1418. L.O'Neill-de Valera, 27 Jan. 1921

7   DCC. Mins. no. 95, p. 84

8   UCDA. Ms. P150/1418. de Valera-Ld. Mayor, 1 Feb. 1921

9   NLI. O'Neill Letters, Ms. 35,294/13. Abp. Dublin-Ld. Mayor, 1 Feb.1921

10 Idem, Logue-Ld.Mayor, 25 Jan. 1921

11 NLI. Mary Spring-Rice papers. Ms. 43,334/3, Correspondence N-O. L.O'Neill, Ld. Mayor- Spring-Rice, 19 Jan. 1921

12 *Revolutionary Woman. Kathleen Clarke, 1878-1972. An Autobiography,* p. 73

13 UCDA. Ms. P 150/1418. de Valera- Ld. Mayor, 11 Feb. 1921

14 Idem. Ms. P 150/1303. Ld. Mayor-de Valera, 15 Feb. 1921

15 Idem. Ms. P 150/1418. de Valera (through Cathleen O'Connell) – Sean (O'Hegarty in USA), 24 March 1921

16 NLI. O'Neill papers, Ms. 35,294/13. Logue-Ld.Mayor, 25 March 1921

17 UCDA. P 150/1303. C.F. France- Executive Commmittee, 30 March 1921

18 Idem. de Valera papers. Ms. P 150/1303. C.F. France- Ld Mayor O'Neill, 2 April 1921

19 Idem. Ms. P 150/1418. de Valera- Smith-Gordon, 6 April, 1921

20 ONFP. de Valera-Ld Mayor, 16 April 1921

21 J.A. Gaughan (ed.) *Memoirs of Senator James G. Douglas, Concerned Citizen,* p. 10. On the attitude of the U.S. State Department, see B. Whelan, op. cit., pp. 336-8

22 Idem, pp. 10-11

23 NLI. O'Neill papers. Ms. 35,294/15, no date. Sent from 'The Business Men's Club, Cincinnati, Ohio

24 Idem. Ms. 35, 294/13. Logue-Ld.Mayor, 15 June 1921

25 Gaughan. *Memoirs James Douglas,* p.11

26 DCC Mins. 7 March 1921, no.166, pp. 139-40

27 INL. O'Neill papers. Ms.35, 294/13. Dr Hallinan-Ld.Mayor, 12 March 1921

28 DCC. 14 March Mins. pp.140f.

29 ONFP. "Six Executions in Mountjoy"

30 DCC., Mins. 2 May, no.321, p. 236

31 DCC. Mins. meeting 9 Feb. 1921, no. 126, p. 102

32 Idem, Mins 13 April 1921, no. 293, p. 212, and no. 294

33 ONFP. Pages on Archbishop Walsh. Also partly cited in newspaper cutting of 14 April (*Freeman's Journal?*) in Archbishop Walsh papers, Dublin Diocesan Archives (DDA), de Valera-Bishop (Byrne?), April 1921, see T.J. Morrissey. *William J. Walsh, Archbishop of Dublin,* p. 352

34 Macardle, op. iam cit., p. 423

35 ONFP. Typed sheet sent from Headquarters, Park Gate, Dublin.

36 Macardle, op. cit., p. 424

37 Idem, p. 426

38 UCDA. de Valera papers. P.150/1451. Letter by O'Hegarty in *Irish Independent,* 21 Oct. 1942

39 Macardle, p. 427

40 Idem, p. 431

41 Idem, pp.432-33

42 *Irish Times,* 5 July 1921

43 Cit. idem

44 ONFP. Unionist Conference and Smuts arrival

45 *Dublin Evening Mail,* 8 July 1921

46 Both cited in *Dublin Evening Mail,* 9 July 1921

47 DCC. Mins. 4 July, no. 427, p. 312

48 Idem, 11 July, no.456, p.334; no.468, p.338

49 UCDA de Valera papers, extract from *L'Illustration* in summary volume, 23 July 1921, no. 4090, Ms. P.150/1472

50 UCDA. De Valera papers, P 150/1467

51 Idem, P. 150/ 1466

52 *Dublin Evening Mail,* 15 July 1921

53 Cit. idem, 16 July.

54 UCDA. de Valera papers, P 150/1466

55 Idem

56 NLI. Art O'Brien papers, Ms. 8425/7

57 *Dublin Evening Mail,* 22 July 1921

58 Idem, 23 July

59 Idem, 29 July

60 *Dublin Evening Mail,* 27 Aug. 1921

61 Idem, 11 Oct. 1921

62 DCC. Mins. no.92, pp.78 ff

63 Idem, no. 173, p.146

64 Idem, meeting 2 May, no. 322, p. 236

65 Idem, meeting 6 June, nos. 422, pp. 303-4; no. 374, p. 276; no. 377, p. 277.

66 ONFP. "The Dublin Horse Show, August 1921", 2 typed pages.

67 NLI. O'Neill papers. Aberdeen-Ld. Mayor, 31 Aug. 1921, Ms. 35,294/13

68 Idem

69 DCC. Mins. 5 Sept. 1921, no. 531, p. 392

70 *Dublin Evening Mail,* 6 Dec. 1921

71 Idem, 8 Dec. 1921

72 ONFP. "The Treaty", 5 typed pages.

73 NLI. O'Neill papers. Bryan Mahon-Ld.Mayor, 8 Dec. 1921, Ms. 35,294/1-19 (18).

74 *Dublin Evening Mail,* 21 Dec. 1921

75 UCDA. Mrs Wyse Power papers. Wyse Power-Sighle, 22 Dec. 1921, Ms. P 106/736

12.
1922 – 1923:
Years of Personal and National Upheaval

As the country waited with foreboding for the Dail Eireann debate on the Treaty to re-commence, Dublin Corporation had its first meeting of the New Year on 2 January. Among its concerns was the proliferation and influence of the cinema. There were more than twenty licensed picture houses in Dublin, apart from the theatres.[1] The councillors expressed disquiet at the possible dangers to moral and social values presented by foreign films. The discussion arose in the context of the appointment for the year, by the Public Health Committee of the Corporation, of honorary censors of cinematograph films. After a number of interventions, the Lord Mayor observed that they 'would be well advised to leave matters to the Public Health Committee'. The censors recommended by the Committee were approved.[2]

The harsh reality of the present re-asserted itself the following day with the re-opening of the Anglo-Irish Treaty debate. It ran from the third to the seventh of January. It is not clear that Alderman O'Neill attended the sessions. Conscious of the tensions and hostilities between the parties, and of his friends on both sides, he may have thought it more appropriate as "Lord Mayor of all the citizens" to stay away. 'Oh, the sorrow of it all', his colleague, Mrs Jenny Wyse Power, exclaimed. De Valera 'broke down and there was dead silence in the chamber'.[3] The vote on 7 January resulted in approval of the Treaty by 64 votes to 57. On 9 January, de Valera resigned as President of the Dail, and was then proposed for re-election by Mrs Clarke. Arthur Griffith was proposed by Treaty supporters, and was elected.[4]

Following the ratification of the Treaty, the British military set about taking down barricades around public buildings, and evacuating those they had occupied such as City Hall. On 14 January, the provisional government of the Irish Free State was elected; and two days later the members of the provisional government were received by the Lord Lieutenant at Dublin Castle. There was a formal transfer of power to Michael Collins as chairman of the government.

Those were tumultuous, consciously historic days for Lord Mayor O'Neill. The Irish provisional government met in the Mansion House to make arrangements for the taking over at Dublin Castle of the executive authority and government of the country. There were numerous callers in the forenoon of 16 January, the day of meeting with the Lord Lieutenant at the Castle.[5] Two days later, the provisional government met again in the Mansion House to plan its various departments. It ordered the continuance of existing services for the present. The continuous coming-and-going put huge pressure on the Lord Mayor and his office. In addition, it is likely that meals had to be provided for the members of the government. The chaotic state of things was conveyed by the *Dublin Evening Mail* of 19 January.

> The accommodation in the Mansion House is taxed to the fullest
> capacity, with the result that "nothing is anywhere", and when
> one meets a member of the government in the hall, or sends him
> a letter, nobody can tell where his office is to be found. The result
> is that callers are in a quandary

And there were numerous visitors worrying each member of the government. They came from the remotest districts in the country with 'every kind of paltry grievance'. The need for offices was obvious. On 20 January it was decided that the government would move to City Hall the following day. There, there was intense activity as the British military and many officials moved out. On 21 January, the City Hall was handed over to the Free State Provisional Government. Ald. Cosgrave, T.D., hoisted the national flag over the Municipal Buildings. At the Mansion House, meantime, there was a flurry of energetic action as the documents and correspondence relating to each ministry was moved from there to the City Hall.[6] A relieved O'Neill was rendered free to give all his attention to the work of the Corporation.

The Lord Mayor and Corporation affairs

A special meeting was held on 25 January to record sincere sorrow at the death of Pope Benedict XV. It was 'resolved to attend in state at the solemn requiem office and High Mass for his Holiness'.[7] Ald. W.T. Cosgrave chaired the meeting, in the absence of Ald. O'Neill. The latter was back as chairman five days later when a deputation from the Irish Volunteers of the Dublin City Brigade met the Municipal Council. Following the approval of the Treaty, those members of the IRA who opposed it reverted to the old title, Irish Volunteers. The deputation, led by Oscar Traynor, a friend of O'Neill, sought employment for its members. He pointed out that they had 500 unemployed members, and the Brigade sought that a percentage of their number be engaged every time the Corporation undertook work entailing the employment of large numbers of men. The Lord Mayor replied that the Council would meet the request as best they could. The request of the IRA was forwarded to all the employing committees of the Corporation.

The election for Lord Mayor of Dublin took place next day, 30 January. For some time there had been speculation that the treaty and anti-treaty parties would challenge for the position, and that O'Neill would be replaced.[8] In the event, there was a mixture of votes supporting the candidates, Laurence (Lorcan) O'Neill and Clr. Sean MacCaoilte.[9] O'Neill was proposed by Clr. Michael J. Moran, seconded by Ald. MacDonagh, T.D... Ald. Sean McGarry proposed that Clr. MacCaoilte be elected Mayor, and Clr. Mrs Wyse Power seconded that proposal. Their amendment was defeated by 41 votes to 27, and the motion in favour of O'Neill was then put and carried. The mixture of allegiances in the voting is indicated by the following examples. MacCaoilte was supported by Sean McGarry, Mrs Wyse Power, Ald Staines, but also by the unionist Ald. Sir A. Beattie, as well labour radical P.T. Daly, and Clrs. Raul and Doyle. For O'Neill were such as Ald. MacDonagh, M.J. Moran, Alfred Byrne, but also Mrs Kathleen Clarke, Hanna Sheehy-Skeffington, Clr. Briscoe, and Mrs Margaret McGarry, as well as the Labour members William O'Brien, and Tom Foran.[10]

Among the messages of congratulation O'Neill received was one from John Dillon, who wondered whether congratulations were appropriate in that he expected O'Neill would have 'a *very* troublesome year of office'. A serious understatement as it turned out. 'But', Dillon added, ' it must have been a source of very great gratification to you to find that after a desperately difficult year you still retained so firm a hold on the confidence of the citizens and your colleagues in the Corporation.'[11]

During February, public concern was generated by uncertainty about people's political allegiance and by the growing militancy of some groups. On 5 February, Cumann na mBan rejected the Treaty. They were alleged to have 'run wild' under the control of Mary MacSwiney[12] (the able sister of Terence MacSwiney), who was also reputed to have de Valera 'under her wing'.[13] That same date, Archbishop Byrne of Dublin, without references to political differences, and clearly wishing to avert civil violence, publicly welcomed the transfer of power and responsibility to Irishmen, who 'may be expected to take a real interest in solving the many problems that concern our people's well-being'. He exhorted his people to pray that peace might be established, and that their native rulers might govern them with wisdom, discretion and justice.[14]

Alderman O'Neill, meantime, was actively fulfilling his assurance to the deputation from the Dublin Brigade that the Corporation would respond as best it could. On 20 February it was agreed that in the case of works to be carried out by the Corporation's committees, 25 per cent of those employed would 'be taken from the unemployed list of the Dublin Brigade IRA', but 'only those who were members of the IRA before the truce', thereby excluding those who had flocked to the standard when the fighting was over.

Two days later, 22 February, the *Dublin Evening Mail* regretted to announce that the Lord Mayor was 'seriously ill with a sharp attack of influenza'. Perfect quiet was essential, but there was no immediate cause for alarm. His indisposition also meant that he missed his formal inauguration as Lord Mayor on 23 February. Ald. Cosgrave, acting as Lord Mayor, expressed on behalf of the Municipal Council their 'sincere sympathy with the Right Hon. the Lord Mayor in his serious illness'[15]. The "serious illness" was the prologue to a future more serious and protracted infirmity. The constant tension and outpouring of energy during troubled years - facilitating IRA and Sinn Féin leaders in the Mansion House while he walked a tight-rope with the Authorities – had weakened his robust constitution. On this occasion, he recovered quickly. He was back chairing the Municipal Council at its next meeting on 6 March, and he would do so during the succeeding agitated months.

Widespread disorder

During March, armed groups, especially those opposed to the treaty, took part in raids, burning property, and exercising intimidation. With a general election to ratify the treaty not taking place until June, and with the Government hesitating to intervene lest it precipitate a civil war, there was a hiatus in which ill-disciplined armed men had scope to rob and to terrorise. The propensity to violence was attributed by Bishop Patrick O'Donnell, later Cardinal, to 'the prestige of physical force used as a remedy in recent years'.[16] As if to underline this, a conference of the anti-treaty members of the IRA, at the end of March, established an executive council which aimed at preventing a free election. Writing from Dublin to his friend, Fr John Hagan, in Rome, on 11 April, Sean T. O'Ceallaigh reported that the state of affairs was much more chaotic than a month ago. The extreme stance taken by the new army executive committee contributed to this. 'They did not think even Brugha or Boland good enough fighting men to join them.' He added that Archbishop Byrne and Larry O'Neill were meeting the heads of both parties to find an arrangement to end the shooting and general disorder.[17]

Bishop and Lord Mayor intervene for peace

The intervention by the Archbishop and the Lord Mayor followed many appeals to both men to do what they could to bring about agreement between the leaders of both parties. The news of their intervention was greeted with widespread relief. On 13 April, O'Neill received appreciative support from (former General) Bryan Mahon, who congratulated him on having succeeded in getting the leaders of the rival parties to meet in conference. He hoped that something satisfactory might come of it. He had made several attempts to see O'Neill, but he was 'too busy these days'.[18]

Getting the leaders to agree to come together in conference made for busy days. O'Neill's personal links with both sides, joined to the archbishop's popularity and his being successor to Dr Walsh, made the conference possible. Their hopes may not have been sanguine, but they were determined to do all in their power to restore peace. The prospects for agreement were undermined by the occupation of the Four Courts on 14 April by IRA militants opposed to the treaty and to compromise.

The Archbishop, in his opening words, sought to create a climate of good will and serious intent. On behalf of the Lord Mayor, Mr Stephen O'Mara (an agreed facilitator), and himself, he thanked those present for attending. They had 'not been invited in the interests of any party or section'. For some time past, recurring incidents had aroused a grave anxiety that the nation was heading straight for civil war. The Lord Mayor and himself, looking on bloodshed amongst brothers as the ultimate calamity thought to stave off such a disaster by calling together the leaders of the people on both sides. 'It is a strange thing', Dr Byrne observed. 'that we should use the first instalment of anything like freedom to engage in fratricidal strife. Already hearts have been made sore enough by the British bullet and British bayonet without Irishmen bringing more sorrow to Irish homes.'[19]

It is difficult to establish the exact course of events. It would appear that Dr Byrne, O'Neill and O'Mara met separately with the different leaders, Collins and Griffith, and de Valera and Brugha. The negotiations ran from 19 to 29 April. O'Neill, O'Mara and Dr Byrne left no detailed account of the negotiations. The archbishop made some passing references in a small diary. On Wednesday, 19 April, his entry read: Mansion House, 3 o'clock'; the following Wednesday, 26 April, it was: 'Mansion House 11 o'clock; and on Friday, 28 April: 'Mansion House, Labour delegates, 11 o'clock.' The following day, Saturday 29 April, was much the same: '11 o'clock Mansion House'[20]. It, however, was the final and critical day.

Meantime, the Labour Party and Trade Union Congress had issued their own manifesto for peace and against "militarism". They called for a general strike on 24 April. At the Municipal Council meeting on 21 April, the Lord Mayor proposed, and Clr. Loughlin seconded, that they endorse the manifesto and, in accordance with its instruction, direct that all Corporation offices and works (except those which are absolutely necessary) be closed on Monday, 24 April. The motion was carried.[21] The general strike was widely supported across the Free State. Subsequently, it would seem that, as the negotiations were not going well, the Archbishop and the Lord Mayor met with a Labour delegation and invited them to join the conference. By the time Thomas Johnson, Cathal O'Shannon and William O'Brien attended the conference meeting on 29 April, it was clear to them that there was little likelihood of any agreement.[22] They were struck by the absolute distrust between the two sides. 'Neither side had any faith in the honour or honesty of its opponents, each believing the other was merely playing for position'. Both were focussed on the coming election.[23] Subsequent to the conference, de Valera issued a press statement in which he announced: 'Republicans maintain that there are rights which a minority may justly uphold, even by arms, against a majority'.[24] Such language provided a platform for the extreme militants who had taken over the republican movement.

It is likely that O'Neill, like Archbishop Byrne[25], had anticipated failure, but he remained open to further interventions to prevent bloodshed. He visited the Four Courts in company with his Corporation colleague, the trade-unionist William O'Brien, and met with the leaders, Rory O'Connor, Liam Mellows, Joe McKelvey, and perhaps Liam Lynch, Sean Moylan, Peadar O'Donnell, and Seamus Robinson,[26] but they could not be persuaded from the course they had taken.

On 9 May, the Municipal Council took the important step of approving a motion put by Ald. Cosgrave 'that it recognises and will conform to the lawful orders and decrees of the Provisional Government of Ireland'. The motion was passed by 44 votes to 11.[27]

Two days previously, Michael Collins, anxious to ensure a trouble-free general election, entered into an election pact with de Valera by which there would be a panel of Sinn Féin candidates drawn from the pro and anti-treaty parties in proportion to their strength in the existing Dail. The pact ensured a largely peaceful election, but was read, perhaps, as a sign of weakness on Collins's part.

From election to civil war

The general election was called for 16 June. Laurence O'Neill, being openly for the treaty, was pressed to go forward for election. Mrs Wyse Power, writing to her friend Sighle Humphreys on 6 June, observed that 'things have calmed down since the "pact", and Larry appears as a treaty card, and of course will head the poll'.[28] The election results gave 58 seats to pro-treaty Sinn Féin, 36 to anti-treaty Sinn Féin, 17 to Labour, 7 to the Farmers' Party, and 10 to Independents. With the assured support of Labour and the Farmers, the pro-treaty Sinn Féin had a clear majority to form a government. The victory, plus pressure from Britain, encouraged a reluctant Collins to move against the Four Courts garrison. The latter's provocative action in kidnapping the pro-treaty General J.J. "Ginger" O'Connell on 27 June proved the last straw. The following day the civil war began with the Provisional Government's attack on the Four Courts.

Lord Mayor O'Neill, nevertheless, was involved in two further attempts to bring about peace. He, Archbishop Byrne, and Cathal O'Shannon approached the Government, through Mr Cosgrave, now Minister for Local Government, with proposals for dealing with the anti-treaty forces. Their proposals were turned down.[29] The second attempt was as chairman of a woman's peace committee formed by Maud Gonne MacBride. She had been in Paris when she read on 29 June of the shelling of the Four Courts. Her son, Sean, was one of the garrison. She returned in haste to Dublin and sought out "that man of peace" at the Mansion House. O'Neill agreed to lead a deputation of women to both sides in an effort to win a truce. Next day, 30 June, the Four Courts went on fire and many of the garrison surrendered; others, however, continued the struggle in vantage points around the city. Maud Gonne determined to continue her efforts for peace. Her Peace Committee included well-known figures such as Mrs Despard, Hanna Sheehy-Skeffington, Nora Connolly, and Louie Bennet. The committee drew up peace proposals: immediate cessation of all hostilities so that the conflict could be settled at the July meeting of the Dail; during the truce all combatants should return home, and there should be no arrests. The Government, meantime, had insisted that the Irregulars, as they termed the anti-treaty militants, must lay down their arms.

The deputation from the Peace Committee, led by O'Neill, first approached the anti-treaty forces at their headquarters in Hamman Hotel. They dealt with Oscar Traynor, a friend of O'Neill, who accepted the proposals on behalf of the anti-treaty IRA, but refused to call on his followers to give up their arms. On visiting the Government representatives, Griffith, Collins and Cosgrave, they met with rejection. The surrender of arms was a basic requirement.[30] On 1 July, Cosgrave declared that the military action in progress against the Irregulars would be vigorously continued[31].

The anti-treaty forces were driven from the Hamman Hotel. The fatalities included Cathal Brugha. Once more Dublin's buildings were destroyed. To Alderman O'Neill it had to be doubly saddening to see former friends in mortal combat and his much loved city, which he had largely protected under British rule, now being destroyed by fellow Irishmen.

In two months, the civil war took the lives of more prominent members of Sinn Féin than had occurred in four years of armed struggle against British forces. Dublin Corporation chronicled the deaths of most of them with, by and large, its customary respect and concern for the relatives. The first to be mentioned was Cathal Brugha, on 17 July 1922.[32] Arthur Griffith followed, from a cerebral haemorrhage, on 12 August, and Harry Boland on the 21st.[33] Then, on the following day, 22 August, the unthinkable happened; Michael Collins was killed in an ambush in his native County Cork. The

Corporation, at a special meeting on 26 August, was still in shock as it put and carried:

> That we the Municipal Council of the City of Dublin, in special meeting
> assembled, place on record an expression of our deep sense of horror
> and grief on the untimely and tragic death of General Michael Collins T.D.,
> Commander-in-Chief of the National Army, and of the irreparable loss
> which it entails to the Irish Nation, and we tender our heartfelt sympathy
> and condolence to his relatives, and to his colleagues in the Government
> and Army, in their sad bereavement.[34]

The grief and loss experienced by Ald. O'Neill was to some degree alleviated by the appointment of his friend and colleague, Ald. William T. Cosgrave, as chairman of the Provisional Government.

The new Dail. O'Neill and inappropriate procedures

On 9 September, the third Dail assembled as a constituent assembly. O'Neill was among the deputies who elected Cosgrave as president of the Provisional Government. In the early sessions of the third Dail, it is evident that there were uncertainties about proper procedures. O'Neill, with his long experience of procedures at meetings, raised three questions during the first meeting. On the election of Ceann Comhairle or Speaker, the Clerk of the Dail took the proposal of Professor Michael Hayes for Ceann Comhairle. O'Neill intervened: 'I think the proper procedure is to elect a temporary chairman for the time being, and then put a motion… for the election of a Speaker, consequently I beg to move'- he was cut off by the Clerk of the Dail stating 'I cannot take any amendment on this. It is only a proposal that Professor Hayes be made Ceann Comhairle. It is proposed by Mr Blythe and seconded by Mr Hogan. No opposition ? I therefore declare… Mr Ginnell interjected: 'You have not waited for (another) nomination'. At this stage, the chair was taken by Professor Michael Hayes.[35]

   With reference to the appointment of members to the Standing Orders Committee, O'Neill, with others, queried the absence of Independent deputies from the committee. Once again, objections were brushed aside[36]. Following the election of W.T. Cosgrave as President, he proceeded to nominate his ministers. The first nominated was Mr Desmond Fitzgerald as Minister for Foreign Affairs. Mr Gavan Duffy then sought assurance that the Foreign Affairs of the Irish Free State would be taken seriously and not be swallowed up in Britain. O'Neill, probably reflecting the confusion of many deputies, queried: 'With all respect, I say a great many knotty points have been raised here today, which I cannot follow. Has the President the power to appoint his own ministry, or is it within the power of the Dail to appoint his ministry?' The Ceann Comhairle responded: 'The President nominates his ministry for the approval of the Dail'. O'Neill then asked: 'If the Dail does not sanction the nominations of the President, where do we stand?' The Ceann Comhairle: 'That will be a matter for the President himself. Is not that right?' The President replied – 'Yes'. At that, the Ceann Comhairle declared: 'I take it the Dail approves the appointment of Mr Desmond Fitzgerald. Approved.'[37]

A Serious and Protracted Illness

There is no record of any further questions or interventions from Mr O'Neill. In fact, shortly after the 9 September, his career as a member of the Dail effectively came to an end. He experienced a serious break-down in health, a massive "burn out" marked by physical and psychological exhaustion. His efforts to keep his office above the struggle and remain courteous and available to all sides, while the Mansion House was frequently used by Collins and de Valera, and raided by the Black and Tans and other Government forces, left him, as the *Irish Times* observed, almost a wreck in health when the Treaty was signed.[38] Thereafter, there were the efforts to prevent civil war, the repugnance to him of the bitterness between friends and of the destruction of his city, and the shock and pain of his wife and life-long supporter being laid low by a malady from which she was unlikely to recover. It all proved too much for an exhausted mind and body.

His secretary, Mary O'Sullivan, indicated the seriousness of his condition in a letter to the Town Clerk, which was read at the City Council meeting of 27 November 1922. She announced that she had had a letter from 'Miss O'Neill', the Lord Mayor's daughter, who was 'away with the Lord Mayor', requesting her 'to convey her father's regrets to his colleagues on the Council at not being able to be with them owing to ill-health'. She regretted 'to have to inform the Council

> that his Lordship is still seriously ill, and far from well, and the
> doctor under whose care he is at present, as well as his own
> medical adviser in Dublin, think it absolutely essential that he
> should remain away for some time longer, as his health is
> completely broken down.[39]

From the letter, it would appear that O'Neill was under special medical care in Britain. The Council was contacted through his secretary, hence no address was provided as to his whereabouts. The reference to the doctor 'under whose care he is at present', as distinct from his Dublin doctor, suggests a foreign location, perhaps a specialist recommended by his son who was, as noted, a physician in England.

By May 1923 Lord Mayor O'Neill was back in Ireland, but not yet at work. On 14 May he informed the Town Clerk that he had hoped to be at that day's meeting, but he regretted that, acting under doctor's orders, he would not be able to attend for the present. He asked him to kindly convey to the members of the Council his gratitude to them for their forbearance during the past six months.[40] Almost four more months were to pass before he returned to chair the Council.

Prisoners and Corporation at odds with Government

During O'Neill's long absence, different colleagues acted in his place, most frequently his long-time friend, Ald. Alfred Byrne. In that time, the harvest of death and fratricidal strife continued. Property was wilfully destroyed, people were shot in action or accidentally or in reprisal. The plight of prisoners became once more a live issue. Already on 17 July 1922, Lord Mayor O'Neill had seconded a motion by Mrs Sheehy-Skeffington that 'prisoners taken recently in action be treated as prisoners of war'. The motion was carried by 24 votes to 16.[41] Later, during O'Neill's illness, the Council set up a committee to inquire into the general treatment of prisoners, sought permission to visit prisons, and complained of ill-treatment of prisoners.[42] President Cosgrave assured Ald. Byrne by phone that while the Government would not permit the visitation of prisons, he could assure the Council that there was no ill-treatment of prisoners but that there was overcrowding due to the very large number of prisoners but that was not the fault of the Government.[43] The issue of the prisoners continued to excite the Council into 1923 and gave rise to strained relations between it and the Government. In the past, the Council perceived itself as speaking for the Irish people in supporting prisoners held by an alien power, now it was a local assembly protesting against the lawfully elected Government of the country on behalf of rebels who had taken up arms against that Government.

Not surprisingly, Government ministers fighting a vicious civil war, and endeavouring to establish law and order and economic survival, displayed impatience at times with the Council. Thus, early in 1923, the Minister for Finance, Earnán de Blaghad, and General Richard Mulcahy sent a letter to the Corporation directing that no monies should be paid to the dependants of Corporation employees then in military custody. The Council had earlier decided to give such dependants half-pay. Following the letter, the previous decision was rescinded by 33 votes to 17 against[44]. By the end of May fears for the future of the Corporation were being felt. On 28 May, the Municipal Council passed a resolution expressing its resentment at recent suggestions that it be abolished. Such a view was 'unwarrantable, unjustifiable and reactionary'. Nevertheless, such suggestions continued to be made.[45] The Corporation had diminished in importance.

Public attention was focussed increasingly on T.Ds rather than Councillors, and the business and unionist communities remained sharply critical.

End of civil war. General Election 1923

During May 1923, the civil war came to an end. The Irregulars dumped their arms. De Valera's self-esteem was a temporary victim of the savage struggle.[46]

In the turmoil of the war, there had been no election in 1923 for Lord Mayor. Alderman O'Neill was seen as continuing in office. A general election, however, was called while he was indisposed and unable to contest it. As a consequence, after the election on 23 August 1923, he was no longer a member of the Dail. The election result gave the Government party, Cumann na nGaedheal, 63 seats, Labour 14, the Farmers 15, Independents and others 17. The Republican side, despite the civil war defeat, obtained 44 seats. Support for them was to grow in proportion to dissatisfaction with the Government.

O'Neill's return to office. Saluting John McCormack

During the summer, Laurence O'Neill's general health and self-confidence improved to the point that he determined to return to office in time for one of the most pleasing actions of 1923, the conferring of the Freedom of Dublin on the renowned Irish tenor, John McCormack, early in September.

The press of the day noted that in the Oak Room of the Mansion House, at mid-day on 6 September, 1923, all present stood and applauded 'while Mr and Mrs McCormack with the Lord Mayor entered the hall'. A little daughter of Ald. A. Byrne presented Mrs McCormack with a bouquet of carnations. Ald. O'Neill said they had come together to pay the greatest compliment that public representatives could bestow on John McCormack. There was no need to state the reasons why his colleagues had decided to confer the freedom of the city on Mr McCormack. Feeling frail to the point of not exercising his natural eloquence, Ald. O'Neill then announced: 'Ladies and Gentlemen, this is my first appearance for some time, but I felt it would be ungracious of me if I did not give my small testimony to what John McCormack has done for Ireland'. He called on Ald. Byrne, 'who had been a noble friend to him during the past eighteen months'. Ald Byrne welcomed the Lord Mayor and expressed his pleasure and that of the citizens on his return. He praised Mr McCormack's energy in raising £50,000, in a series of concerts, for the sufferers of the recent wars in Ireland. He spoke of his elevation of the name of Ireland in the theatrical world, and that he had killed 'the stage Irishman' by refusing to go on the same platform where such was played. His would be the first name on the roll of the city in its new freedom. Having signed the roll, Mr McCormack expressed his appreciation that 'a free Dublin in a free Ireland' had made him 'a free man', and he gratefully acknowledged Dublin's support of him down through the years.[47]

Political prisoners and criticism of the Government

It was a gentle and auspicious occasion for O'Neill's return. Other Municipal Council occasions were to be contentious. He took several weeks to regain his former confidence and control. The question of political prisoners became a persistent issue. On 24 September, a motion was passed calling for the release of all prisoners detained for political offences. In October leave was sought for representatives to visit certain Dublin prisons. On 29 October, the Lord Mayor read to the Council General Mulcahy's refusal of permission; a response that evoked the angry comment that they were being refused 'a right accorded to them even during the Black and Tan regime'.[48]

The influence of anti-treaty members of the Council was evident in many of the resolutions put forward. The reception the resolutions received from the Council as a whole, however, indicated a growing alienation from the Government. The trend continued in November when some anti-treaty members moved 'the release of Mr de Valera and all imprisoned or interned Republican deputies as the first step to national unity, peace and prosperity'.[49] Even more provocatively, the Council sought to apply to the Dail a privilege pertaining under British rule, namely a right of appeal to the Bar of the House of Commons. The appeal in this instance for the release of the political prisoners, was passed unanimously. Not surprisingly, Lord Mayor O'Neill, on 3 December, read to the Council a letter from the Ceann Comhairle of Dail Eireann, dated 20 November, which announced that there was 'no procedure at present by which petitions can be presented to the Dail'.[50]

In October and November there was also criticism of the Government on other issues. The Council protested not only against the Government's reduction of the old age pension ; but also protested 'in the strongest possible manner' against any change that would reduce the number of members in the Municipal Council, and held 'that the present method of area representation' was the only way in which to give all sections of the citizens fair representation. A copy of the resolution was to be sent to the General Council of County Councils for support at their annual meeting'.[51] To President Cosgrave, so long a proud member of the Corporation, the hostility of the Municipal Council must have been difficult to accept with equanimity.

On 15 October, the Council had expressed sympathy with the family of republican activist, Noel Lemass, whose body had been found in the Dublin Mountains. A motion was passed nominating the Lord Mayor and the Law Agent to represent the Council at the inquest 'and to assist in every possible manner to discover and punish the murderers'.[52] It is unlikely that O'Neill attended the inquest, but he may have sent a representative. The still fragile state of his health and his need to nurse his energy was indicated by his absence from the funerals of Philip Cosgrave, brother of the President, and of the greatly esteemed trade union leader, Senator Thomas McPartlin, whose burials also took place in October.[53] A month later, however, O'Neill may have been able to attend the funeral of a long-time colleague, Ald. Sir Andrew Beattie, concerning whom he moved the vote of sympathy at the Council meeting of 26 November. Around this time he began to noticeably exert his authority at Council meetings.

Renewed energy

On 29 November, 1923, on the occasion of the report of the Electricity and Public Lighting Committee, there was a recommendation for revised rates of pay for two types of employees. When Clr. Raul, who was strongly anti-treaty and had moved a number of motions critical of the Government, proposed that the report be adopted, the Lord Mayor 'ruled that any increases of salary chargeable against the rates, and not provided in the estimates, were out of order'. A number of failed amendments later, it was decided to defer further consideration of the report pending a statement from the Town Clerk stating the names of the officials affected by the Lord Mayor's ruling, and the extent to which it applied in each case[54]. On the 17 December, the Town Clerk, John J. Murray, gave a lengthy response regarding the Electricity and Public Lighting Report and those to whom the ruling applied. As his response went on and on covering matters outside his brief, the Lord Mayor intervened and 'ruled the whole report out of order'. Again, at the same meeting, with respect to the report of the Streets Committee, no. 367, with its recommendation of increased salaries for the inspectors in the Paving Department, 'the Lord Mayor ruled the report out of order'.[55] In neither case was there a recorded protest. His strong stance suggested that matters relating particularly to expenditure had been allowed to drift in his absence.

Occasions for rejoicing

During the autumn, on the wider national front, there had been some positive, encouraging developments. On 10 September, the Irish Free State was formally acknowledged internationally by being admitted to membership of the League of

Nations. On 1 October, W.T. Cosgrave addressed the opening meeting of the Imperial Conference in London. And public esteem was raised in a different way on 14 November, when W.B. Yeats was awarded the Nobel Prize for literature (presented in Stockholm on 10 December). On 5 December, the *Dublin Evening Mail* celebrated: 'The last day of Provisional Government. To-Morrow, the Birthday of the First Irish State. To-night the Royal Assent will be given to the Irish Constitution Bill.' The 6 December was described as a day of quiet rejoicing in Dublin. 'Flag-waving greeted the birth of the Irish State.' In the temporary euphoria, the highest hopes were expressed of complete re-unification of North and South. Even the weather seemed to conspire to uplift the spirits as Christmas approached. By 18 December the foggy and wet weather had given way to sunshine. Flowers were blooming and trees budding as if it were spring. Christmas crowds were gathering holly and mistletoe.[56]

Yet the following day there was the sombre news of seven executions in Dublin for the 'illegal possession of arms'. All the executed were labourers.[57]

Christmas was also a sombre time in Laurence O'Neill's household. His much loved wife, companion, and mother of his children was in the final stages of her illness.

Notes

1   Dublin City Council (DCC), Mins. meeting 6 Feb. 1920, n.120, p. 106

2   *Dublin Evening Mail,* 2 Jan. 1922

3   UCDA. Mrs Wyse Power papers, P. 106/737, Wyse Power-Sighle (Humphreys), 8 Jan. 1922

4   *Dublin Evening Mail,* Monday, 9 Jan. 1922

5   Idem, 16 Jan. 1922

6   Idem, 20, 21, 22 Jan. 1922

7   DCC. Mins. 25 Jan. no. 74, pp. 57-8

8   UCDA. Wyse Power papers, P. 106/737. Wyse Power-Sighle, 8 Jan. 1922

9   He was to lose two sons during the year, and was to die himself in Sept. 1922. DCC. no. 552

10   DCC. Mins. 30 Jan. 1922, no. 78, p. 61

11   UCDA. de Valera papers, P. 150/607, in section 11, re anti-conscription fund, p. 165; John Dillon-Lord Mayor O'Neill, 31 Jan. 1922

12   UCDA. Mrs Wyse Power papers, Ms. 106/744, Wyse Power-Sighle, 26 Feb. 1922

13   Idem, 24 Feb.

14   *Irish Catholic Directory* (ICD), 1923 (1922 summary), pp. 551-2

15   DCC Mins, no. 204, 205

16   Irish College Rome Archives(ICRA), Hag. 1/1922/194. O'Donnell to John Hagan, rector, 10 April 1922

17   Idem, Sean T. O'Ceallaigh- Hagan, 11 April 1922

18   NLI O'Neill papers, Ms 35,294/14. Mahon-Ld. Mayor, 13 April 1922

19   DDA. Archbishop Byrne papers, box on Govt.Politics (1). Opening address at peace conference,1922

20   Idem. "Diaries and Personalia", small diary for 1922

21   DCC Mins. 21 April 1922, no. 280, p. 204

22   See T.J. Morrissey. *Edward J. Byrne, 1872-1941,* pp. 82-83

23   Report of the Irish Labour Party and Trade Union Congress, 1922, p. 30, and see William O'Brien. *Forth the Banners Go,* pp.219-20, and T.J. Morrissey. *William O'Brien, 1881-1968,*pp. 203-4

24   T.P. Coogan. *De Valera,* p. 315

25   ICRA.Hag 1/1922/230(1), Byrne-Hagan,1 May 1922: 'The effort, as I more or less anticipated, resulted in failure.' See T.J. Morrissey. *Edward Byrne…,* p. 84

26   NLI. O'Brien papers. Ms. 15,704 (iii). O'Brien recalled visiting the Four Courts with the Lord Mayor. He mentioned two visits, in one of which he met with all those mentioned. He does not specify whether this last was the one with the Lord Mayor. See also A.J. Gaughan. *Thomas Johnson,* p. 200, f. n. 15

27   DCC. Mins. 9 May, n. 345, pp. 258 ff

28   UCDA. Wyse Power papers, P. 106/750. Jenny Wyse Power-Sighle, 6 June 1922

29   NAI. NAS Dept. of Taoiseach, S 1437, 1 July 1922

30   Nancy Cardoza. *Maud Gonne,* pp. 350-51. See A.MacBride, White, and A Norman Jeffares (eds.). *Always Your Friend. The Gonne-Yeats Letters, 1893-1938,* p. 522 f.n.

31   NAI. Taoiseach's Dept. S 1437, 1 July 1922

32   DCC.7 July 1922, no. 38, p.34

33   Idem, 12 Aug., no. 491, p. 368

34   Idem, 26 August, no. 492, p. 370

35   NLI. Irish Parliamentary Debates, vol.1, 9 Sept.-4 Dec. 1922, p. 10

36   Idem, p. 61

37   Idem, pp. 30-31

38   *Irish Times,* 29 July 1943, obituary.

39   DCC Mins. 27 Nov. 1922, no. 626, p. 482. Mary O'Sullivan-Town Clerk.

40   Idem, 14 May 1923, no.283, Letter no. 2,154:1923

41   Idem,, no. 439, p. 335

42   Idem, meetings of 9 and 23 October 1922

43   Idem, no. 576, p. 436

44   M. O'Neill. "Dublin Corporation in Troubled Times, 1914-1924" in *Dublin Historical Record,* vol. 47, no.1, 1994, p. 68

45   Idem, and DCC meeting of 28 May 1923

46   UCDA. de Valera papers. P. 150/657. "Correspondence between de Valera and Mary MacSwiney, Sept. 1922 – 9 August 1923, n.657, p. 181. During this time, without a precise date, de Valera wrote a remarkable letter to Mary MacSwiney. He was evidently harried by her uncompromising republican stance and ideological logic: 'Nature never fashioned me to be a partisan leader in any case, and I am sorry that I did not insist on Cathal's (Brugha) assuming the leadership when the party was being formed. For the sake of the cause, I allowed myself to be put into a position, which it is impossible for one of my outlook and personal bias to fill with effect for the party. Every instinct of mine would indicate that I was meant to be a dyed-in-the-wool Tory or even a bishop, rather than the leader of a Revolution.' The self-depreciation did not last long. Even in his self-humbling he thought of himself as 'a bishop', not as a simple curate or even parish priest.

47   *Dublin Evening Mail,* 6 Sept. 1923

48   DCC. Mins. 29 Oct. no. 617, p. 398

49   Idem, 5 Nov., no. 659, p. 421, and no. 660

50   Idem, 3 Dec., no. 703, pp. 454-5

51   Idem. Mins. 29 Oct., no. 635, p. 408

52 Idem. Mins 15 Oct., no. 613

53 *Dublin Evening Mail* 24, 29 Oct. 1923

54 DCC. Mins. 29 Nov. 1923, no. 699, pp. 447-50

55 Idem, 17 Dec. 1923, no. 769, p.496

56 *Dublin Evening Mail,* 18 Dec. 1923

57 Idem, 19 Dec. 1923. The executed men were: Patrick Bagnel, Joseph Johnston, Patrick

58 Mangan, Brian Moore, Patrick Nolan, James O'Connor, and Stephen White.

13.

1924:

Bereft. The End of an Era

On 16 January 1924, the *Dublin Evening Mail* announced the death of the Lady Mayoress at her residence, Bridge House, Portmarnock. 'She was a member of a respected North County Dublin family', and 'as Lady Mayoress she had engaged in much philanthropic effort up to about two years ago, when she was stricken down by the malady which has now terminated in her death at a comparatively early age. Her illness has affected the Lord Mayor, who suffered a serious breakdown last year.' 'A few weeks ago she became steadily worse, and the end came peacefully this morning.' On Friday, 18 January, the funeral took place.[1] 'It was attended by official representatives of the State and the Municipality as well as a great concourse of Dublin citizens. The remains were removed from Baldoyle Church to St Marnack's cemetery, Portmarnock, amidst numerous manifestations of public sorrow.'

Messages of sympathy poured into the Mansion House. President Cosgrave, it appears, did not attend the funeral, nor did any of his ministers. Moreover, no message of sympathy from them remains among those preserved by Laurence O'Neill. He did retain, however, messages of condolence from the Municipal Council,[2] from Count Plunkett,[3] from Cardinal Logue,[4] from Padraigh O'Riuttledge,[5] 'acting president of the Government of the Republic of Ireland', who conveyed the sympathy of Mr de Valera, then in jail, from William O'Brien, on behalf of the Irish Transport and General Workers' Union, and finally from Alfred Cope, 18 Abington Street, Westminster, London. Of these, the most informative to the biographer and, perhaps, the most meaningful to the bereaved Lord Mayor, were those from colleague, William O'Brien, and from the former Assistant-Secretary of Ireland, Alfred Cope, who, with O'Neill, was among the key architects of the truce.

'The Union has always felt itself under a deep obligation to your Lordship', O'Brien wrote, 'since the days when it had very, very few friends outside its own ranks, for the stand which you then took when the employers, with the help of the Government of the day, sought to crush the union and outlaw its members. In all the critical years that have passed since then, you have at all times been ready and willing to come to our assistance whenever required, and so it is was with deep sorrow that we learned of the latest blow, after all you have gone through during the past eight eventful years. It is our earnest hope that you will be given strength to bear up against this latest and most severe loss of all.'[6]

The letter from Alfred Cope,[7] although not written until 1 April 1924, was in many ways the most empathetic to O'Neill's loss, and the most appreciative of what he and his wife had accomplished. It was also a most informative letter in relation to Cope as well as to the Lord and Lady Mayoress, and merits wider attention.

'My dear Lord Mayor,

I hear with great regret that some short time back you had the great misfortune to lose dear Mrs O'Neill. I am very sorry indeed and offer you my sincere sympathy. I had the privilege and pleasure to meet your dear wife on several occasions – on one memorable occasion at your private house when she was in the midst of her family, and I saw clearly the deep affection her family had for her and she for them. I realise therefore how heavy the loss must be to you and your family.

The Lady Mayoress was exceptionally kind and thoughtful to me in rather trying times, and particularly on the occasion I mention. She gave me a very warm and homely welcome which I appreciated and have not forgotten.

I am sure the Lady Mayoress shared your burdens in a very onerous office during most difficult times. Burdens which you carried so successfully, and you must miss her. But you have the satisfaction of knowing that hand in hand with her, you fought a great fight and that you steered your ship through many rocks in a very troubled sea. Your dexterous handling of the vessel amazed me, *and I am sure that when the true history comes to be written (and it will be some day) you and your Lady Mayoress will stand out in strong light among the few who worked wholeheartedly and disinterestedly to promote your country's welfare.* Your great work for moderation and the avoidance of hardship and bloodshed on all sides will be fully recognised one day. *I know of no other man who, in your exalted position, would have worked so strenuously or who could have overcome so successfully the almost overwhelming difficulties of your office in so perplexing a period.* And yet at the same time you retained the full confidence of your people. It was a great accomplishment. You must have had great support from the Lady Mayoress or you could never have carried through.

The loss of your helpmate and consoler is a sad blow but you have the great consolation of knowing that the Lady Mayoress lived a life of great usefulness and great service, and that, unlike many, she did not live in vain. This, I am sure, must ease the blow.

There is still much to do, and I feel you will be following her wishes if you keep a stout heart to carry on. I hope you have quite recovered from your illness.

Yours Very Sincerely,
A. Cope

The death of his wife was not the only occasion of pain and loss experienced by the Lord Mayor during 1924. Criticism of the Corporation had greatly increased, much of it from business interests but also finding expression from Jim Larkin and his followers.

An Official Inquiry into Dublin Corporation

The Minister for Local Government, James A Burke, on 20 February 1924, addressed a formal letter to the Town Clerk stating that in response to 'serious complaints' (not specified) he was ordering an inquiry, under section 12 of the Local Government (Temporary Provisions) Act 1923, into the administration of the Corporation. Two days later, the *Evening Herald* welcomed the minister's decision and gave vent to an extravagantly bitter attack on the Corporation and its members. Deeply annoyed by the unfairness of the attack, O'Neill made a strong response at the next Municipal Council meeting, on 25 February; even though some members thought it might further antagonise the press.

The *Evening Herald* had asserted that 'jobbery and corruption' were 'rampant in City Hall', that all Dublin had 'been disgusted at the action of this gang in refusing to accept the Government's grant of £10,000 for the benefit mainly of ex-soldiers of the National Army', and that 'corrupt and unscrupulous brutes is the only description we can apply to a large proportion of the members of the Corporation'. O'Neill declared that he welcomed criticism provided it was substantiated. But he believed that the *Evening Herald* had over-stepped the line of decency and fair criticism and he strongly objected to its tone. He went on to defend the record of the Corporation during the years of the Troubles, and to direct in passing an indirect accusation at Mr Cosgrave, who had been a colleague for years and now subjected them to an inquiry. 'With an experience of what my colleagues went through in the Black and Tan regime of three or four years ago, when the men and women of this Council faced prison, and even assassination, and when they loyally stood behind President Cosgrave, then a member of the Corporation and Minister of Local Government, it is my belief that if this Corporation faltered then, and did not take up a stand in giving a lead to the country, it is questionable whether you would have a Free State Government in power to-day.'

Having expanded on the disadvantages under which the Corporation had worked during the past few years, with its ranks depleted by death and by tragedies, the Lord Mayor concluded: 'Although I do not agree with many of the things done by my colleagues, not agreeing with the majority of my colleagues on their action in connection with the much-talked-of grant – and it does not follow that I am right and they are wrong – I must say I have never yet found anything in their actions which would merit the designation applied to them by the *Evening Herald* as being "corrupt and unscrupulous brutes".'[8]

The hearings of the Official Inquiry commenced on 12 March under an engineer of the Local Government Board, Nicholas Dwyer. The Lord Mayor, and a number of other council members, attended the hearings. Two senior barristers, Messrs Lardner and Lynch, appeared for the Municipal Council. At a special meeting of the Council, the members were of the view that as the authority had produced no complaints serious or otherwise, the barristers were only to take part in the proceedings to defend 'such charges as may be made against the Corporation'.[9]

Demise of a historic institution

On 20 May, however, the Minister for Local Government announced that, arising from the inquiry, he was satisfied 'that the duties of the Council of the County Borough of Dublin' were ' not being duly and effectually discharged by them' and that, therefore, he declared the Council hereby dissolved, 'the property, several powers and duties of the Council (are) hereby transferred to the Commissioners, Seamus O Murchadha, Dr Dwyer, and P. J. Hernon'. He was careful to add that members of the Council who had been elected or appointed by the Council to public bodies, prior to the dissolution of the Council, would continue to be members of such public bodies, until he should otherwise direct.[10] In a covering letter, the Minister stated that he had been impressed by the sense of duty and civic spirit displayed by individual members of the Corporation but that it was evident 'that the efforts of such members to secure efficient and economical management of the business of the city were unavailing in the absence of support from the majority of the Council'.[11] Each member of the Corporation, apart from the Lord Mayor, was notified that their functions came to an end at 6.0 p.m. that day, 20 May. O'Neill, as will appear, received word some days earlier.

The dissolution of such a historic institution gave rise to some lively exchanges in the Dail. Thomas Johnson described the unceremonious dissolution as 'a very extraordinary and unprecedented action' suggesting that 'we are rapidly going towards oligarchy and dictatorship'.[12] Many believed that the Government's action was political. As has been noted, the Dublin Corporation during 1922-23 had become a public platform for the Government's political opponents. Alderman Alfred Byrne, T.D., during the Dail debates made the point in relation to the Corporation that 'very many resolutions emanated from that body – resolutions which, I think, did good work for the city recently, resolutions asking for the release of prisoners, proper treatment of the prisoners, examination of the jails, inspection by our medical officer – all these probably the Government have taken into consideration, and not the inspector's report'.[13]

Maire O'Neill, in her "Dublin Corporation in Troubled Times, 1914-1924" noted that although the Minister had power to order such a dissolution, it was surprising that there was no government decision to take such a step. Perhaps the problems which the Government faced that spring, following the army mutiny and the resignation of two ministers (Joseph McGrath and Richard Mulcahy), and concerns about the Boundary Commission, may have diverted attention from Dublin Corporation.[14] Apart from questions in the Dail, there was no public outcry against the dissolution. The contrary was the case. The *Irish Independent* and the *Irish Times* welcomed the Minister's decision, and a leading article in the *Irish Builder and Engineer*, of 31 May 1924, observed that 'it is doubtful whether any other step taken by the present Government has proved so generally endorsed as the appointment of commissioners to administer the affairs of the city'.[15] The *Evening Herald*, characteristically, welcomed the sweeping away of 'a mighty civic parasitic institution'.[16] The *Irish Times* was an entrenched critic representing unionist business interests, and the *Independent* newspapers reflected the criticism of Catholic businessmen and that of members of the public who, presumably, believed the charges of incompetence and corruption and, in some instances, resented the Municipal Council's attitude towards the lawfully elected Irish government.

Reaction of the Lord Mayor

For Laurence O'Neill with his dedication to his native city and his deep awareness of the long history of the Corporation, the whole question of dissolution was extremely painful. Even though it was made clear to him that his honour was in no way impugned, he claimed to see no grounds for the appointment of commissioners. The President, W. T. Cosgrave, days before the dissolution, offered that he continue as Lord Mayor and chair the commission, but O'Neill declined briefly – even though it meant forfeiting a much-needed salary:

> Although appreciating very much the compliment you have
> suggested paying me, I regret I cannot see my way to accept same.
> I presume if the Order is issued, you have no objection to me
> making it known the compliment you have paid me.
>
> With kind regards,[17]

The day after the Minister's order, Lord Mayor O'Neill, responding to an *Irish Times* reporter, declared that he would be staying on at the Mansion House. It was not a personal matter, nor was he being antagonistic to the Government, it was a matter of his official position – 'Are the citizens to be deprived of a civic head?' He would continue in the Mansion House until he had an opportunity to hand back his chain of office to those who elected him. This would be after an election. 'I want', he proceeded, 'to maintain for the citizens the position of Lord Mayor …The office dates back for hundreds of years, and I think it is not fair to the citizens that any Government with the scratch of a pen should destroy that office. I could understand it if a man occupying the position of Lord Mayor committed any offence.' In the course of further conversation, the Lord Mayor said that within the next few days he would summon a meeting of his colleagues to discuss the matter. He repeated the statement made in an earlier interview that the Government had offered to leave him in the position of Lord Mayor and invited him to act with the commissioners but that he had declined the offer.[18]

Three days after the act of dissolution, O'Neill sent letters[19], with a black border of mourning, to former colleagues in the Corporation inviting them to a meeting in the Mansion House on Monday at 3.0 p.m. At the meeting the Lord Mayor stated that he had invited to the meeting only those to whom he owed allegiance, the members of the Council. He would abide by their majority opinion. 'To the Council and to the Council alone would he hand in his gun.' (hear, hear) Obviously moved emotionally, he declared that 'he did not come before his colleagues with a swan song, but he would be false to his position if he sat down without protesting in the strongest manner possible at the gross insult that had been offered to the citizens of Dublin. He sat through the inquiry, and if there was anything in that inquiry, why were they not made aware of it – why had the citizens not got an opportunity of criticising the Council and saying whether they erred or not! Barely concealing his anger, he concluded: 'The policy he would respectfully suggest to the meeting as that which should be followed would be to get the Government by the throat and demand an election, so as to give the Council an opportunity of rendering an account of their stewardship to the citizens. It is for the citizens and the citizens only to decide.'

Clr. P.T. Daly moved – 'that the meeting instructs the Lord Mayor to call a public meeting of the burgesses to consider the situation arising at the undemocratic action of the Government and to press for an immediate election for members of the Corporation; and, further, to take such steps as may be considered necessary to place the facts before our fellow-countrymen.' The motion was passed by the meeting. Concluding, the Lord Mayor congratulated the meeting on the dignified manner in which their protest had been made, and their unanimous support of the resolution. He reminded the meeting, however, 'that they had no funds to enter on an elaborate campaign in the country'.[20] As reported in the press, there was an aura of futility about the meeting.

The meeting proved to be, in effect, a swan song. The report of the meeting coincided with the publication of the Report of the Inquiry, thereby lessening the publicity afforded their protest. Nothing further seems to have taken place about demanding and contesting an election.

Report of the Inquiry

Presenting his report, the inspector, Nicholas Dwyer, remarked significantly that the evidence at the Inquiry 'points to a rather extraordinary change, which was not for the better, in the performance of their duties by the Corporation. When they first came into office in 1920, it would appear they accomplished great things for the better management of the city administration, while last year (while O'Neill was absent?) they apparently made little attempt to suit the administration to prevailing conditions.' Notwithstanding the neglect, 'administration had in general maintained a very high standard, and many members, including chairmen of the standing committees, have diverted much time and energy to their public duties.'[21] All of which served to confirm that the drastic step of termination was taken, as Ald. Byrne indicated, because of the Municipal Council's hostile criticism of Government policy and decisions.

The reign of the Commissioners and the Lord Mayor

The first meeting of the commissioners took place on 29 May 1924. They were to continue administering the city for six years, leaving a notable gap in the succession list of Lord Mayors of Dublin which went back to the middle ages. For O'Neill, at first, little seemed to change. He continued undisturbed in the Mansion House and served on a number of public bodies. On 5 June 1925, however, the ministry for local government announced that Mr Laurence O'Neill had not held the office of Lord Mayor since the Minister's order dissolving the Corporation. Questioned by a reporter, O'Neill replied circuitously: 'I feel not a little puzzled that such a letter should have been sent after 13 months, since the Order suspending the Corporation specially provided that the Lord Mayor and his colleagues who are nominated by the Council to act on other boards as members of the Corporation should be allowed to do so. During the last 13 months I have acted as Lord Mayor at the Port and Docks Board, at the National University, and on other bodies, and no exception has been taken. I am still in occupancy of the Mansion House and have not been interfered with by anyone.'[22]

Reflection

It is not clear when he vacated the Lord Mayor's residence. It is clear, however, that the year 1924 marked the end of the traditional form of Dublin Corporation and the end of one of the most dramatic decades in the country's history. For the elected Corporation the pressures of coping with the many convulsions during the years 1918-1921 had been intense. That harmony was preserved, and some balance of judgement, manifested the sturdiness of the institution, the general good sense of the members, and the leadership of its Lord Mayor; concerning whom the senior politician, William O'Brien, M.P., observed: -

> The Lord Mayor of Dublin can truly be described as the only
> Irishman of our time who lived through long years of civil war,
> belonging to no party, but gave noble service to them all.[23]

O'Neill, who enjoyed the limelight, was to find that once out of public office his name and achievements were soon forgotten. Public appreciation, he was to lament more than once, was fickle and short-lived. To some extent he found himself tarred with the ill reputation ascribed to the Corporation; and business rivals, who kept their distance while he was Lord Mayor, now felt free to undermine his ailing firm, which had been neglected both by his absence through illness and by his various municipal activities and expenditures, and also by the decline in customers for corn products with the withdrawal of the British army and the decrease in the number of horses. Before long, he was to find himself in financial difficulties.

Notes

1   *Freeman's Journal,* Sat. 19 Jan. 1924

2   DCC. Mins. 21 Jan. Expression of condolence moved by John T. O'Kelly. The Council adjourned in sympathy.

3   ONFP. Plunkett- Ld. Mayor, 17 Jan. 1924

4   Idem, Card. Logue- Ld Mayor, 18 Jan.1924

5   NLI. O'Neill papers, 17 Jan. 1924; Ms 15, 294/15

6   NLI. O'Neill papers, Ms 15,294/15; Wm O'Brien – Ld. Mayor, 29 Jan. 1924

7   Idem, A Cope-Ld. Mayor, 1 April 1924.

8   DCC. Mins. 25 Feb. 1924; no. 101, pp. 78-9

9   DCC. Meeting on 24 March, no. 145, pp 118-20; and cf. Marie O'Neill. "Dublin Corporation in the Troubled Times, 1914-1924" in *Dublin Historical Record,* vol.47, No.1 (1994), p. 69

10   DCC. May 1924, no. 321, pp. 296-7

11   Idem, p. 296

12   Dail Debates, 7, p. 1874; cit. Ruth McManus. *Dublin 1910-1940,* p. 81

13   Idem, p. 1880, cit. McManus, p. 81

14   Maire O'Neill, art. cit., pp. 69-70

15   p. 483, cit. McManus, p. 82

16   28 May 1924

17   NLI. O'Neill papers. O'Neill- President Cosgrave, 16 May 1924; Ms. 15, 294/15

18   *Irish Times,* 22 May 1924

19   For example, letter to Hanna Sheehy Skeffington, 23 May 1924, NLI. Sheehy Skeffington papers, 1922-1924, Ms. 24091.

20   *Irish Times,* 27 May 1924

21   Idem, 28 May

22   *Irish Independent,* 6 June 1925

23   ONFP., under heading "William O'Brien, M.P.", no further source for the observation.

Laurence O'Neill, 1864-1943
Lord Mayor of Dublin, 1917-1924
Patriot and Man of Peace

PART III

A Long Epilogue, 1925- 1943

"No memory of having starred

Atones for later disregard

Or keeps the end from being hard."

[Robert Frost. 'Provide. Provide' in *Poetry of Robert Frost* (London 1971)]

Laurence O'Neill, 1864-1943
Lord Mayor of Dublin, 1917-1924
Patriot and Man of Peace

14.
1925 – 1936

From the time of his first election as Lord Mayor until 1925, Laurence O'Neill resided at the Mansion House, and thereafter at the family home, Bridge House, Portmarnock, County Dublin. That rather large house, still standing and occupied, was part of an estate of more than thirty acres. In 1908, as noted previously, he gave land for a local golf course, which became known as the "Riverside Golf Course". It was, in effect, a grade three course for the local people, who could not afford to join the prestigious Portmarnock Golf Links, which had opened in 1894 and hosted open championships and international tournaments.[1]

O'Neill, during his time as Lord Mayor, was described as a small, sturdy, dapper figure, with a little brown moustache, and a bowler hat.[2] In the years after leaving office, he was careful to keep up appearances.

Seeking re-election to Dail

In 1927 he put himself forward for election to the Dail as an Independent. His election leaflet indicated his lack of resources. 'I have never belonged to any political party. I refuse to join one now; but if you elect me I shall support whatever group that aims at the restoration of our lost nationhood, and whose policy is to promote peace and good will amongst all our people – North, South, East and West.' He promised to move to have restored the shilling taken off the old-age pension, and that he would support whatever group that prevented extravagant expenditure and squandering of the people's money. He added: 'As I have no organisation or financial help behind me, I will be unable to indulge in the usual electioneering campaign.' He stood on his record as a public representative for over 20 years, and as Lord Mayor from 1917-1924, and he asked for the continuity of the public's support and influence.[3]

He received a sharp reminder of the short-lived nature of public memory. He did not have the required financial backing for his campaign and, hence, failed to get public support. But he did not just lack financial backing for an election campaign; his personal financial situation was such that he felt obliged to make a number of attempts to meet with President Cosgrave to seek his assistance.[4]

A plea for assistance

Eventually, he was in such straitened circumstances that, on 15 May 1928, he wrote a begging letter to Cosgrave, his former friend and colleague. It revealed his critical situation and, in effect, his failure as a business man. Writing it must have been a humiliating experience.

> I am dreadfully pressed at the moment. I had hoped an account
> due me for £900… but again disappointed, and you would hardly
> believe it I have received a writ for my Corporation rates,
> consequently for old times sake, I will be frank with you, you are
> the only one in this world I would approach, as the bank has
> turned me down. If you … give me a sum between £250 to £500
> to tide me over my present pressing difficulties I shall make every
> effort possible to have it paid back as soon as I can collect what
> is due to me. I know I am asking a great deal, but I think you
> know me sufficiently well in the past to know only it is a case of
> absolute necessity I would not trespass on you otherwise.

On 21 May, it was necessary to write once more, seeking a meeting with Cosgrave. On 23 May he received an appointment for the following day.[5] The day after their meeting, on 25 May, Cosgrave authorised Mr W. O'Hegarty to 'pay out of the Dail Special Fund to Mr Laurence O'Neill, Bridge House, Portmarnock, the sum of £250, which is repayable'. On the same date, there was a receipt from O'Neill, and an undertaking to re-pay. A month later, on 25 June, President Cosgrave authorised O'Hegarty to pay a further £250 out of the Special Dail Fund to Mr O'Neill. Once again, O'Neill signed a receipt and promised to re-pay.[6]

At home in the Senate

Matters improved in 1929. An opening occurred in the Senate on 20 June, following the resignation of the Marquis of Lansdowne, Henry Petty-Fitzmaurice. With the support, it appears, of President Cosgrave, O'Neill was one of three candidates in a by-election for the position. The other two were Major-General Sir George Franks, County Limerick, and Arthur K. Maxwell, Lord Farnham, County Cavan. In the first vote, O'Neill scored highest. Franks was lowest and was eliminated. In the further contest, O'Neill was successful by 26 votes to 23

In the Senate, he soon made his presence felt: speaking on the Juries Protection Bill, 1929, on 3 July;[7] the Game Preservation Bill, 1929;[8] the Local Government (Dublin)

Bill, 1929;[9] the Military Service Pensions Bill, 1929;[10] and the Volunteer Reserve Bill, in December 1929. On this last, he spoke to a motion by Mr Thomas Johnson, the Labour Senator, which he felt was not receiving a proper hearing. The motion expressed disapproval of the procedure adopted by the Minister for Defence in the formation of a Volunteer Reserve as being an abuse of ministerial power and an encroachment upon the authority of the Oireachtas (the Parliament).

After some debate, Senator O'Neill moved 'the adjournment of the debate until the next meeting of the Seanad'. Senator Dowdall seconded O'Neill's motion, in the light of the importance of Mr Johnson's motion and the small attendance. The Cathaoirleach (Speaker) concurred if Senator Johnson accepted the adjournment. Johnson accepted, and O'Neill, sensitive about procedure, interjected: 'I had Senator Johnson's consent before I moved the motion. Otherwise I would not have dreamed of doing so'.[11]

On the Local Government Bill, 1929, during the second reading on 28 May 1930, O'Neill made what was termed his maiden speech. He spoke at considerable length and with much feeling, his contribution running to 13 columns or 9 pages. He attacked the section in the Bill dealing with the commercial franchise in the local government elections, and the granting of special provisions for the benefit of the larger property owners. In the process, he introduced his background, and his views, ranged over the history of the years of struggle for political independence, and provided a spirited defence of Dublin Corporation in defiance of slighting remarks by business men and others both in the Dail and the Seanad. He reminded his hearers that when the Corporation was dismissed and vilified, its members were traduced – men like President Cosgrave, Sean T. O'Kelly, Dr Myles Keogh, Aldermen James Moran, Alfred Byrne, and Thomas Kelly, and women such as Mrs Sheehy Skeffington, Mrs Margaret McGarry, and Senators Mrs Clarke and Mrs Wyse Power. 'I speak as one', he declared, 'who for seven and a half long, sad, and weary years helped in a small way to frame the destinies of this city as its civic head. I was helped by courageous and honourable colleagues, who never shirked their duty or responsibilities to the city or to the country – not like now, not like the time of the Commissioners; those were the days of actual danger. No Lord Mayor at any period... – a position which goes back for close on a thousand years – was ever flanked by more faithful friends or more loyal colleagues as Lord Mayor than I was during that period. Out of their loyalty to me, and my loyalty to them, I refused at the hands of my friend, President Cosgrave, the chairmanship of the Dublin Commissioners, while retaining the title of Lord Mayor with emoluments and salary of £1,600 a year. That may be a personal matter. I appreciated the kindness of President Cosgrave at the time, but as I have said, out of my sense of loyalty I felt bound to refuse the offer. I wonder how many of the Corporation traducers would do the same?'[12]

In the course of his long speech, O'Neill had flattering words for President Cosgrave, Arthur Griffith, and the Minister of Local Government, General Richard Mulcahy, but also for Sir Henry Robinson, head of the British Local Government Board, and very particularly for 'My great friend, Senator Bryan Mahon, commander-in-chief of the British forces in Ireland in 1917, only for whose tact, bravery and humanity, the citizens of Dublin would have been butchered in cold blood. I have documents in my possession to prove that some permanent officials were anxious for that'...[13] In his parade of past events, O'Neill referred to the responsible Dublin evening newspaper that described the members of the Corporation as "a gang of corrupt and unscrupulous brutes"; and he disclosed 'that the largest owner of that newspaper, which his father (William Martin Murphy) had founded, called upon me at the Mansion House in evident distress and produced a resolution that was passed by himself and his co-directors condemning the article that I have mentioned and, further, apologising to me as Lord Mayor of Dublin on behalf of my colleagues'. That was an honourable act but it 'was spoilt by the fact that not a line of apology or regret appeared in the columns of the newspaper'.[14]

O'Neill made contributions to other Bills during 1930: the Public Charitable Hospitals Bill, second stage, 14 May 1930, where, as he sometimes did, he kept his intervention to near the end of the debate; the Military Services Pensions Bill, final stage, 9 April 1930;[15] and on "The Safety of Irish Missionaries in China". In this last debate, he requested permission to speak 'outside the domain of mundane affairs'. One of the members of the House, who has endeared himself to them all by his quiet, unassuming manner, Senator Linihan, had gone through the maddening anxiety of suspense concerning the safety of his son in China. O'Neill thought it not out of place now for the Cathaoirleach to extend to Senator Linihan how happy they felt at the good news that his son, and his colleague, had been released from captivity. The Cathaoirleach, in response, felt sure that Senator O'Neill's words would convey to Senator Linihan the feelings of the House on the matter.'[16]

Sadly, Senator O'Neill was faced with the death, on 24 September 1930, of Senator Sir Bryan Mahon. The Senate's motion of sympathy, on 19 November, was put by the Earl of Granard, and seconded by Colonel Moore. The only other speaker was Laurence O'Neill, who stated briefly: 'Having been associated in many transactions with Senator Sir Bryan Mahon during times of peril, I can say that I found him always courteous, and always honourable. I consider it an honour to be associated with the motion.'[17] The senators stood as the motion was passed.

By the close of 1930, it was evident that Laurence O'Neill was at home in the Seanad, quite unfazed by the unfamiliar presence of titled gentlemen, generals and literati.

Municipal politics re-visited

It had been a significant year for him. Dublin Corporation was re-constituted, though in a much attenuated form. He stood for election in the ward – Electoral Area No. 3, and topped the poll. His long-time friend and colleague, Alfred Byrne, was elected Lord Mayor, and subsequently had struck a large silver medal for the benefit of Laurence O'Neill:

> 1930. Corporation Dublin Member
> Presented to Senator Laurence O'Neill
> Elected Alderman in the First Election
> Of the City Council
> By
> Alderman Alfred Byrne
> First Lord Mayor
> Of Greater Dublin[18]

In that year, too, O'Neill, who could not afford to give away any possessions, contributed some of his land to the local community for the building of a church, requesting only that it be known as "St Anne's Church" after his wife Anne. It was to serve the people of the area for almost fifty years and, in the early days of aviation, became a landmark for aeroplanes approaching or departing from what was then known as Collinstown Airport.[19]

At the first meeting of the new Corporation, on 14 October 1930, the newly-appointed city manager took the chair until the Lord Mayor was elected. Senator Laurence O'Neill was one of six aldermen and twenty-two councillors who heard the city manager announce that 'to-day there is not merely a new City Council created, but a new system of civic government is inaugurated, and these two great changes are accompanied by the inclusion of large areas not hitherto within the city limits... In solving the many problems which confront me in my new position, I confidently count upon your sympathetic assistance'. The new era having been announced, the election for Lord Mayor took place. Ald. Senator O'Neill proposed Senator Alfred Byrne, and was seconded by Clr. Belton. The Fianna Fail members supported Clr. Sean T. O'Kelly, who was proposed by Clr. Tom Kelly, and seconded by Clr. Senator Mrs Clarke. Alfred Byrne was elected by twenty votes to thirteen.[20] O'Neill attended the next meeting on 3 November, at which draft standing orders were adopted, and he was appointed to a committee concerning the provision of suitable alternative accommodation for street traders.[21] The final meeting of the year was on 12 December, at the usual time of 6.30 p.m., in the City Hall.

Political priorities. Threat to the State

The year 1931 highlighted O'Neill's priorities as a public representative. He supported a Government that was freely elected and therefore represented the will of the majority of the people – (His expressed grievance concerning the dissolution of the Corporation was that its members were freely elected by the citizens and the citizens were not consulted on the dissolution). He opposed violence, especially violence aimed at undermining the lawfully elected Government; and he determined to remain independent politically. In 1931 he had reason to believe that the continuation of the new Irish State was seriously being threatened.

The Soviet Comintern had infiltrated some Irish unions, Irish labour bodies, and the IRA by the end of the nineteen-twenties. In 1931, Communists found a major opening in the IRA by means of Saor Eire, an organisation founded that year to achieve an independent republic, overthrow Irish capitalism, and provide an independent revolutionary leadership for the working class and working farmers.[22] There was a surge in IRA recruitment. Violence and crimes increased; and as shooting and intimidation of juries became more frequent there were reports from Garda sergeants that they were losing control of the countryside.[23] On 17 September, President Cosgrave presented detailed facts to the Irish Catholic hierarchy indicating that he and his colleagues viewed 'with grave anxiety the rapid growth ... of subversive teachings and activities. A situation without parallel as a threat to the foundations of all authority has arisen'.[24] To less biased observers such as Labour Senator Tom Johnson, the IRA appeared 'to have been captured by the communist wing'.[25] Dail Eireann enacted a Public Safety Bill on 17 October; and next day a pastoral letter was read in Catholic churches deploring 'the growing evidence of a campaign of Revolution and Communism' and declaring Saor Eire and the IRA sinful and irreligious.[26]

Laurence O'Neill had been one of the first to speak up in favour of the Anglo-Irish Treaty, now he also appears to have spoken out strongly in support of the Government and law and order. So much so that he was placed under Garda protection. He wrote in praise of the members of the Garda protecting him, and, on 17 November, Garda Commissioner Eoin O'Duffy thanked him for his reference to the members of the Garda who were detailed to look after him for some weeks.[27]

In the Seanad of 1934-1936

O'Neill stood as an Independent candidate in the 1931 Seanad elections. He topped the poll. The first meeting of the new Seanad took place on 6 December 1931. The early weeks of the New Year were taken up with preparations for a general election. Cumann na nGaedheal had many of its election meetings violently disrupted by the IRA. In response, on 9 February, the Army Comrades Association was formed, an organisation of ex-members of the Irish Free State army, later known as the "Blue Shirts" because of the colour of their shirts. The distinctive shirts evoked comparison with the Brown Shirts in Germany and the Fascist Black Shirts in Italy. On 16 February, Fianna Fail proved the most successful party in the election. It obtained 72 seats. Cumann na nGaedheal got 57, Labour 7, Farmers 3, Independents and others 14. O'Neill was happy to give his support to the new Government: it was the choice of the electorate; he greatly admired de Valera; and there was a residual sense of grievance against the previous Government because of its termination of Dublin Corporation. He was to prove a sturdy supporter of the new administration in a senate weighted strongly against government policies.

During 1932, Alderman Senator O'Neill busied himself once more in support of prisoners. It seems likely that he welcomed the Fianna Fail Government's release of 20 political prisoners during March. In June, an extant letter from O'Neill to Fr Dunne, the Archbishop of Dublin's secretary, requested the archbishop to use his influence to have the death sentence of Mrs Jane Cousins commuted.[28] She had been convicted of the murder in March 1932 of her nephew at Killinick, County Wexford. Whether or not the archbishop used his influence, the death sentence was commuted to imprisonment for life following an appeal.

O'Neill's combined work in the Corporation and the Seanad provided him with what he called 'pin money', something greatly welcomed. Of the two bodies, however, his preference was very much with the Seanad.

Seanad debates

He spoke on Bill after Bill, sometimes garrulously, but with a debating skill that handed-off all interruptions. A blend of humour and acerbic comment, often personalised, gave pause to opponents. Features of his contributions from 1932 to 1934 were defence of Government proposals, defence of popular democracy, opposition to violence, a tendency to drag in the unjust suppression of the Corporation and to recall the celebrated figures with whom he had had contact.

On 22 August 1933, in the debate on The Executive Council and the Preservation of Peace, Sir John Keane criticised the Government on its handling of order and peace in face of IRA violence. O'Neill chose to view the motion and its supporters as turning the Senate into a platform for party warfare. He questioned the motives of Sir John

Keane, was dismissive of interventions from opponents, Miss Browne, Mrs Costelloe and Colonel Moore, and proved highly critical of the Army Comrades Association. He opposed the motion because he believed that the Government were 'doing their best... to maintain order and were endeavouring, according to their lights, to deal with dangerous organisations'.[29] At the close of the debate, Sir John Keane withdrew his motion.

One of the concerns of the Government was the capacity of the Seanad to delay measures approved by the Dail. This was addressed in a Constitution Amendment Bill. In the Seanad debates, a number of speakers, including Senators Milroy, Crosbie, and Counihan, were highly critical of the Bill. O'Neill, in turn, was highly critical of them, and supported the Bill because the Government had received a mandate from the people to do certain things, including the curtailment of the powers of the Senate.[30]

Next day, 12 July, dealing with the Local Government (Extension of Franchise) Bill, which gave franchise to every citizen over 21 years who was 'not subject to legal incapacity', O'Neill declared that he supported the Bill on the broad principles of equality and democracy: one man, one vote.[31] Six days later, on 18 July, there was a further Bill – on Public Services (temporary economics) – on which O'Neill diverged somewhat from the Government. An amendment was moved against cuts in the wages of the Garda Siochana. O'Neill defended the Government's policy on cuts because of the economic condition of the country during the current economic war, but then stated that he would vote for the amendment because what the Garda earned was not over-generous and a tremendous amount depended on a contented Garda force. He suggested, very respectfully, to the Minister, Mr Sean MacEntee, T.D. (Finance), that he might consider allowing the amendment to pass! The amendment was carried by 28 votes to 9.[32]

During the debate on the Loans and Funds Bill, Report Stage, on 26 July, aspersions were cast on Mr de Valera's motives during the collection of funds in the United States. O'Neill rallied to his defence. 'Speaking as one who in days of danger was in very close proximity to President de Valera', he declared that whatever de Valera's political sins, he never committed the sin of acting for personal gain. 'He is an ennobling spirit doing what he can for the people of this country, and particularly the lowly people...'[33]

Adopting the role of the senior figure in the House, which he did from time to time, O'Neill, referring to the Minister for Industry and Commerce, Mr Sean Lemass, T.D., on 7 February 1934, announced that he took 'more than a passing interest in the present Minister, because his father and myself have been lifelong friends'.[34]

One of Senator O'Neill's more impressive speeches was in relation to the Wearing of Uniforms (Restriction) Bill, 1934, Second Reading, on 21 March 1934. The Bill, put forward by the Minister for Defence, Mr Ruttledge, forbade the wearing in public of any uniform, or part of a uniform, belonging to a political group. The Bill, in effect, was directed against the Blue Shirts. It gave rise to a very heated debate.

O'Neill's speech was marked by respect for both sides and by an appeal to move away from old hatreds and division. It was delivered with feeling. Having commenced by stating that he enjoyed the great advantage of belonging to no political party, he went on to admit that he was 'really a Government man', meaning by that – 'I am in favour of any Government that purposes to maintain law and order'. O'Neill referred to President de Valera's comment that all arms in the possession of unauthorised people should be melted down and a statue erected similar to the statue of Christ which stands on the peak of the Andes; and he quoted what was engraved on the pedestal of the great symbol of peace between Chile and the Argentine. Drawing to a close, his mind went back almost twenty years, 'when these men who are warring now met around the table in the Mansion House – de Valera, Cosgrave, Griffith, Collins, Harry Boland, Austin Stack, Paddy Ruttledge, Dick Mulcahy, Sean T. O'Kelly, Kevin O'Higgins, Cathal Brugha and many others – thinking out the best means of regenerating their country, each sworn to the other'. Why not come together like that now? He appealed to the Government, if the Bill passed, that they forego putting it into operation unless they felt it was a case of absolute necessity to do so, and he appealed to the leaders of the Blue Shirt movement, 'in particular Deputy Cosgrave, a dear old friend of mine', to discard the blue shirts because they would bring about a most dreadful civil war, and they would be back once more to the beastly faction fights. And the sadness and the bitterness of the ten or fifteen years past would be revived. In making this appeal to the leaders of the Blue Shirts, he would not have the presumption to suggest to them that they should not go on with their movement as they were going but, 'without any disrespect', in his opinion the blue shirt was a red rag to the country.[35]

The next speaker, Senator Comyn, usually in disagreement with O'Neill, acknowledged that he had 'been greatly moved by the eloquent sentences with which Senator O'Neill concluded his speech'.[36]

Also with reference to the Blue Shirts, but on a lighter note, O'Neill sought vainly to intervene during the debate on Privileges of the House, on 28 February 1934.[37] The particular issue was visitors being allowed entry to the Oireachtas, which was aimed at the exclusion of Blue Shirts as being a danger to the House. The Cathaoirleach, Senator Bennet T. Westropp, declared that there would not be a debate on the matter in the Senate. This was too sweeping for Senator O'Neill, who, 'with all due respect' kept endeavouring to make a speech on what he considered 'a most Gilbertian situation'. The patient Cathaoirleach eventually mixed reproof with irony, remarking: 'I think you are not judging the matter accurately, Senator. You talk so interestingly that I find it hard to stop you, but you may not go outside the rules of debate'.[38]

Abolishing the Seanad

Perhaps the longest and most vigorous debate in 1934 was on the Constitution Amendment Bill, which carried out one of the objectives announced by the Government at the last election, namely the abolition of the Seanad as presently constituted and an examination of the case for the retention of a second chamber.[39]

O'Neill's contribution was long, with favourable asides relating to the personality and history of other speakers such as Senator the Earl of Granard and Senator Andrew Jameson, and was generally rambling and provocative. He was not afraid of being abolished. He, like Senator Mrs Wyse Power and Senator Staines, had been abolished already in another body 'with the joyful consent of this House'. 'The former Government', he persisted, 'abolished a body which … was a more important body than the Seanad, and did far more national work for the country than the Seanad. To use an expression for which, perhaps, you, A Cathaoirleach, might haul me over the coals, I would be inclined to say that for abolishing the Dublin Corporation', it serves you damn well right to be abolished now.' Following this outburst, he conceded that few 'would join in a prayer of thanksgiving at their own wake', and some, though it might appear vulgar to mention it, 'would find it difficult to wear a smile at the destruction of our pin money in these hard, perilous, material times'. He had a perfectly open mind as to whether the country wants a second chamber or not, but he was not impressed by the argument that a Seanad was needed as a rein on the Government. To hold that view was a reflection on the elected representatives to the Dail and a gross insult to the intelligence of the people of the country who sent these members to the Dail.[40] The Seanad to be respected and effective had to be impartial. This Seanad had not been impartial. When the late Government was in power, only one Bill sent to this House was thrown into the waste paper basket; during the two and a half years that the present Government had been in office four Bills had been, practically speaking, thrown into the waste paper basket. On that score, the President was fully justified in his action towards the Seanad as at present constituted.[41]

Senator Milroy, perhaps O'Neill's chief antagonist in the Seanad, commented that listening to his friend Senator O'Neill, he was reminded of Goldsmith's river – "remote, unfriended, melancholy, slow". 'Senator MacLoughlin would describe Senator O'Neill's utterances as that of a lachrymose banshee waiting for the revolution with which we are to be presented as a result of the action of this House.'[42] He subsequently observed that Senator O'Neill, in his rather peculiar kind of advocacy of this Bill, seemed to indicate that so far as he was concerned it was a reprisal for the abolition of the Dublin Corporation.[43]

The descriptions of his speech by Milroy and MacLoughlin registered with O'Neill, and he made his response on the next appropriate occasion, which was on 15 June 1934, when dealing with the Committee on Procedure and Privileges. The first recipient of his response, however, was another regular protagonist, the very earnest and serious Miss Browne, whose speech before his he described as 'most peculiar'. 'Senator Miss Browne', he declared, was like a kind of Lady Godiva 'naked of' political emblems 'while her only blue blouse was out in the wash'.[44] He continued his delivery despite interruptions, until Senator Milroy interjected. O'Neill then observed: 'When I look at my friend Senator Milroy, the lines from Goldsmith's "Traveller" come to me – "remote, unfriended, melancholy, slow"; and he noted that the Senator had settled beside him 'his bosom friend Senator Mac Loughlin, whom he is pleased to quote as an authority in name calling. The other day he referred to me as some kind of banshee – a "lachrymose banshee". I am going to be more respectful to Senator Milroy than he is to me. I should like it to go out to the world and appear on the pages of Irish history that Senator Milroy, in love or war, is

> The grandest, the brightest, the loveliest-minded man that has
> appeared on the horizon of Irish politics since the time of Brian
> Boru. We will leave it at that.

'As I was saying, Sir,' he added, ' I take delight in Senator Milroy interrupting me because, no matter what he says about me or no matter what I say about him, with all our faults we love each other still.' But to get back to 'the serious part …'

It was difficult to get the better of Senator O'Neill in debate, or indeed to take serious offence at his manner of riposte.

The final debate for the summer was on the Constitution Amendment no. 23 Bill, which provided for the deletion of article 27 from the Constitution. That article entitled each university in the Free State to elect three representatives to Dail Eireann. Strong voices were raised against the Amendment, including past Trinity College men like Oliver St John Gogarty, who accused the Government of being anti-intellectual and anti-minority. O'Neill, true to form, supported the Bill in an inimitable manner. Dublin University, he argued on 18 July, had 3,260 voters, the National University 4,655, that was 8,000 all told, and they had six representatives, while in the city of Dublin there were only six representatives for over 100,000 voters! Moreover, in the case of Dublin

University, many of the 3,000 voters were scattered all over the world and knew nothing about what was going on in Ireland. He, therefore, supported the Bill and congratulated the Government on setting their hand to this anomaly, one of the many which existed.[45]

Meanwhile in the Corporation

While all these meetings were proceeding, Laurence O'Neill continued to serve on Dublin City Corporation. In 1932 he was a member of the committees on Housing and General Purposes and on Old Age Pensions. He was present for most meetings but was rarely recorded as speaking. On 4 April he moved that letters in praise of the Fire Brigade and the Garda, in relation to a fire at the Central Catholic Library, 18 Hawkins Street, be recorded in the minutes. At the same meeting a letter from Sean T. O'Kelly announced his retirement from the Council because of his appointment as Minister for Local Government and Public Health. He had been a member of the Corporation from 1906.[46]

That year, 1932, was an auspicious year for the city and country. Political stability was sufficient for Ireland to be chosen as the venue for the 1932 International Eucharistic Congress. On 27 June, O'Neill was present when the Municipal Council bestowed Honorary Freedom of the City on the Papal Legate, Lorenzo Cardinal Laure; and on 8 August he shared in the councillors' pride in the overall success of the Congress and the over all morale boost it had given the country, when they expressed, 'on behalf of the citizens of Dublin, the universal feeling of appreciation and admiration evoked by the manner in which the various ceremonies and functions associated with the recent International Eucharistic Congress were planned and executed', and they further conveyed their 'wholehearted congratulations' to Archbishop Byrne, the sponsor of the Congress, 'on the outstanding success which marked the occasion, not alone from the magnitude of the undertaking but also in perfection of detail'.[47]

It was down to life's ordinary demands soon afterwards. On 22 August, O'Neill seconded a motion of sympathy by the Lord Mayor to the widow and family of the late former alderman Ernest Bewley.[48] A week or so later, there was the drama of a mayoral election. O'Neill proposed Ald. Alfred Byrne and, despite the challenge of two other candidates, Ald. Byrne was re-elected by twenty votes to eleven.[49]

Also at the above meeting, O'Neill had proposed the names of various representatives to boards and bodies, but avoided being on any board himself. He was absent from the next two meetings, was present on 3 October, absent again on 7 November, and present at a significant meeting on 5 December when Clr. Larkin, Junior, moved, and Larkin,

Senior, seconded, that the Lord Mayor be condemned for refusing to them the use of public rooms at the Mansion House. The proposer was known to have been educated in the Soviet Union, and his father had previously claimed to be a member of the Soviet Comintern. The last thing the Lord Mayor and the vast majority of councillors wished in that tense period was to be associated with Communism. Hence, presumably, the refusal of the premises, and the resounding defeat of the proposal by twenty-eight votes to two.[50]

During 1933, Senator O'Neill again attended regularly, but, apart from voting, seldom took a prominent part. He was appointed, however, to four committees: Housing and General Purposes, Housing, Old Age Pensions, and School Meals. He was also appointed , on 12 June, to a small committee of the Council in a conference between the city manager and representatives of producers and factors regarding the establishment of a distinct market for the sale of potatoes, and outlining regulations to ensure that all potatoes entering the city for consumption should pass through such a market and be subject to such tolls as should be fixed.[51] On the completion of business, the members were reminded that as this was the last meeting of the first Council elected under the Local Government (Dublin) Act, 1930, the Council should place on record 'its appreciation of the services of the City Manager and the various officers of the Corporation during its term of office'. This was agreed, and among the supporting speakers was Ald. Senator O'Neill. [52]

In the election for the new council, O'Neill was elected for Borough Electoral A, but did not top the poll. Henceforth, he was Clr. O'Neill, and continued with the same committees. He voted for the re-election of Alfred Byrne as Lord Mayor on 7 July and attended almost all the remaining meetings in 1933, but he was not recorded as making an active contribution except in connection with a number of messages of condolence.

In 1934 he attended only two meetings from May to December, and for whatever reason, ill-health perhaps or, more likely, business problems, he was present for only three meetings during 1935. The first of these involved the re-election of Alfred Byrne as Lord Mayor on 1 July, the other two related to O'Neill's interest in art and history. On 12 August, following news that the City Manager had accepted, on the recommendation of the Municipal Art Gallery Advisory Committee, thirty-three paintings by Sir John Lavery, R.A., R.H.A., presented by him in memory of Lady Lavery, Clr. O'Neill moved, seconded by Ald. Breathnach, T.D., 'that the best thanks of the Council be and are hereby tendered to Sir John'. This was put and carried, and was succeeded by a proposal from Lord Mayor Byrne, seconded by Clr. Senator O'Neill, that the City Council, in gratitude for 'the important historical group of his pictures', confer on Sir John Lavery the Honorary Freedom of the City of Dublin.[53] O'Neill's only other attendance was for the conferring of the Honorary Freeman on Sir John at a special meeting of the City Council on 17 September.

In 1936, he missed meetings in January and February but was present on 2 March, when he twice supported the Lord Mayor on the minority side in a division. From then until 8 June he attended every meeting but does not appear to have spoken. There was a municipal election on 30 June. He never attended the Corporation thereafter. He had, in effect, been easing out of municipal life for the previous two years. The Council that he knew and loved had changed greatly in power, scope, and in personnel; and he was in business and financial difficulties.

The Seanad 1934-1936

In the Seanad, by comparison, he waxed eloquent up to its dying day. On 6 September 1934, he was even more outspoken, some would say more outrageous, than usual. On a motion by Sir John Keane expressing concern at the reported intention of the Government to grant to one firm the monopoly of manufacturing motor tyres in Saorstat Eireann, O'Neill declared sweepingly:

> Monopolies have been the curse, the ruination of Ireland for the
> past three or four hundred years. First the land monopolists, who
> drove out the previous owners; monopolies destroyed the milling
> trade – the ruins of mills are silhouetted along the banks of our
> canals and rivers.

He went on audaciously to denounce the monopolies in the brewing trade. In his youth there were seven or ten breweries in Dublin, now there was only Guinness, 'one of the greatest curses ever created in this city'. Monopolies in the bakery trade destroyed many little bakeries. Then, embarking on one of his asides, he remarked that Senator Dowdall's reference to pneumatic tyres brought back memories, and if he might mention a personal matter – 'I remember that the Minister's (Lemass) father and I were the first to ride pneumatic tyres in this part of the country. When a little tyre industry was started in Westland Row there was the prospect of the creation of a good industry, but the monopolists from the other side of the water, and the objections of the good people of Merrion Square, destroyed the industry'. After all this, he proceeded to presume that the new factory in Cork was not a monopoly, but the re-creation in Ireland of a former industry! Sir John Keane, not for the first time, withdrew his motion.[54]

Three days later, 9 September 1934, in relation to shootings in Cork, the usual harmony in debate dissolved into heated party exchanges. The motion before the House, condemned members of the Special Branch of the Garda for firing on unarmed citizens in Cork, killing one and seriously wounding others, and called that they be put on trial. The motion against the Garda, in O'Neill's view, was proposed solely for the set purpose of political propaganda . Accordingly, he opposed it, but the motion was put and carried.[55]

Towards the end of the year, on 12 December 1934, the triennial election for the Cathaoirleach took place. There were two candidates, Westrop Bennett, the incumbent, with whom O'Neill had had some exchanges, and Senator Michael Comyn, K.C. In the election, Senator O'Neill voted for Comyn. Each candidate received 28 votes. The casting vote was given to Westropp Bennett by the acting-chairman, Sir William Bernard Hickie.[56]

In the New Year, the Seanad debated the Irish Nationality and Citizen Bill, second stage. On 17 January 1935, O'Neill quoted his frequent critic, Senator Brown, as an authority on international law, to the effect that the Bill was "an absolute necessity".[57] De Valera, as Minister for External Affairs as well as Taoiseach, presented the Bill. At the fifth stage, on 3 April 1935, O'Neill criticised the efforts of those who sought to undermine the friendship which existed between the mass of the people of Ireland and Britain. This, inevitably, evoked speeches for and against. Then, in the presence of de Valera, O'Neill made a most partisan avowal of his hopes and allegiances, which may have embarrassed de Valera himself.

In his lifetime, O'Neill stated, he had seen many leaders pass away, but he wished to express the hope, 'shared by millions of our scattered race, that the man who sat before us, President Eamon de Valera, may be spared to go on, and to reach for our country that goal, which every man and woman in this country with any spark of patriotism should stand behind him in his endeavours to attain, that goal for which so many of our people suffered and died in their efforts to attain, in the words of that noble young patriot, "that Ireland should take her place among the nations of the earth". I am a fairly old man, and I may not live to see the realisation of these hopes, but I am satisfied that President de Valera and those associated with him are on the right road, and, as the son of a Fenian, I want to say that I thank President de Valera and those associated with him for the efforts they are making to re-establish the nationhood of this country.' [58]

The hortatory style and the unalloyed rhetoric of support for de Valera must have been as salt in the wounds of many senators who recalled the start of the civil war and now wilted under the suffering and deprivation of the economic war. O'Neill's much vaunted pride in being independent of all parties had been exchanged, as a senator, for de facto allegiance to Fianna Fail, and particularly to de Valera, whom he revered.

A further debate on a germane topic, National Policy, provided further outlet for eloquence from Senator O'Neill. On 20 February 1935, he challenged a motion that a select committee be set up to consider and report to the Seanad 'on the national policy at present being pursued, with particular regard to its economic and social effects'. The motion, he declared, was an indirect way of getting the Seanad to give the Government a stab in the back, and would give new strength to English statesmen and the English press to pursue the economic war to the end. [59] The motion was defeated after a long debate.

On 12 February 1936, the Constitution (Amendment no 23) Bill 1934 was again brought before the Seanad. It had previously been defeated there. Much of the debate focussed on the removal of the special parliamentary franchise for university representatives. Again, a number of senators – the Unionist and Fine Gael representatives combining together – depicted the Bill as an attack on the Protestant minority. Many speakers ranged far and wide. O'Neill did so also and was charged by the Cathaoirleach with being irrelevant, off the central topic, to which O'Neill replied that so had many others but they got away with it.[60] He also dealt with interruptions in his usual half-amused, salty manner, though in the case of the formidable Senator St. John Gogarty he was caustic. Gogarty, a fierce critic of de Valera ever since the civil war, tended to identify himself with the common man and in younger days as a competitive cyclist, as noted in an earlier chapter, he had once been disqualified by O'Neill for inappropriate language. In the course of the debate on the Constitution Bill, he made some comment supportive of O'Neill, perhaps in a derisory way, and was told – 'When I want defence, it is not to Senator Gogarty I shall go; God help the poor fellow!'[61] And at another juncture, 'I humbly give him a little advice now, and that is for a man of his exceptional abilities to try to keep away from aping the position of the mediocre. He should also try to give up belittling his own countrymen at home and belittling them in the colonies'.[62]

Earlier, he had not spared a former acquaintance during his years working for prisoners. When Senator Blythe accused Labour Senator Farren of using catch-cries, O'Neill observed that he had been a long time listening to speeches but had 'never heard so many catch-cries used in a speech in his whole life' as he had heard 'in the speech that Senator Blythe made'.[63]

Senator Miss Browne, as noted, tended to evoke a quick response from O'Neill. This occurred again on 4 March 1936, during the debate on the Imposition Duties Bill.

She expressed the view 'that this country should owe allegiance to the English King'. O'Neill was roused to a quietly devastating response: 'I am not as great a student of history – political, historical or any other sort of history – as Senator Miss Browne, but I would not like it to go out from this Seanad that Miss Browne's version of Irish history is correct. When Senator Miss Browne was speaking, my mind went back to

> The time of Conscription, when each and every one of us
> took a solemn oath that Ireland was a nation separate
> and distinct. However, I shall leave it at that.[65]

His warmest and proudest memory was the unity achieved against conscription and his prominent role in that achievement. He was conscious that it was a critical moment in modern Irish history.

As the Seanad wound down in its final session on 19 May 1936, tributes and appreciations were recorded to various officials and finally to the Cathaoirleach. Senator Mac Loughlin paid tribute to his tact, skill, courtesy and impartiality, and then could not resist criticising those who voted for the destruction of the Seanad as a stronghold of feudalism and West-Britainism. He hoped they would 'enjoy their well-earned obscurity'.[66] The final speaker before the concluding words of the Cathaoirleach was Senator O'Neill. 'I cannot help joining in this tribute,' he began. 'I do not go to the length of saying, as was said by one of the senators, that you have been a perfect chairman. I suppose no member of the Seanad has fallen foul of you oftener than I have. I recognise now that, in the words of Senator O'Farrell, we are cutting asunder old associations. Although at times I felt aggrieved at your decisions, I was convinced, deep down in my heart, that there was no personal animosity on your part, that you were guided solely and entirely according to your lights. I regret some of the remarks made by Senator MacLoughlin, but I should like to join with other members in expressing my gratitude to you for many kindnesses, and as we are now about to separate, I trust you may live long, enjoy your life, and have many years of prosperity.'[67]

It was a not unworthy valediction, and, so far as he knew, it was also a valediction to his own public life. For a man who loved the public arena and the sense of public service, it was a sad occasion; an occasion made all the more desolate by the fact that his business, once so prosperous, had collapsed. But as ever, anguish was concealed by a cheerful exterior and an almost debonair manner. His was a generation that believed in homespun aphorisms such as: "Smile and the world smiles with you, weep and you weep alone".

Notes

1   T. Kennedy. *The Velvet Strand.A History of Portmarnock with part of Malahide, Kinsaley, Balgriffin, and Baldoyle . (NLI. Ir. 94133, K.6, pp. 135-9)*

2   Marie Comerford. "Laurence O'Neill: Lord Mayor of Dublin, 1917-1924" in *Irish Press* 18 February, 1960.

3   Printed election leaflet. Polling date 15 Sept. 1927. NLI. ILB 300, p. 3 (no. 39)

4   L. O'Neill- President Cosgrave, 10 Feb. 1927, 19 March, 2 May 1927. NAI. Taoiseach's Dept. Taois/ S 7474.

5   NAI. Taois/ S 7474. O'Neill-President Cosgrave, 15 May, 21 May; clerk of President – O'Neill, 23 May

6   Idem. Cosgrave-O'Hegarty, 25 May, 25 June 1928

7   Seanad Debates, Official Report, vol. 12, p. 831, pp.1029-1030

8   Idem, vol. 13, p. 584

9   Idem, pp.1280-1303, 1381, 1414-024

10 Idem, pp. 721, 962

11 Idem, vol. 13, Volunteer Reserve, 18 Dec. 1929, pp. 539, 546, 548

12 Idem, 28 May 1930, p. 1281

13 Idem, p. 1288. No such document appears to have survived.

14 Idem, p.1286

15 Idem, p. 962

16 Idem, vol. 14, 3 Dec. 1930, p. 50

17 Idem, vol. 14, 19 Nov. 1930, p. 3

18 In Kilmainham Jail Historical Museum, alongside the Thomas Ashe showcase.

19 T. Kennedy. *The Velvet Strand...,* memoirs of P. J. Ryan, p. 137

20 DCC. Mins. 14 Oct. 1930, pp. 220-21

21 Idem, no. 452, pp. 239-242

22 F.S.L. Lyons. *Ireland since the Famine,* p. 502

23 23 NAI. Dept. of Taoiseach, Memo Sept. 1931. S. 5864; cit in Emmet O'Connor. *Reds and the Green,* p. 172

24 Cosgrave- Abp.Byrne of Dublin, 17 Sept. 1931. DDA. Abp. Byrne papers, Box, Government Politics (1), file "Office of President to the Executive Council"

25 E. O'Connor. *Reds and the Green...,* p. 173

26 Idem, p. 174

27 ONFP. Duffy-O'Neill, 17 Nov. 1931

28 DDA. Abp. Byrne papers, O'Neill- Fr Dunne, 24 June 1932

29 Seanad Eireann, vol. 17, 11 July 1933- 14 Dec. 1933, "Executive Council", pp. 130-136

30 Idem, 11 July. Constitution Amendment Bill, pp. 43-45

31 Idem, Local Govt. (Extension Franchise) Bill, 12 July, p. 143

32 Idem, Public Services Bill, pp.319-20

33 Idem, Loans and Funds, p. 740

34 Idem, vol. 18, 1934; Workmen's Compensation, p. 311

35 Idem, Wearing of Uniform Bill, pp. 807-12

36 Idem, p. 812

37 Idem, on The Privileges of the House, pp. 465-7

38 Idem, p. 467

39 Idem, vol. 18, 2nd stage, 30 May 1934, pp. 1215-6.

40   Idem, pp. 1311, 1313
41   Idem, p. 1315
42   Idem, p. 1319
43   Idem, p. 1321
44   Idem, vol. 18, p. 1620
45   Idem, 18 July, pp. 1990-1991
46   DCC. Mins. 4 April 1932, n.71, pp. 40-41
47   Idem, 8 Aug. 1932, n. 160, p.111; also n.131, p. 101
48   Idem, 22 Aug. n.172, p. 116
49   Idem, n.176, p. 124
50   Idem, monthly meeting on 5 December 1932
51   Idem, n.102, pp. 67-8
52   Idem, 12 June, n. 102-3, pp. 67-8
53   Idem, 12 Aug. 1935, n. 145, p. 115
54   Idem, vol. 19 (22 Aug 1934 – 22 May 1935), 6 Sept. 1934, pp.722-23
55   Idem, 9 Sept. 1934, pp.749ff
56   Idem, 12 Dec. 1934, pp.768-770
57   Idem, 17 Jan 1935, p.1076
58   Idem, vol. 19, 3 April 1935, p.1575
59   Idem, pp.1265-1266, 1322
60   Idem, vol. 20, 12 Feb. 1936, pp. 2041-2
61   Idem, p.2235
62   Idem, p.2019
63   Idem, p.1978
64   Idem, pp.1980-81
65   Idem, vol. 20, 4 March 1936
66   Idem, 19 May, pp. 2431-2
67   Idem, p.2433

Laurence O'Neill, 1864-1943
Lord Mayor of Dublin, 1917-1924
Patriot and Man of Peace

15.

1936 – 1943: The Last Lap

"There is no prize in this race; the prize is elsewhere,

Here only to be run for."

[E. Muir. 'The Journey Back', no.7, in *Selected Poems* (Faber, London 1965)]

In 1936, Laurence O'Neill was seventy-four years of age. On 23 August 1943, his son, John, wrote of his father – 'almost seven years ago, owing to his stand for labour, he was forced to close down'. At this stage it is not clear what the circumstances were that "forced" him to close down. Was it, as in the past, that he had alienated the local business community by pressing for better wages and conditions for employees, or was there a wider issue that also influenced his customers? His son's further words might suggest just that – 'for standing behind the Labour people he lost everything'.[1]

Defending Labour

The Labour movement in 1936 was accused of being Communist. Its "Workers' Republic" Constitution made it a ready target for Catholic actionists. Episcopal Lenten pastoral letters denounced socialism and radical republicanism; and early in 1937 the Labour Party leader, William Norton, T.D., in response to an article in the influential Catholic newspaper, *Osservatore Romano*, felt obliged to declare that 'the Labour movement never had any relations with the Communist Party in this country',[2] a statement which did little to convince people who associated the Larkins, father and son, with both Labour and Communism. In this scenario, it would not be surprising if Laurence O'Neill publicly defended the reputation of labour friends whom he knew were not Communists but were being accused of being so. In the charged, almost hysterical atmosphere of 1936 and 1937, when 5,000 gathered in College Green to prevent a Communist Party rally on Easter Sunday 1936, and Cardinal MacRory had described General Franco as 'fighting the battle of Christendom against the subversive powers of Communism',[3] such an action by O'Neill might, conceivably, have led to a boycott of his business and resulted in his son John's observation – 'For standing behind the Labour people he lost everything'. It has to be said, however, that so far no other evidence has come to hand regarding the actual circumstances of the collapse of his business.

Bad financial circumstances

There is clear evidence, nevertheless, that by 1938 Laurence O'Neill was in a parlous financial condition. That year, for some reason, perhaps because he was catalogued as not having paid back his loan to the Taoiseach's department, he was one of a number of people subjected to a discreet Garda inquiry. A Garda report, headed "Secret and Confidential", was sent to the Secretary, Department of the Taoiseach, on 29 December 1938. It left no doubt about O'Neill's situation:

> With reference to your minute S 1811 of 25 ultimo, I am directed by
> the Commissioner to say that confidential inquiries have been
> discretely made regarding the persons in the list which you
> enclosed. Results are as follows.

'No. 8. Mr Laurence O'Neill still resides at Bridge House, Portmarnock, County Dublin. He is the owner of the house in which he resides and is also the owner of three other small houses in the locality, which are let at a weekly rent and bring in about £100 per annum. He is the rated occupant of 24 acres of land which is left out for grazing.

'Mr O'Neill is known to lie in very bad financial circumstances for a number of years past, and all his property is heavily mortgaged and practically owned by a bank.

'His daughter resides with him, and she kept a motor car up to about 18 months ago, when she was obliged to dispose of it.'[4]

It is noted subsequently, that the Taoiseach approved the waiving of the amount still outstanding.[5]

Outwardly unperturbed, O'Neill continued to present his confident public image, to live in reasonable comfort, and to take an active interest in the fortunes of others. Thus, in November 1936, he sent a letter of congratulation and kindly sentiments to Oscar Traynor, T.D., on his appointment as Minister for Defence. In return, he received a grateful appreciation of his remarks – 'all the more coming from a man of your own sterling qualities who thus expressed himself after thirty years of friendship'.[6]

Memoirs manqué

Laurence O'Neill had been tempted to write an account of events during those "thirty years". He had been putting recollections together during 1929 and the early nineteen-thirties, and a number of these have been quoted or referred to in this book. In 1935, he had been in communication with John MacDonagh, productions director in Radio Eireann, about providing a script for a title such as "Mansion House Memories". On 30 August 1935, MacDonagh got back to him saying they were sure he would have much of interest to say and perhaps he might concentrate 'on some of the highlights' of his time as Lord Mayor.[7] A talk of twenty minutes was envisaged. It is not clear that anything emerged from this. Concentrating material into 20 minutes might have proved less than attractive to a man as voluble as Mr O'Neill.

In October 1937, he was in touch with Leslie Luke at the *Mail* office in connection with publication.[8] On 5 January 1938, Mr Luke contacted him once more. He was 'very sorry to hear in December' that O'Neill had been 'rather unwell' and he hoped that the New Year had brought him new health. He reminded O'Neill that the latter had said 'very kindly' that he would permit Luke 'to glance over the undoubtedly interesting data' he had 'prepared, with, perhaps, a view to Memoirs now or later'. He would be happy to call on Mr O'Neill at his home on any evening that suited him.[9] Again, there is no evidence of the outcome, beyond the fact that no memoirs were published.

A Senator once more

A new Seanad was formed in April 1938. Laurence O'Neill was not a member. Two years later, however, de Valera, as was his way, remembered old friends and, on the death of one friend, Patrick T. Keohane, he personally nominated Laurence O'Neill to the Seanad. He took his seat on 4 January 1940.[10] He is not recorded as speaking during his three years in the new body, but from the divisions for voting he appears to have a good attendance record. He was present and voted on more than nine Bills, in the flood of legislation from the Emergency Powers Bill on 4 February 1942 to the Army Pensions Bill on 20 April 1943.[11]

He was in the Seanad during the most dramatic years of the Second World War and, like so many, became interested in self-sufficiency and in the emphasis on "back-to-the land". He appears to have had some work done on his own land. By the spring of 1943, the British had won in El Alemein and the Russians in Stalingrad. The danger of invasion appeared to be over in Ireland. In the general election of June 1943 there was a reaction against the hardships and shortages endured under the Fianna Fail Government. The party received 67 seats, and the combined seats of Fine Gael, Labour, Clann na

Talmhan, Farmers, Independents and others, came to 71. There was widespread interest as to what would happen next. Would de Valera be ousted from leadership? The first meeting of the new Dail was the focus of intense attention. Laurence O'Neill came into the city to view proceedings.

Last visit to the Dail

Kathleen O'Brennan recalled in the *Irish Times* how she met him when 'he came into the press gallery in the Dail during the division on the question of the Taoiseach'. He told her 'that he had come in from Portmarnock, although he was busy with the haymaking, since he was interested in seeing Mr de Valera re-elected as chief of the Government.' 'While he had retired from politics and was enjoying a much deserved rest, he still felt that we should not have changed horses at the present time, and he waited anxiously until the verdict of the new House was given, chatting about the old days when the Dail met underground, and always prepared for a hurried dispersal. He laughed as he recalled the many amusing incidents in the Mansion House, and the well-known personalities, cleverly disguised, who came to visit the Lord Mayor. They included tramps, frock-coated gentlemen, and fashionable ladies. It was a source of interest to him, he said, to look down on the new House, a meeting without incident.' [12] De Valera was re-elected as Taoiseach that day, 1 July, by 67 votes to 37 for Cosgrave, with Labour and Clann na Talmhan abstaining.

Less than a month later, Laurence O'Neill was dead. He died on his own, on Monday 26 July, sitting on a chair in his summer house in the garden of Bridge House, Portmarnock. He was seventy-nine years of age. [13]

The obsequies and the irony

The funeral took place on 28 July from Baldoyle parish church to St. Marnock's cemetery, Portmarnock. Requiem Mass was celebrated by the parish priest, Rev. W. Field, assisted by curates Frs J. Dillon, C. Skehan, J.F.Tarpey, and by Rev. Charles Molony, S.J. 'The chief mourners were: 'John (son), Miss A. O'Neill and Mrs M Carrig (daughters), Mrs J. O'Neill (daughter-in-law), Miss B. Carrig (grand-daughter), and Donald and Laurence Carrig (grandsons). The attendance included: An Taoiseach, Mr de Valera, Mr Sean T. O'Kelly (Tanaiste), Mr Oscar Traynor (Minister for Defence), Mr W.T. Cosgrave, T.D., the Lord Mayor, Ald. M. O'Sullivan, T.D., Senator Margaret Pearse, Cormac Breathnach, T.D., Ald. A. Byrne, T.D., Senator M. Hayes, a number of other senators, members of the Corporation, and various acquaintances.' [14]

It was an impressive send off, but thereafter Laurence (Larry) O'Neill was virtually forgotten. As if symbolic of that, he rests in a cemetery that is unmarked from the public road and has to be accessed across a field; and much of the lettering on the plinth of the Celtic cross marking his grave, and that of his wife, Anne, is blotched by lichen. Laurence O'Neill used to talk of the ironies of Irish history. Among them was the honour given to men of violence while the contributions of men of peace were neglected. And there was the further irony in his case: the warmest appreciation of his achievements as Lord Mayor came not from his active republican friends whom he assisted, but, as has been seen, from a British General and an English Assistant-Secretary.

A Reflection;

Laurence O'Neill was a small, unprepossessing-looking man, but he had a rare gift of personality that was open to all, irrespective of creed, political adherence, or nationality, and was combined with an eloquence and charm that won friends and disarmed enemies. With it all went a strong social conscience, courage, ambition, and determination; and a sense of history that assured him that he had played an important secondary role in the struggle for his country's independence, had been a key figure in creating national unity through his initiation and chairing of the anti-conscription campaign, and had been involved in developing the truce that brought conflict to an end. He was not, however, a successful businessman, and one of his major concerns in his later years had to be the future prospects of his unmarried daughter, who lived at home with him and had no special qualifications to make her way after his death, and of his son, John, mentioned earlier, who was married, had an unsatisfactory job as storekeeper/timekeeper, and depended on whatever little his father could send him.

John, indeed, less than a month after his father's death, was seeking a job and availing of his father's achievements to smooth the way. He had heard that there was a vacancy for the position of acting warrant officer. He wished to be considered for the job, even though labour people would argue that there were 'others more entitled to it on the point of service'. His letter, although aimed at furthering his own quest, conveys something of his personal estimation of his father's career.

> I was born and have lived all my life in the city of Dublin. I entered
> my father's business (one of the most flourishing of its kind in
> Ireland) when very young. My father entered public life and was
> connected with it for over 35 years. He was Lord Mayor of Dublin
> from 1917 to 1924 during the most strenuous years in the history of
> the country. He sacrificed his business, his health and his

happiness for everyone. For standing behind the Labour people he
was forced to close down. Mr de Valera out of gratitude for his past
services appointed him as one of his personal nominees to the Senate,
and he would have been re-elected again only for his death a few
weeks ago.

John then went on to make his appeal. 'With his help and a very worrying job as
storekeeper/timekeeper … on the various relief schemes, I have been trying to live and
support my family for the past seven years. Now he is gone and surely it is not too much
to expect that his son, who indirectly has been a victim also of circumstances connected
with his political and labour activities should be given a chance.'[15]

John was not successful in his application. He lived out his life and cared well for
his family in a job similar to the one mentioned in his letter. His sister, Anne, left
Portmarnock and went to stay with her married sister in Co. Mayo. Their father had
devoted much of his life to helping others. That was forgotten when it came to assisting
his children, and the money owed to his business remained unpaid. It says something of
the personality of their father, that his children felt no bitterness towards him. They had
had a good life with him as they grew up and afterwards.

Finally, there is a certain appropriateness in the case of this unusual ordinary
Irishman, who as cyclist, administrator, and in public life, made friends across national
and religious boundaries, to leave the last word to an Englishman, confidant of Lloyd
George, Under-Secretary at Dublin Castle, Alfred Cope, who, on 1 April 1924, assured
Laurence O'Neill:

> When the true history comes to be written… your great work for
> moderation and the avoidance of hardship and bloodshed on all sides
> will be fully recognised …I know of no other man who, in your exalted
> position, would have worked so strenuously or who could have overcome
> so successfully the almost overwhelming difficulties of your office
> in so perplexing a period. And yet at the same time you retained the
> full confidence of your people. It was a great accomplishment.'[16]

An accomplishment, perhaps, that merits wider recognition in an Ireland that
gradually has learned to celebrate the achievement of peace-makers in a European
context and within its own island.

Notes

1   ONFP. John O'Neill- T. Andrew Kavanagh Esq., writing from 47 Grosvenor Square, Rathmines, 23 August 1943.

2   T. J. Morrissey. *William O'Brien,1881-1968,* pp. 285-6

3   Idem, pp. 281-6; and see Emmet O'Connor. *Reds and the Green,* pp 212-13

4   NAI. Taoiseach's Office, S 7474, 29 Dec. 1938

5   Idem, S 1811

6   ONFP. Oscar Traynor- L. O'Neill, 9 Nov. 1936

7   ONFP. MacDonagh-L. O'Neill

8   Idem. L. Luke- O'Neill, writing from 8 Longford Place, Monkstown, 18 Oct. 1937

9   Idem. Leslie A. Luke- L. O'Neill, 5 Jan. 1938

10   Seanad Eireann Debates, vol.24, 4 Jan. 1940, p. 421

11   Idem. Among the Bills on which he voted were: The Emergency Powers Bill, 4 Feb. 1942; the Minimum Price for Wheat Bill, 11 Feb. 1942; on the Dairying Industry, 6 March, 1942; and the Central Bank Bill, 8 Oct. 1942 [vol. 26, 5 Nov. 1941-14 Oct. 1942]. In the session from 18 Nov. 1942-14 July 1943, he voted on the Censorship Publications motion on 9 Dec. 1942; on the School Attendance Bill, 13 Jan. and 3 Feb. 1943; on Intoxicating Liquor Bill, 28 Jan. 1943; St Laurence Hospital, 10 Feb. 1943; and in the final division of the session, the Army Pensions Bill, on 20 April 1943 [vol. 27]

12   *Irish Times,* 29 July 1943, in "An Irishman's Diary" by Quidnunc.

13   Most newspapers got his age wrong, having him 69 years rather than 79.

14   *Irish Press,* 29 July 1943

15   ONFP. John O'Neill- Andrew Kavanagh, iam cit.

16   NLI. O'Neill papers, Ms. 35 294/15. A. Cope- Ld. Mayor O'Neill, 1 April 1924

Laurence O'Neill, 1864-1943
Lord Mayor of Dublin, 1917-1924
Patriot and Man of Peace

Index

Compiled by Julitta Clancy